W9-BLS-063

Friendship Counseling

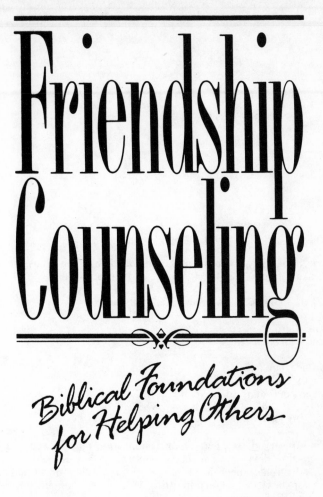

Friendship Counseling

Biblical Foundations for Helping Others

CAROL LESSER BALDWIN

PYRANEE
BOOKS

Zondervan Publishing House
Grand Rapids, Michigan

FRIENDSHIP COUNSELING
Copyright © 1988 by Carol Lesser Baldwin

Pyranee Books is an imprint of Zondervan Publishing House, 1415 Lake Drive, S.E., Grand Rapids, Michigan 49506.

Library of Congress Cataloging-in-Publication Data

Baldwin, Carol Lesser.
  Friendship counseling.

  "Pyranee books."
  Includes bibliographies.
  1. Peer counseling in the church. I. Title.
BV4409.B35   1988   253.5   87-37272
ISBN 0-310-39041-9

All rights reserved. No part of this publication may be reproduced, stored in a retrieval system, or transmitted in any form or by any means—electronic, mechanical, photocopy, recording, or any other—except for brief quotations in printed reviews, without the prior permission of the publisher.

SOME OF THE CASES IN THIS BOOK ARE TRUE. ALL THE NAMES HAVE BEEN CHANGED EXCEPT FOR REFERENCES TO THE AUTHOR.

All Scripture quotations, unless otherwise noted, are taken from the *Holy Bible: New International Version (North American Edition).* *Copyright © 1973, 1978, 1984 by the International Bible Society. Used by permission of Zondervan Bible Publishers.*

Edited by Linda Vanderzalm
Designed by Louise Bauer

Printed in the United States of America

88 89 90 91 92 93 / AF / 10 9 8 7 6 5 4 3 2 1

CONTENTS

Grateful acknowledgement is expressed to the following for permission to use copyright material:

American Psychiatric Association

Material reprinted with permission from *The American Psychiatric Association Diagnostic and Statistical Manual of Mental Disorders,* 3rd Edition, 3rd Edition Revised, Copyright © 1987.

Brooks-Cole Publishing Company

Excerpts from *Face to Face* by Gerald Egan, Copyright © 1973.

Christian Marriage Enrichment

Excerpts from *Training Christians to Counsel* by H. Norman Wright, Copyright © 1977.

The C.V. Mosby Company

Paraphrased material from *Crisis Intervention: Theory and Methodology* by Donna C. Aguilera and Janice M. Messick, 5th Edition, Copyright © 1986.

Christian Helpers, Inc.

Adapted material from *Amity: Friendship in Action* by R. P. Walters, Copyright © 1980.

Herald Press

Adapted material from *Peer Counseling in the Church* by Paul Miller, Copyright © 1978.

Random House, Inc.

Paraphrased material from *Parent Effectiveness Training* by Dr. Thomas Gordon, Copyright © 1970.

Regal Books

Excerpts from *Caring Enough to Hear and Be Heard* by David Augsburger, Copyright © 1981.

Excerpts from *How to Be a People Helper* by Gary Collins, Copyright © 1976.

Research Press

Excerpts from *A Couple's Guide to Communication* by J. Gottman, C. Notarius, J. Gonso, and H. Markman, Copyright © 1976 by the authors.

ACKNOWLEDGMENTS

It's impossible to thank each person who has contributed to this book. My ideas have come from interaction with my colleagues, friends, clients, and students, as well as from numerous sermons over the last fourteen years. For those of you who read this book and see an incident or example that you told me, I hope you'll smile and remember I warned you that one day you might see your words in print!

I do want to thank a few specific people whose help has been invaluable. Dave Powlison has been my friend, editor, and critic extraordinaire. He has shared my vision for peer counseling in the church and has stretched me as a Christian, counselor, and writer. When we first talked about this book, we thought we might write it together. But then he jokingly said, "Carol, I don't have time to write it. I'll tell you what. I'll help you with the ideas, and you can write it." To a large extent that's what happened. Although the book you now hold has my name on it, many of the thoughts, ideas, and even some of the words are Dave Powlison's.

Second, I want to thank my dear friend, Jane LeBeau. My second-best editor, she sharpened my writing and encouraged me to work toward excellence. But even more than that, she stood alongside me after my first husband died and helped me to make the transition to being single. She was often the type of helper described in this book.

My special thanks to the Riggall, MacQueen, and Priestley families for loving me, feeding me, praying for me, and basically keeping me going while I wrote this book. They welcomed me into their families and helped me to combat the double loneliness of being both single and a writer. A special thanks to Linda Riggall for going above and beyond the call of duty as a secretary.

To the people of Maple Glen Bible Fellowship Church, who first gave me the opportunity to teach this material; to the Roslyn discipleship group for reading each chapter; to Rod Robinson and the staff at the Counseling Center in Abingdon, Pennsylvania, who taught me about Christian counseling; and to Dick Keyes of L'Abri Fellowship for helping me clarify many of my ideas for Part I; and to Brian Eck for his help on the evaluation forms in Part II—I thank you all.

Thanks to Jim Ruark, my first editor at Zondervan, who didn't abandon me but encouraged me to "hang in there" when I thought I would never finish the manuscript; and to Julie Link, Martha Manikas-Foster, and Linda Vanderzalm, whose editorial input were greatly appreciated. And thanks to Mike Smith, who helped to get me going in the beginning.

And finally to Creighton Baldwin, who took seriously his responsibility as my husband by reviewing the manuscript with me and making numerous, helpful recommendations.

INTRODUCTION

Whenever someone asks me what this book is about, I say, "lay counseling in the church." Then I add, "It's really about how to be a good friend."

Specifically, this book has been written so that Christians can learn a systematic, biblical approach to helping their friends. Although the focus of the book is on helping believers, many of the skills described also may be helpful with nonbelievers. I hope that as a result of reading this book, you'll become a better equipped Christian who is more able to confront, accept, love, and care for your friends.

Many of the skills described in this book basically are good relationship skills. That's because helping and counseling skills (and I use these two words interchangeably) are essentially the same skills we need to relate well to another.[1] Effective helpers must be able to approach a person in pain or in trouble, listen accurately and empathically, and then speak words of hope and confrontation that will encourage that person to take appropriate action.

As members of the body of Christ, we have the opportunity and responsibility to relate closely to one another. Throughout His Word, God calls us to bear one another's burdens, to love one another, and to encourage one another (Rom. 12:10–13; Gal. 6:2; Heb. 3:12–15). In fact, Scripture teaches us that when one member of the body suffers, the whole body suffers (1 Cor.

12:26). Since we are touched by the problems that our brothers and sisters experience, we must be prepared to minister to them. We also are affected if a fellow member of the body sins, and therefore we also must be ready to apply God's Word to those who are not living the way He commands.

But we are called not only to serve the church but also to demonstrate God's truth to the whole world. Acts of love and mercy are powerful declarations to an unbelieving world that Jesus is the Christ (John 17:21).

The question for many Christians today is not *whether* to love, minister, or confront a friend, but *how* to translate those desires into effective counsel. We need to know what to say to a neighbor who always seems depressed. We need to learn how we can help a friend who blows up all the time.

If we don't know what to say or do in these kinds of situations, one of two things happens: we either avoid the situation, allowing our fear of saying the wrong thing to dictate our response, or we say something that we regret later on. We can prevent both responses by equipping ourselves with good helping skills.

Our helping equipment begins with an understanding of how God helps us: He righteously *confronts* our sin and calls us to repentance, and then He mercifully *comforts* us with His forgiveness. This twin theme—confronting, comforting—is the backbone of the helping model presented in this book. Part I will discuss how God the Father, God the Son, and God the Holy Spirit illustrate this model in various ways. Part II will help you evaluate yourself as a helper. Part III will help you study the counseling process and learn how to help your friends. Each of these later chapters includes biblical principles, case examples, and practical exercises.

Before we begin this study, let's look at a few definitions. Particularly, let's consider what makes counseling "Christian" and what "lay" counseling includes.

WHAT IS CHRISTIAN COUNSELING?

Anytime we influence another person toward a particular attitude or action, we are counseling. When a mother speaks to her daughter who is upset over a friend's betrayal, she is counseling her with encouragement and love. When a pastor preaches that husbands need to love their wives as Christ loved the church, he is counseling by admonishment and encouragement. Since we are each engaged in a variety of family, work, or church relationships, we probably are already involved in counseling one another. Our challenge is to influence our friends in meaningful and effective ways.

Christian counseling distinguishes itself from secular counseling in that its direction is taken from God's Word. The Christian counselor helps a person both to apply biblical principles to the problems that he or she is facing and to see these problems from God's perspective. The goal of Christian counseling is that each Christian be made complete in Christ (Col. 1:28b), becoming more like Him in the ongoing process of sanctification (Rom. 8:29; 1 John 3:2). Furthermore, Christian counseling is characterized by God's love, communicated through a caring and committed relationship. The Christian helper uses this relationship to communicate the gospel message of God's righteous confrontation of sin, His loving forgiveness for the sinner, and His directives to obey His Word.

WHAT IS LAY COUNSELING?

Lay counseling generally refers to help that is given by a person who has not received professional training. Friends are often in the best position to help one another since they already know and trust each other. Sometimes friends may have had similar experiences and can share what has helped them. In addition, concerned friends who know how to effectively intervene during a time of trouble can help prevent small problems from developing into major crises.

Lay counseling goes beyond just meeting our friends' needs. God's call to "love your neighbor as yourself" (Lev. 19:15–18) expands our concept of neighborhood. In response to the lawyer's question, "Who is my neighbor?" Jesus told the parable of the Good Samaritan (Luke 10:30–37). His answer challenges us to minister to anyone we meet. Opportunities to counsel often lie at our doorstep: in our jobs, schools, and neighborhoods.

If you work in a people-helping position—police work, social work, teaching, or childcare—you handle people's problems daily. But helping isn't limited to the "professionals." Often accountants, secretaries, lawyers, taxicab drivers, and hairdressers are the first to hear someone's problems. All of us share the responsibility of people helping.

If you have a position of leadership in your church, you may be asked to counsel someone. As a youth group leader, Sunday school teacher, Bible study leader, or elder, you may be seen as someone who can help with difficult problems. If you are the type of person in whom others easily confide, you may end up feeling overwhelmed by the responsibility of many confidences. This book not only will help you recognize and evaluate the help you are already giving, but it also will teach you additional skills to handle difficult situations.

Remember that the training offered in this book is limited; it's not intended to create (or eliminate) professional helpers. The experience and education that professionally trained counselors acquire is often needed for certain types of problems. We can think of helping as a continuum, with professional counselors such as Christian psychologists and psychiatrists at one end and trained laypersons at the other. The people at the ends of the spectrum are separated by experience and education but joined by their commitment to serve fellow members of the body of Christ. (The particular types of problems that lay counselors are equipped to handle are reviewed in chapter 5.)[2] Furthermore, lay counselors don't replace or usurp the authority and responsibility of church elders. Like Dorcas (Acts 9:36) and Phoebe (Rom. 16:1–2), well-trained helpers should assist the work of the church.

In summary, we can say that Christian lay counselors are people who help others find a biblical perspective on their problems. Christian lay counselors attempt to bring God's truth to others while standing alongside them. With sensitivity, understanding, and knowledge of God's Word, Christian lay counselors encourage their friends to godliness and obedience. They also urge their friends to use the resources God has provided: the promises of His Word, the guidance of His Spirit, and our minds, emotions, wills, and abilities.

HOW TO USE THIS BOOK

This book can be used in four different ways. *First, it can be used as a foundational course to train lay counselors in the church.* These lay counselors would be selected, trained, and recognized as "official" lay counselors. The leader for this kind of group should be a trained professional counselor. The leader's guide at the end of the book will help leaders become good helpers to the people in their groups.

Second, this book can be used by people who want to become better helpers but don't intend to become recognized lay counselors. Groups such as a neighborhood Bible study, a college fellowship group, a social action group, or the elders and deacons of a church could decide to study this book together. The leaders in these small groups do not need to be professionally trained, but they should be sensitive to the group learning process.

Both kinds of groups—the lay counseling trainees and the other small groups—can meet for an hour or two a week to discuss each chapter and to complete the various group activities outlined in the leader's guide. Since there are thirteen lessons, a church could use the Sunday school hour for the course. Each group member should prepare for the group meeting by reading the assigned chapter and completing the exercises in the Personal and Practical section at the end of each chapter. Although the size of the group can vary from two people to twenty-five people, the recommended size for maximum participation and interaction is ten to fifteen people.

Third, this book can be used for individual study. If you aren't a member of a specific lay counseling study group, you still will profit from reading each chapter and completing the Personal and Practical section yourself. Your study will be limited, since a group provides opportunities (for sharing ideas and practicing your helping skills) that individual study does not. Since you really need only one other person to form a "group," encourage a friend or family member to study the book with you! If that isn't possible, then ask a friend if you can practice the counseling skills in Part III with him or her. You both will profit: you will gain the experience that you need, and your friend will be helped in the process.

Fourth, this book can be used by pastors and professional counselors who want to enrich their knowledge of biblical counseling. Although many other books have been written about Christian counseling,[3] this book is unique in that it derives practical counseling skills from a study of *who* God is and *how* He has dealt with His people. This emphasis on obedience to God also separates this book from secular counseling texts, which fail to acknowledge our need for salvation through Jesus Christ.

However you use this book, I encourage you to keep a notebook or journal. Use it to record your responses to the Personal and Practical sections, your goals, your insights, your questions, your growth, and your problems.

It is my hope and prayer that you will be challenged, inspired, and equipped as you study this book. In the years of teaching and writing that have gone into its preparation, God has demonstrated to me the truth of Hebrews 13:6: "The Lord is my helper; I will not be afraid." I pray that He will demonstrate that truth to you and to all the friends with whom you will counsel.

For Further Reading

Read R. Paul Stevens, *Liberating the Laity* (Downers Grove, Illinois: InterVarsity Press, 1985).

NOTES

[1]Gerard Egan, *The Skilled Helper: Model Skills and Methods for Effective Helping* (Monterey, California: Brooks-Cole Publishing Co., 1975), p. 10.

[2]If you need to consult a professional Christian counselor, be sure to choose one who uses the Bible, not psychology, as his or her final authority. Although many professionals call themselves "Christian counselors," not all of them counsel from a biblical perspective. For a good description of a biblical psychologist, see Lawrence Crabb, *Effective Biblical Counseling* (Grand Rapids: Zondervan Publishing House, 1977), pp. 47–52.

[3]The following books also discuss Christian counseling:

Jay Adams, *Christian Counselor's Manual* (Phillipsburg, New Jersey: Presbyterian and Reformed Publishing Co., 1973).

Gary Collins, *How To Be a People Helper* (Santa Ana, California: Vision House, 1976).

John Carter and Bruce Narramore, *The Integration of Psychology and Theology* (Grand Rapids: Zondervan Publishing House, 1979).

Everett Worthington, *When Someone Asks for Help* (Downers Grove, Illinois: InterVarsity Press, 1982).

INTRODUCTION TO PART I: LOOKING UPWARD

Helping people through their problems can be a very complicated job. Fortunately, we don't assume this responsibility ourselves. Jesus assures us that we aren't on our own, for the Holy Spirit has been sent to guide us into all truth (John 14:16–17; 16:13).

What are the spiritual truths we need in order to help others? Primarily, we must be grounded in a knowledge of *who* God is, *what* He has done for His people, and *how* He has promised to help us. These three truths are examined in the first part of this book.

In chapter 1 we'll study who God is, who we are, and how Adam's Fall is the source of all our problems, both personal and interpersonal. In chapter 2 we'll see how God provided the ultimate cure to these problems through the work of Jesus Christ. We'll also see how Jesus, the master counselor, is the model for helping our friends. In chapter 3 we'll become acquainted with the Holy Spirit's role as the helper—enabling us to be effective helpers and coming alongside our friends as the encourager, comforter, and advocate.

This material will shape us in two different ways. First, we'll strengthen our knowledge of God. Second, we will learn that the way God helps us provides the model for how we can help our friends.

CHAPTER 1

WHO IS GOD AND WHO ARE WE?

The counsel of the Lord stands forever.

—Psalm 33:11a NASB

We are social beings. We have spiritual, emotional, psychological, and physical needs that can be met only within the context of our relationships. Our need to be redeemed, to have purpose, and to be loved unconditionally are met in our relationship to God. Our need to be loved, to be affirmed, to be valued, and to be part of a group are met in relationship to other people. Relationships are vital to our emotional and psychological well-being.

But if we take an honest look around us, we see people whose lives are characterized by broken relationships. We see whole societies that don't know God and live as if He were only a myth (Rom. 1:25). We see men and women who drink, worry, overeat, spend too much money, or get depressed because they know no peace. We see children who grow up mistrusting the world because of their inconsistent or abusive parents. We see husbands and wives who are devastated when their life partners leave because they feel bored or unfulfilled. We see people who are separated from God, from themselves, and from each other.[1]

In a world marred by broken relationships, the Bible provides a much-needed answer—God's word on reconciliation.

17

In a nutshell, the gospel of Jesus Christ is about restoration: restoring our relationship to God, to ourselves, and to others.

As helpers, we are invited to participate in this process of restoration. To prepare ourselves appropriately, let's look at God (the one who has restored us), ourselves (the people who need restoration), and the Fall (the event that precipitated all these broken relationships).

WHO IS GOD?

One of our biggest problems is that we often don't perceive all of who God is; we see only an incomplete and distorted picture of Him. Although it's beyond the scope of this book to provide an in-depth study of the character of God, we'll look at four aspects of His nature: His power, His knowledge, His holiness, and His love.[2]

God Moves Powerfully in Our Lives

God's power is limitless. In Psalm 33, David describes many ways that God reveals His strength. God created the world and sustains it (vv. 6–7, 15); His word alone brings things to pass (v. 9). His plans are always fulfilled (vv. 10–11). God considers the whole earth, and by His power provides for the needs that He observes (vv. 13, 19b). And most of all, His power saves us from our greatest enemy, death (v. 19a).

Seeing God's power reminds us that we are made *to depend on* and *trust in* God. We discover our weaknesses in the light of His strength, and we discover our strengths in the light of leaning on Him. As helpers, we must draw our guidance and wisdom from God and encourage our friends to seek His power. Ultimately, it's His strength that will enable them to solve their problems.

God Knows All Things

David wrote about God's absolute and intimate knowledge in Psalm 139: "O LORD, you have searched me and you know me. You know when I sit and when I rise; you perceive my thoughts from afar. You discern my going out and my lying down; you are familiar with all my ways" (vv. 1–3).

David marvels that God knew him in his mother's womb

and ordained his days before he was born (vv. 15-16). David concludes his testimony to God's omniscience by entrusting himself to Him: "Search me, O God, and know my heart; test me and know my anxious thoughts. See if there is any offensive way in me, and lead me in the way everlasting" (vv. 23-24).

David's response shows us that we were made *to be honest* before God. We can trust Him with the darkest corners of our sin, failures, and weaknesses.

God Defines Perfection for Us

The Bible often describes the character of God with the word *holy,* which literally means "to be set apart." Moses rejoiced in God's holiness when he sang: "Who among the gods is like you, O LORD? Who is like you—majestic in holiness, awesome in glory, working wonders?" (Exod. 15:11). God's absolute holiness sets Him apart from His creation: He is exalted above us in infinite majesty.

Since God is holy, He is also absolutely just and righteous. In other words, there is no evil in Him. His righteousness is the standard for His own perfection, and He opposes anything that contradicts His character.[3] Furthermore, God's absolute holiness determines the moral standards for the world (Lev. 19:2).

What are the implications of God's holiness? First, since we were created in His image, we were made *to be holy.* His beauty and perfection characterize the lives He intended us to lead. Second, because of the Fall, we don't measure up to His standards and are therefore separated from Him (Isa. 59:2; Rom. 5:12). Third, His justice demands that He must deal with our sin; He can't ignore it (Rom. 2:1-16). God's holiness is a mirror by which we come face to face with our guilt and shame; it confronts us with our sin.

If we see God's holiness but don't trust in Him for forgiveness, we sink into despair. This can surface as unrelenting personal criticism ("Such a perfect God could never love a worthless person like me"), as frustration and anger ("I know I can never be good enough for God. It's unfair that He asks me to do the impossible"), or as fear ("If God is so holy, I'm sure He'll punish me horribly").

Such depression, frustration, and fear often result from an incomplete knowledge and trust in God. But God's holiness is full of glory, beauty, and goodness because it is combined with

His perfect love. If we know God for all of who He is, we will be able to stand honestly before Him, trusting in His merciful love.

God Values Us

God's love ensures us that He seeks our good, not our harm. His love demonstrates that He values and esteems His elect. For God's love is unique because it's unmerited: "[God's love] is not at all a response to that which is lovely. Rather, God sets His love upon us, esteems and cares for us, despite the fact that we in our sinfulness are most unlovely."[4] God's love is a gift that is independent of our works, efforts, achievements, or performance (Eph. 2:4–8).

The result of God's holy confrontation and His loving comfort is the Cross of Jesus Christ. For it is there that God's grace meets the unyielding demands of His holiness with regard to our sin; and it is there that we are both *judged* for who we are, *guilty sinners,* and *loved* for who we will become, *redeemed sinners* (Rom. 1:18, 32; 2:2; 3:23; 6:23a). The good news of the gospel is that the King of the universe, the one who could rightfully condemn us, saves us instead.

To summarize, honest self-examination must be carried out within the context of God's merciful and powerful love. What freedom is ours when we realize that we are both totally known *and* totally loved! How wonderful it is when we recognize this as the complete picture of what God has given us in Christ. And as helpers, we then have the privilege of leading our friends to a total understanding of who God is: completely perfect and righteous, absolutely loving and merciful, and One who commands a response of trust and obedience.

WHO ARE WE?

Preparation for the job of counseling needs to include a study of the nature of mankind. Our understanding of *why* a person behaves as he or she does will affect the help that we give. As Christians, we must find our understanding of personhood in the Word of God. In other words, our theology should determine our psychology. An understanding of human nature helps us appreciate the spiritual needs and problems that people face as well as the solution that God gives. Dr. Sinclair Ferguson, noted author and theologian, says it well: "Only as we begin to appreciate what we were before we became Christians (or what we would be naturally were we not Christians), do we begin to sense something of the immense grandeur of being new creatures in Christ. . . . We will never properly understand the work of God which takes place in the Christian life unless we first of all have some kind of grasp of *why* we need the grace of God" (italics added).[5]

With this in mind, let's take a look at the biblical picture of mankind.

Created in God's Image

Our study begins with the Creation and Fall of mankind. In Genesis 1–2 we discover an amazing fact: Adam and Eve were made in the very image of God (Gen. 1:26–27). What does this mean? First, it means that the essence of who we are is a reflection of our Creator. We human beings are not great in ourselves; rather our uniqueness, nobility, dignity, and value are derived from being like God.[6]

Second, since we "participate in the divine nature" (2 Peter 1:4), some aspects of who God is will be mirrored in who we are. At Creation, Adam and Eve perfectly imaged God's moral nature (Gen. 1:27; 5:1), and their minds, wills, and emotions echoed God's personality.[7]

The core of being made in God's image was that Adam and Eve had the potential of living life in perfect relationship to God. They could depend on God instead of trying to rely on their own power and strength. They could know God's truth and not hide from Him in fear. They could love and worship their Creator, and in that way mirror His glory. They could obey Him instead of striking out in rebellion. In other words, they could believe and act on all that God had revealed.

Fallen from God's Intention

But what happened? If God intended us to be like Him and to be in perfect relationship to Him, why aren't our lives full of truth, love, and righteousness? In fact, it seems as if our lives are the total opposite. We put ourselves first and get angry if we don't get our way. We become preoccupied with what others think of us and work to gain their approval. We need only read the daily newspaper to realize that this world and the people in it don't match the picture of God's intention for His creation.

Genesis 3 helps us to understand why the world is different from what God originally pronounced as good. God's world has been horribly scarred by the Fall. Adam and Eve broke their relationship to God when they disobeyed Him and ate from the fruit of the tree of the knowledge of good and evil. Trying vainly to grasp equality with God, our spiritual parents set the precedent for all subsequent sin. No longer was Adam in perfect fellowship with God, at peace with himself, or in harmony with his wife. Adam and Eve's actions began a pattern of separation and alienation that apart from God's grace inescapably leads to the ultimate separation from God—eternal death (Gen. 2:17; Rom. 6:23; Rev. 20:14–15).

Because of the Fall, Christians still must constantly contend with their sinful nature (Rom. 5:12; 7:21–22). Like Adam and Eve, we also find a variety of ways to tell God: "I want to be master of this area of my life, not you." I don't need *you* to tell *me* what to do." We decide that our thoughts, feelings, and plans are more important than His. In this way we misuse our minds, wills, emotions, and freedom. In the remainder of this chapter, we'll look at the various problems that have developed, directly or indirectly, because we sin and don't live up to God's original design for us.

EXPERIENCING THE CONSEQUENCES OF THE FALL

Sin: Our Personal Evil

The Fall means sin is normal in the world. In today's do-your-own-thing society, sin is not a very popular notion. But as one author writes: "Christianity doesn't make sense without sin. If we are not sinners, turned away from God, then there was no reason for God to become a man, and no reason for Him to die. . . . It follows that if you have no consciousness of sin, you simply won't be able to see the point of Christianity."[8]

We must be prepared to recognize our selfishness, lying, or greed for what it is—sin. Just like a patient who refuses treatment because he or she won't accept the diagnosis of cancer, we'll be unable to receive God's "cure" (forgiveness through Jesus Christ) if we don't acknowledge and confess our sins.

What is sin? The most common word for sin used in both the Old and New Testaments means "missing the mark" or "falling short of God's standards" (Ps. 53:2–3; Matt. 15:18–19; Rom. 3:23). Sin twists what is good into something evil. For example, it's not sinful to want to be loved. But when these desires are expressed in an extramarital affair, something has gone wrong. In the same way, the desire to achieve success in one's job is not wrong in itself. But left unchecked, this desire can grow into a ruthless thirst for power.

At this point you might be thinking, "But that's not me! I'm just a quiet Christian, minding my own business. I never sin like that!" Let's take a closer look. God's Word lays bare the true condition of our hearts. Have you ever grumbled and complained when your plans were interrupted? Have you ever told a "half truth" in order to create a good impression? Have you ever snapped irritably at your spouse or children? Actually, the variety of ways that we have sinned and broken our relationship to God is endless (Rom. 1:29–31; Col. 3:5–9). None of us is without sin. We all need the saving grace of Jesus Christ.

When we realize the full impact of our own sin and the affect it has on others, we feel like the apostle Paul, who looked at himself and concluded, "What a wretched man I am! Who will rescue me from this body of death?" (Rom. 7:24). But like Paul, we can also discover the solution: "Thanks be to God—through Jesus Christ our Lord! . . . [For] therefore, there is now no condemnation for those who are in Christ Jesus" (Rom. 7:25–8:1). As we'll see in the next chapter, the good news of the gospel is that although God confronts and hates our sin, He also has mercifully delivered His people from its penalty and has restored us to a right relationship to Him.

And this is our hope. When we have a proper view of *who God is* and *who we are,* then we can experience total freedom. For when we honestly admit and confess our sin, God will forgive us.

Hiding: The Great Cover-up

Adam and Eve responded to their sin by hiding from God and from each other. Ashamed and guilty, they didn't want to take responsibility for their behavior. Hiding became the opposite of honesty. Unfortunately, we often adopt a similar pattern of deception by denying our mistakes, rationalizing our failures, or blaming others for our disappointments.

Why do we hide? First, we're afraid of being known and being held accountable for who we are: men and women who are at times proud, critical, jealous, bitter, spiteful, demanding, suspicious, untrustworthy, lazy, impatient, greedy, or selfish. Second, we're afraid of being seen as weak, dependent, or insecure. We think we'll be rejected or condemned if we let others see us "warts and all." Third, our pride keeps us from facing our sin and limitations. We want to avoid seeing our *guilt* when we sin, and want to hide from the *shame* of our weaknesses.

Each one of us has different ways of hiding, and we use various "defense mechanisms" to cover up our sin.[9] Some people shift the blame for their problems onto others, refusing to see their own responsibility. Others pretend to have it all together: with a facade of control, they deny the despair, confusion, or anger hidden inside. Still others sink into excesses like alcoholism, promiscuity, or overeating in order to numb their sense of personal failure.

Christians must learn to come out of hiding. We need to speak the truth, even though our honesty won't always be welcomed. "It is only as we honestly see who we really are before God, ourselves, and others that there can be a foundation for God's character to be developed within us."[10]

Honest confession is the crucible God uses to lead us toward change. When we honestly see ourselves and confess our sins to God, He can begin to reshape us.

When our friends see our willingness to look honestly at ourselves, they'll feel free to begin to look at themselves. As Christian helpers, we can give our friends permission to be totally honest with themselves first by accepting our own sin and weaknesses and then by communicating that same acceptance to them. As we encourage our friends to face their personal sin and failures, we'll help them assume personal responsibility and set the stage for action.

Guilt and Shame: What's Under the Cover?

Although the church should be the most obvious place where people can be open, honest, and vulnerable with one another, the opposite is often true. Confusing forgiveness with perfection, too many of us labor under the burden of "Now that I'm saved, I should have it all together." Consequently, we put on a veneer of composure when we're anxious, or we wear a facade of joy when we're feeling miserable. Our pride keeps us from facing the fact that we don't measure up to God's standards of perfection. If we honestly faced ourselves, we would experience pangs of both guilt and shame.

Guilt is the objective experience of failing to meet God's moral standards. Our daily lives demonstrate that we constantly fall short of who God intends us to be. Each time we tell a "white lie," deceive an employer, or hold a grudge against a friend, we fail to live up to our responsibility as divine image-bearers. Guilt is concerned about how God sees us.

Shame or embarrassment, on the other hand, are more personal and subjective. If you've ever suddenly become aware of something that you did and thought, "That couldn't have been me! I'm not the type of person who does things like *that*," then you've experienced shame. Shame worries about how other people see us.[11]

When we see ourselves for who we really are, we respond in one of four ways: we experience true guilt; we ignore our guilt; we experience false guilt; or we have no guilt.

True guilt. When we break one of God's commands and feel guilty, our feelings reflect a true state of affairs. For example, let's say that I promise to meet my friend Susan for lunch at 12:30, but I stop to do some errands on the way. I think to myself, *Sue won't mind if I'm late.* As a result, I don't arrive until 1:00, thereby breaking my commitment to her. I will experience both guilt in not keeping my word and embarrassment when she sees that I'm not a very punctual person.

Ignored guilt. The second response is to ignore the guilt when we've done something wrong. Let's say that when I arrive at the restaurant, I try to cover up for my lateness by making excuses. I blame the traffic, the weather, or the baby-sitter, trying to find a way to rationalize my failure to Susan. I might even lie to hide the embarrassment I feel. It's easier to put up a false front of innocence than face my failure and guilt. If this were a repeated pattern, my conscience could even become dulled to my sin and guilt.

False guilt. The third response is to experience false guilt; we feel guilty even though we haven't disobeyed one of God's laws. False or misdirected guilt is a result of false standards. Let's imagine that as I drive to the restaurant, I tell myself that I'm really stupid to be getting there late and that because I'm such a lousy friend, Susan will never want to go out with me again. I'm now exaggerating the situation. On top of not keeping my commitment, I'm dumping the "sin" of being a bad friend. In fact, I'm feeling guilty for the wrong thing. My true guilt is an underlying pride that says, "I should be a perfect person who is never late."

When we create standards that are not directly set down in God's Word, we set up a breeding ground for false guilt.[12] Many Christians experience tremendous guilt over what they think is sin but what really is an expectation they have set for themselves or one they have adopted from others.

No guilt. The fourth response is to experience no guilt. We can be "not guilty" in only two ways: if we don't sin or if our sin is forgiven. I wouldn't be guilty if I had arrived at the restaurant on time. Susan and I would have had a pleasant, enjoyable lunch uncomplicated by my lateness, excuses, or profuse apologies. On the other hand, if I had arrived late and acknowledged my failure to keep our appointed time, apologized, and received Susan's forgiveness, then I also wouldn't be guilty. Her forgiveness would set me free and put my sin into the past.

The only way to truly stand as "not guilty" is through the atoning work of Christ. This is the position and privilege for all those who confess their sins and ask for God's forgiveness. Our consciences are clear, and we aren't ashamed to face others either.

The Problem of Pride

Ever since the Fall, human beings have been motivated by pride. Our pride interferes with our relationship to God, to ourselves, and to others.

Pride as selfishness. Just as Adam and Eve elevated their will above God's, we also try to have things our way. And when God doesn't do what we want Him to, we conclude that He isn't fair. Disappointment can infiltrate our relationship to God so that we end up doubting His wisdom and His will.

Pride as false piety. It may sound surprising, but underestimating ourselves also demonstrates a type of pride. When we put ourselves down ("I always fail at everything. I'm not good enough to merit God's love") or berate ourselves ("I'm no good; no one likes me"), we replace God's criteria with our own standards. We make God's love academic by saying to our Savior, "I'm unredeemable; not even Your love can save me." This pride keeps us from relying on God's mercy. In fact, this kind of self-hatred can even be a form of self-worship.

Pride as superiority. If we think we are better than others, we often communicate this through a proud, haughty attitude. Pride can be the motivation for criticism and faultfinding, or pride can surface as a stubborn refusal to admit wrong. If you find yourself constantly arguing your point of view and refusing to acknowledge other people's opinions, you're probably guilty of overestimating yourself! Pride also expresses itself in a facade of toughness that refuses to admit weakness or personal need.

Is there ever room for pride in the Christian's life? When we honestly examine ourselves, we find the talents with which God has blessed us and which He expects us to use.[13] We can feel "proud" of what, by God's grace, we can do. At this point we can agree with Paul that "by the grace of God I am what I am" (1 Cor. 15:10a).

Pride usually reflects our weak attempts at making ourselves appear better than we really are. Unable to face our sin, guilt, weaknesses, and shame, we pretend to be someone we're not.

The Problem of Acceptance

Like Adam and Eve, we experience shame when we fail. We feel the same fears and insecurities that drove them into hiding. If we honestly face ourselves, we wonder how God could possibly accept us. But God is merciful. He sees us at our worst and doesn't turn His back on us. In fact, He does the reverse. Like the father in Luke 15, He welcomes us, even with the dirt of sin muddying our feet. In His love, God sees our sin and gives us a way to be cleansed and forgiven. By sending Jesus as a sacrifice for us, God shows His perfect love and acceptance.

Can I accept myself? If we don't know God's acceptance, we look to ourselves or to others for approval and affirmation. Often these sources prove unreliable and disappointing. Trying to compensate for feelings of worthlessness or self-hatred, we set up a list of "ifs" that we vainly hope will guarantee acceptance. For instance, one person may think "I'll be respected and loved if I'm successful at work." Another concludes, "I'll be admired for my strength if I control my emotions." Both people are mistaken about the nature of true self-acceptance. They are idolizing other people's approval.

Shame and lack of self-acceptance are also felt when people fail to attain their dreams: the single person who isn't married by thirty-five, the "company man" who is fired after twenty-five years of service, the high school dropout all share the same feeling of "I'll never be the person that I hoped to be." Feeling this despair, some people give up on themselves entirely. In extreme situations this can lead a person to suicide—the final act of self-rejection.

The gap between who we are and who we want to be is one that we all face. Our efforts to close this gap can mean the difference between a life of despair and a life of contentment. As Christians, our search for peace and self-acceptance must find its satisfaction in God.

Can I accept you?   In blaming Eve for his sin, Adam rejected her, breaking their relationship of trust and intimacy (Gen. 3:12). In this way Adam established a pattern not only of self-rejection but also of rejecting others.

Similarly, when we fail to accept ourselves, we often fail to accept the people around us. There is a gap between who our friends, children, employees, or roommates *are* and who *we'd like them to be*. Our unmet wishes and expectations often result in conflict. Our shame over who someone else is (or isn't) becomes the breeding ground for rejection and broken relationships.

The Problem of Ignorance

A lack of information isn't sinful in itself, but ignorance often is compounded by sin. Although we are meant to learn as we grow and develop, sin often interferes with that learning. For example, a young girl who doesn't learn how to control her temper may grow into a woman who always wants her own way. A boy who hears from childhood that he is dumb and stupid will grow up believing that he can never accomplish anything. In these cases the children are victims not only of their own ignorance but also of their parents' lack of information on how to raise their children.

A lack of basic "how-to" information can be very frustrating. A Cambodian family who doesn't know how to operate within the American culture, a retired accountant who doesn't know what to do with his time, or a couple who don't know how to communicate with each other are all handicapped by their lack of skills and information. Anger, discouragement, depression, and apathy can follow on the heels of ignorance.

The Problems of Evil, Sickness, and Death

We must recognize that we're constantly involved in a spiritual battle against the rulers, the powers, and the forces of darkness and wickedness in the heavenly places (Eph. 6:12). Although Satan's power was ultimately defeated at the Cross (1 Cor. 15:55–57; Heb. 2:14), God has allowed Satan, the author of evil, limited influence in the world. Scripture teaches that Satan continuously tries to tempt us away from God (Gen. 3:4–5).

We see Satan's grip on the world influencing every act of rebellion. He is in the background, ensuring that spiritual battles will continue until Christ returns. On a global level, we see his influence in a world marked by wars, corruption, and poverty. On a personal level, as Christians, we see him tempting our remaining, indwelling sinful desires. Although God has permitted Satan a limited influence, we're still responsible to resist his temptations (James 4:7).

We also are not shielded from the full range of sickness and disease. From colds to measles, from an infant born with Down's syndrome to a father dying of lung cancer, we are constantly reminded of our mortality. Occasionally we even experience some emotional problems that have a distinct physiological origin.[14]

Medical problems can be a great source of stress for people and their families. The more serious the problem is and the more it limits a person, the more far reaching its effects will be. All serious illness represents some type of loss. The accompanying grief is especially intensified in the experiences of terminal illness, death, and bereavement.

Each of us has experienced evil, has fallen sick, or has lost a loved one. Although we can't always control the events in our lives, God does call us to control our *response* to those events.

Summary

Where does this leave us? We're faced with the fact that in a fallen world, people experience pain, problems, and struggles. We can't escape it. We can't hide from it. This could leave us feeling overwhelmed and helpless. But as Christians, we must look upward and see that we're not alone. God promises that our weaknesses will be the pathway for His strength (2 Cor. 12:10). As we embrace that promise, we'll receive the power we need to help ourselves and others.

Before going on to the next chapter, work through the questions in the Personal and Practical section. These questions will help you apply what you have just studied.

PERSONAL AND PRACTICAL

Study the Scriptures

1. Name several aspects of God's nature. What are our basic needs? How do these truths influence how you help others?
2. What does 1 John 1:8–10 teach about human nature? How does this relate to helping others? Think of a personal situation when you could have applied the truth of these verses. What hindered this application?
3. Read 1 John 2:3–6, 9–11. What effect should holiness and love have on your Christian life? List at least three ways you can demonstrate these characteristics.
4. What are the main promises found in Romans 5:1–2 and Romans 3:21–28? What does this tell you about who God is? How can you apply this to a Christian friend who feels that he or she isn't good enough for God's love?
5. Read Romans 5:6–8 and 8:1–3b. How could you use this passage in counseling a girl who had an abortion before she became a Christian?
6. What would you say to a co-worker who tells you that he has falsified his expense account? He attends church occasionally and sees himself as basically a good person. What Scripture passages would you refer to in your conversation?

For Thought

1. When have you experienced guilt? Read Psalm 90:8 and ask God to show you some of your secret sins.
2. When have you experienced shame? When do you have difficulty allowing others to *really* know you?
3. What types of pride do you experience?
4. What problems do you have accepting yourself or others?
5. Write down three goals for your training as a lay counselor. How will you be able to tell when you are helping others more effectively? Be prepared to share these goals the next time your study group meets.
6. Look up the following Scripture passages and meditate on God's personal knowledge of you: 1 Samuel 16:7; Jeremiah 17:9–10; Amos 4:13; Ps. 139:1–4; Romans 11:33–34.

For Further Reading

1. Read chapter 6 of William Kirk Kilpatrick's *Psychological Seduction* (Nashville: Thomas Nelson Publishers, 1983) for a description of the Christian's need to confront sin honestly.
2. Read chapters 2 and 4 of William Kirwan's *Biblical Concepts for Christian Counseling* (Grand Rapids: Baker Book House, 1984) for his view of the biblical perspective of mankind and the loss of personal identity.
3. Read chapter 5 of Rebecca Pippert's *Out of the Saltshaker: Evangelism As a Way of Life* (Downers Grove, Illinois: InterVarsity Press, 1979) for an application of living out holiness in your life.
4. Consult John Carter and Bruce Narramore's *The Integration of Psychology and Theology* (Grand Rapids: Zondervan Publishing House, 1979) or William Kirwan's *Biblical Concepts for Christian Counseling* for more information about the integration of psychology and theology.
5. Read Bruce Narramore's *No Condemnation* (Grand Rapids: Zondervan Publishing House, 1984) for a deeper analysis of the experience of guilt.
6. Read Elizabeth Skoglund's *Growing Through Rejection*

(Wheaton, Illinois: Tyndale House Publishers, 1983) for a discussion of how we grow through the experience of self-rejection and shame.

NOTES

[1] William Kirwan, *Biblical Concepts for Christian Counseling* (Grand Rapids: Baker Book House, 1984), p. 81.

[2] See J. I. Packer's *Knowing God* (Downers Grove, Illinois: InterVarsity Press, 1973) for a complete discussion of God's nature.

[3] Barry Seagran, "Who is God?," *What in the World Is Real?* (Champaign, Illinois: Communication Institute, 1982), p. 300.

[4] Ibid.

[5] Sinclair Ferguson, *Know Your Christian Life* (Downers Grove: Inter-Varsity Press, 1981), p. 9.

[6] Seagran, "Who is Man?," *What in the World Is Real?*, p. 307–8.

[7] Randall Grossman, "Humanism—Christian or Secular?," *Fellowship News* (March/April 1984): 3.

[8] William Kirk Kilpatrick, *Psychological Seduction* (Nashville: Thomas Nelson Publishers, 1983), p. 74.

[9] Larry Crabb in his book *Encouragement* (Grand Rapids: Zondervan Publishing House, 1984) refers to this concept when he talks about the "layers" people use to protect themselves. See pp. 33–37 and 85–91.

[10] Greg Pritchard and Betsy Page, "Sharpen Your Thinking Through Discussion," *Insight* Vol. 2, No. 1 (Champaign, Illinois: Communication Institute, 1983), p. 33.

[11] For an excellent discussion of guilt and shame, see chapter 2 of Dick Keyes' *Beyond Identity* (Ann Arbor: Servant Books, 1984).

[12] Bruce Narramore, *No Condemnation* (Grand Rapids: Zondervan Publishing House, 1984), p. 20.

[13] See the parable of the talents in Matt. 25:14–30.

[14] For more information about the relationship of emotional problems to physiological causes, see Richard Lechtenberg's *Guide to Diseases of the Nervous System* (New York: Wiley, 1982).

‡

CHAPTER 2

JESUS, OUR MODEL COUNSELOR

Thou didst reach forth thy hand and mine enfold;
I walked and sank not on the storm-vexed sea;
'Twas not so much that I on Thee took hold,
As Thou, dear Lord, on me."
—*from "I Sought the Lord, and Afterward I Knew"*

God *re-cognizes* our sins: *he knows them again* from scratch as it were and, seeing us only in Jesus, sees us as his beloved Son. God *re-members* our iniquities: in his divine knowledge *he puts back into a living unity* the broken and dishonored fragments of the lives we lost in death and, holding as Jesus has *re-collected* them in his resurrection, clasps us to himself.[1]

The distinguishing characteristic of Christian counseling is that it's rooted in the person and work of Jesus Christ. This truth shapes the help that we give in three distinct ways. First, we *apply* Jesus' work on the Cross to our own lives. Second, we model our lives and behavior on the *person* of Jesus, thus becoming tangible evidence to others that God exists. Third, we help our friends apply Jesus' *work* to their lives and then help them to live like Him.

All four Gospels describe ways that Jesus is a unique person who represents all that is *morally* right and who embodies all virtue, truth, and goodness. Since His life was sinless (Heb. 4:15), Jesus is also the *model* of the perfect person. As

33

Christians, it is our privilege and responsibility to imitate Him (1 Cor. 11:1; Eph. 5:1). What does this mean? Should we wear sandals on our feet, hold conversations in Hebrew or Aramaic, and give up our homes or marriages in order to live as Jesus did? Imitating Christ means more than copying His outward behavior. Instead, we must examine Jesus' life story for a total picture of how to relate to others.

When we read the Gospels, we can listen to how Jesus talks and can ask ourselves, "What does this teach me about how to speak to others?" We can consider each time He listens compassionately, confronts sin, or gives hope. We can use each parable or anecdote to learn how God incarnate helped others. As Rebecca Pippert has written: "In Jesus, then, we have our model for how to relate to the world. . . . We must learn then to relate transparently and genuinely to others because that is God's style of relating to us."[2]

We face one danger in considering Jesus as our model counselor. We can feel overwhelmed as we compare His wise counsel with our weak attempts at helping others. If we understand His love for us, then His model will be an *inspiration* for us, not an *infliction* on us. Although we can't be absolutely like Him, we must try to follow the helping pattern that He established.

As a helpful friend, we can point others to Jesus' model. A friend did this for me by giving me a T-shirt on which was printed: "Want to meet super counselor?" in large, colorful letters. Then, in much smaller letters underneath, she had embroidered, "You'll find Him in the Gospel." We all need constantly to point our friends to the one "super" counselor—Jesus.

WHAT WAS JESUS' WORK ON THE CROSS?

Central to a Christian helper's job is the ability to communicate how the incarnation of Christ is meaningful to us today. We can find its relevance by looking at two different aspects of Christ's work: what He accomplished on the Cross and how He interacted with the people He encountered.

What Happened at the Cross?

In chapter 1 we saw how our sin separates us from God. Because of the Fall, we are incomplete vessels, broken by sin, failure, and weakness. If this were the final picture of mankind, it would be a gloomy one indeed. But, praise God, He has taken pity on our spiritual and emotional needs and has provided reconciliation, forgiveness, and acceptance through the work of Jesus Christ. How did this restoration take place?

Jesus' death on the Cross demonstrated God's absolute holiness and His perfect love. Paul explains this in Romans 3:

> There is no difference, for all have sinned and fall short of the glory of God, and are justified freely by his grace through the redemption that came by Christ Jesus. God presented him as a sacrifice of atonement, through faith in his blood. He did this to demonstrate his justice, because in his forbearance he had left the sins committed beforehand unpunished—he did it to demonstrate his justice at the present time, so as to be just and the one who justifies those who have faith in Jesus (vv. 22b–26).

This is an amazing fact: our God is both *just* and the *justifier*. But how can a holy, just God look with favor upon sinful men and women?

Paul states that we're "justified freely by his grace" (Rom. 3:24). Dr. Sinclair Ferguson, a noted theologian, writes that the word *justification* means "being made righteous," or "being in a right relationship." He goes on to say that, "The glory of the gospel is that God has declared Christians to be rightly related to him in spite of their sin."[3]

We're restored to a right relationship to God because of Christ's death. As Paul wrote to the Ephesians: "But now in Christ Jesus you who once were far away have been brought near through the blood of Christ" (Eph. 2:13; see also Rom. 5:1–2, 6–9). He *is* our righteousness (1 Cor. 1:30). We receive this righteousness as a gift—unearned, unmerited, and undeserved (Rom. 3:28; Eph. 2:4–5, 8–9).

Thus, the separation that occurred at the Fall is restored at the Cross. The debt for our sin has been paid. The wrath of God that we deserve has been placed upon Jesus (Heb. 9:22, 28a; 1 Peter 3:18a; 1 John 4:10). Through His work of atonement, our relationship to God is healed.

As repentant sinners we have this extravagant hope: God has freely delivered us from the justly deserved consequence of hell. In place of condemnation and eternal separation, God gives us justification and eternal life. We are totally forgiven and received (Ps. 103:8–14; Rom. 6:23b). As Christian helpers, we must know this hope and healing ourselves in order to communicate it, by word and deed, to our friends, neighbors, and all whom we meet.

What Are the Results of the Cross?

In chapter 1 we saw how as a result of the Fall we suffer from various problems. Let's look at how the Cross answers each of these problems.

We can come out from hiding. One of the first things Adam and Eve did after they disobeyed God was hide. They were guilty and ashamed of their sin, and they chose to hide rather than to face God, themselves, or each other. Following in their footsteps, we also tend to hide because of our feelings of guilt and shame. We try to cover up by blaming, rationalizing, denying, or making excuses.

The good news is that God has provided a way for us to come out from hiding. Jesus' work on the Cross helps us honestly and openly *confront* ourselves since we are assured of the *comfort* of His forgiveness and acceptance. Because Jesus is our adequacy, we are free to face our inadequacy.

Jesus is the answer to our guilt. When we sin, we fall short of God's standards and are guilty. Knowing this, King David looked forward to a time when those who trusted in God would not be found guilty: "The LORD redeems his servants; no one will be condemned who takes refuge in him" (Ps. 34:22). Paul shows us that this promise was fulfilled in Christ: "Therefore, there is now no condemnation for those who are in Christ Jesus" (Rom. 8:1). Christ's atoning work obtains freedom from condemnation. Our guilt is removed—God's forgiveness has freed us from guilt's paralyzing power.

Jesus is the answer to our shame. Shame on the other hand, is the embarrassment we feel when we, along with the people around us, see our mistakes or failures. In the same psalm, David also looks forward to a time when he will look upon God without being ashamed. The pages of the New Testament unfold how Jesus fulfills this prophecy and removes our shame.

The Incarnation itself demonstrates that God is not ashamed of us. Jesus was not embarrassed by His humanity. In fact He chose to become like us in flesh and blood, calling us His brothers (Heb. 2:11–17). Second, like the father who embraced the rebellious son when he returned home, Jesus also welcomes us in spite of our rebellion (Luke 15:11–24; see also Rom. 15:7). It's as if He's saying, "I know you are sinners. I see your failures, faults, and weaknesses. *And* I have determined to love you in spite of them all." The final proof that God is not ashamed of us is that He uses the weak and broken vessels of our lives for His kingdom work. In fact, our weaknesses are often the very thing He uses to glorify Himself (2 Cor. 12:9–10)!

Jesus is the answer to our pride. When we stand before the Cross, we are able to see ourselves for who we really are: self-centered and proud sinners. As we understand the full implications of Jesus' death, we become convinced that His way is the only way of doing things; we see that we are no better than anyone else; and we admit that though we don't deserve it, God has loved and forgiven us. The Cross humbles our proud hearts.

Jesus teaches us how to accept ourselves and others. Guilty and ashamed, we have a problem accepting ourselves and others. Since the Cross restores our relationship to God, it also gives us the only true source of self-acceptance: our heavenly Father's approval. His love ends our struggle to accept ourselves, to be valued, and to have purpose. As Dr. Larry Crabb has written: "True significance and security are available only to the Christian, one who is trusting in Christ's perfect life and substitutionary death as his sole basis of acceptability before a holy God."[4]

Then as we realize and receive Jesus' love, we can become channels of His love to others. As Christians, we receive new eyesight that allows us to see our friends (and enemies) as God sees them—guilty and imperfect people, in need of His grace. Our standard can be nothing less than what Christ said to His disciples: "Love each other as I have loved you" (John 15:12b) and "Love your enemies" (Matt. 5:44).

Jesus is the truth. In the last chapter we saw that sometimes our friends' problems are a result of a lack of information. In our fallen world we don't have access to every fact or detail that we need to live peacefully. But Jesus has come to break that bondage to ignorance. He *is* the truth. His words guide us into a real understanding of Himself, ourselves, and the world around us. Through relationship to Him we can see and know things for what they really are.

Jesus has won the victory over evil, sickness, and death. What does the message of the Cross say to you as you help your friend whose wife was raped or another whose life is wracked by physical pain or another whose son died a tragic death?

Jesus came into this world *specifically* to destroy Satan's works and to defeat his power (1 John 3:8b–10). The rule, reign, authority, and dominion of sin were broken at the Cross. Jesus shared in our humanity so that "by his death he might destroy him who holds the power of death—that is, the devil—and free those who all their lives were held in slavery by their fear of death" (Heb. 2:14; see also 1 Cor. 15:54–57). Then through the powerful act of His resurrection, Jesus showed that He conquered sin and death (Rom. 6:4, 6–7). The effects of the Fall have been reversed forever.

This hope of ultimate eternal deliverance also provides comfort for those who are sick and ill. For no matter how painful, terrifying, or degenerating a sickness is, it doesn't have ultimate control over the believer. We can look forward to the time when our decaying earthly "tents" will be removed and when we'll receive eternal bodies that are perfect in immortality (2 Cor. 5:1–5).

Every one of these victories is already fulfilled in Christ. We experience a taste of them now. What joy will be ours when we see their complete fulfillment when Jesus returns!

What Is Our Response to the Cross?

We take our first step back to God when we confess that we stand as guilty sinners before Him. With sorrow, humility, shame, and hatred for our sin, we repent and seek God's pardon and power to renew us. By repenting, we show our desire to change from a life-style of sin to a life-style in which we trust and obey Christ (2 Cor. 7:8–11). Repentance is both a response *to* God's love and a response generated *by* His love.

Similarly, obedience is also a love response to what God has done for us. As we obey God, we'll find ourselves becoming more like Christ. When we submit our lives to God, He gives us new identities as his sons and daughters (John 1:12; 1 Cor. 15:49; 1 John 3:2). What value and worth is given to us through Jesus' death! What love God invested in us at the Cross!

Dr. Ferguson summarizes this beautifully: "As I look at myself, I see failure, sin, sometimes shame and disgrace. But that is neither the ultimate nor the whole truth about me as a Christian. No! I am united to Christ, a joint-heir of his riches, a child of God. Knowing this to be the real truth about me lends grace and power to my life."⁵

Our identity as forgiven sinners is the cornerstone of Christianity. The privilege and reward of Christian helping is leading our Christian friends to discover their full identity in Christ and helping them apply God's grace, love, and forgiveness to their lives.

Let's look at the specific ways that Jesus helped the people He met. In studying His relationships, we'll find a pattern of how we can help our friends.

JESUS, THE WONDERFUL COUNSELOR

The threads of Jesus' counseling role can be traced from the Old Testament through the New. The prophet Isaiah gives us several glimpses of what our heavenly counselor is like. First, we find a list of His names. "For to us a child is born, to us a son is given, and the government will be on His shoulders. And he will be called *Wonderful Counselor,* Mighty God, Everlasting Father, Prince of Peace" (Isa. 9:6, italics added).

Isaiah writes that this man will have the "Spirit of the Lord" and be full of wisdom, understanding, counsel, power, knowledge, and the fear of God (Isa. 11:2). Isaiah 53 describes Him as a humble servant who will be wounded for our transgressions and crushed for our iniquities (Isa. 53:5, 10). This wonderful counselor will preach the good news to the poor, bind up the broken-hearted, release the prisoners, and comfort the mourners (Isa. 61:1–2).

Turning to the New Testament, we find these promises fulfilled in the person of Christ. We read in Luke how as a child, Jesus amazed the rabbis and teachers with His understanding (Luke 2:47). As an adult, He constantly startled the religious leaders with His wisdom, authority, and teaching (Matt. 7:28–29; Mark 6:2; Luke 4:16–21). Wherever Jesus went, He ministered, healed, and comforted. And then at His death, we see a man so concerned for our sin, that He gave His life as a sacrifice for us (Heb. 2:12). Here, then, is our Messiah, the wonderful counselor promised in the Old Testament and incarnated in the New.

Looking through the accounts of His ministry, we find that Jesus related to the people as a prophet, priest, and king. As the *prophet,* He spoke words of *confrontation;* as the *priest,* He spoke words of *comfort;* and as the *king,* He spoke words of *direction.* In chapter 1 we saw how God *confronts* us with His holiness and *comforts* us with His love. Now we'll see how Jesus carried out these functions in ways that directed people to change.

Jesus, the Prophet

In His prophetic role, Jesus *confronts* us with the truth about ourselves and calls us to repentance.[6] Jesus proclaimed that mankind has sinned and needs reconciliation with God.

How does Jesus confront us? First, He confronts us simply by *who* He is. His life of perfect obedience and holiness is like a mirror into which we see how much we fall short of His divine example. Second, Jesus confronts us by *what* He says. His parables and words disarm His listeners. Without condemnation, Jesus' words of truth provoke and challenge those who listen to His message (Matt. 7:24–29). Third, more than any other person, Jesus sees us and speaks the truth to each one of us. He confronts us because He cares enough to be honest with us.

Confrontation involves two actions: identifying problems and then speaking the truth about these problems. Consider how Jesus used both of these actions in confronting His friend Martha (Luke 10). Here we find Martha trying to do a good job, running around getting the house and meals ready for Jesus and His disciples. Upset that her sister Mary had left her alone in order to listen to Him, Martha complained to Jesus.

How did our Lord respond? First, He identified Martha's problem: she was worried and upset about many things (Luke 10:41). In this way, Jesus confronted Martha's self-righteous attitude, her jealousy toward her sister, and her decision to make her work more important than listening to her Savior. Second, Jesus spoke the truth to Martha: the most important thing at that moment was for Martha to listen to Jesus. Meals and housework would come and go, but caring for her soul should never be abandoned.

Jesus never hesitated to communicate the truth when someone sinned (Matt. 15:1–14), but He was also quick to minister forgiveness and to point the person in the right direction. Jesus' confrontation, combined with His comfort, encouraged people toward change.

Jesus, the Priest

In His role as priest, Jesus personally *comforts* us by forgiving, strengthening, and sympathizing with us. Because of His deep concern for our problems and pain, He involves Himself in our lives, listens to us, hears our confession, and forgives us.[7]

The first way that He comforts us is by being our advocate. He is the one who speaks to God in our defense (1 John 2:1–2). But our heavenly attorney does something that no earthly lawyer is willing to do: He steps in and pays the penalty that we owe. In His love, Jesus covers all of our sins. What comfort is ours when we're touched by this cleansing forgiveness!

Jesus also brings comfort by understanding and sympathizing with us. Jesus walked where we walk. He was tempted (Matt. 4:1–11), suffered physical pain (Matt. 27:29–31; John 20:25), and felt emotional heartaches (John 11:35). He experienced pleasure in celebrating life's joys (John 2:1–10), anger when facing sin (Matt. 21:12–13), and anguish over disappointments (Matt. 23:37).

Jesus acted as a priest to those whom He met by becoming involved in their lives. He went to where the needs were and took the initiative to help others. He went out of His way to dine with the tax gatherers, to visit the sick and dying, and to minister to those possessed by demons. Jesus was accessible to the prostitutes and lepers. He cuddled children and mourned with the bereaved. He forgave and showed mercy. Jesus demonstrates to us a compassion void of fear or hesitation. No trace of disinterest, apathy, or detachment is found in our Lord's life and work.

Jesus, the priest, also took people's problems seriously by listening to them. He didn't ridicule people for their awkwardness, failures, or mistakes. He responded to people's doubts and questions. By His sincere listening, Jesus showed that He compassionately received the other person. This is demonstrated clearly in His interactions with Nicodemus (John 3:1–21). Jesus neither ridiculed Nicodemus for coming to Him at night nor did He laugh at his questions about being born again. Because Jesus desired Nicodemus' good, He welcomed his inquiry, listened patiently, and took his questions seriously. Furthermore, Jesus used the conversation as an opportunity to instruct Nicodemus about the spiritual truths he needed to hear.

Jesus, the King

Not only is our counselor a prophet and a priest, but Jesus is also our king (Jer. 23:5; Matt. 2:2; John 18:37; Rev. 1:5). In this role as ruler, Jesus dynamically *directs and guides* us. Although He commands our obedience, Jesus is not a merciless tyrant, demanding something we can't possibly give. His lordship is the tender authority of a shepherd who cares for his sheep by guiding them and protecting them.

Unfortunately, our first response, in many instances, to Christ's lordship is often not submission. Like stubborn sheep, we want to wander and run at will, unhindered by fences that confine and limit. We struggle with obeying His commandments, and we resist conforming to His direction. But ideally, submission is a love response to our master (John 14:23).

Coming under Jesus' authority demands a desire to change. We see this when He exhorted the man with the shriveled hand to rise, come forward, and stretch out his hand (Luke 6:8–10). The fact that the man rose in response to Jesus' words indicates that faith was taking root and that change had already begun inside his heart.

The desire to change always must be followed by action. When Peter was confronted by Jesus' demonstration of power, Peter called Him Lord, fell down, and recognized his own unworthiness by confessing to be a sinful man (Luke 5:1–11). Jesus responded to Peter's desire to change by challenging him to take action: "Come, follow me . . . and I will make you fishers of men" (Matt. 4:19). Scripture relates that at once Peter and his brother Andrew left their nets and followed Jesus. What a clear demonstration of faith followed by action!

Our Lord knows it's difficult for us to make changes in our lives, but He never stops encouraging us. When people lost hope, He showed them possibilities they had dismissed (Luke 24:25–26). When they lacked faith, He pointed out God's power (Matt. 19:26). And when they feared following Him, He showed His trustworthiness (Luke 8:22–25). With loving encouragement and honest confrontation, Jesus enables people to take action and change.

Summary

What do we learn then from Jesus, our model counselor? First, we learn that Jesus' life and death restores our broken relationship to God. The Cross either directly or indirectly answers all of the problems incurred by the Fall.

Second, we need to respond to *all* of who Jesus is. We can't take Him as our forgiving priest without also receiving Him as the prophet who confronts us and the king who directs us. Like the strands of a rope that are incomplete when separated, Jesus' holy confrontation is incomplete without His comforting love and His ruling power.

Third, we see that confrontation, comfort, and direction are all integral parts of relating to others. Jesus gives us a complete model of helping others. We follow His example each time that we listen attentively, speak the truth in love, or encourage a friend to action. Sometimes we may comfort, confront, or direct our friends at different points in their lives; other times we will exercise all three roles in one conversation.

Finally, let's remember that Jesus has made us prophets, priests, and kings. We have a responsibility to act toward each other in each of these three ways.

PERSONAL AND PRACTICAL

Study the Scriptures

1. Read Mark 2:1–12. How did the paralytic's friends help him? What characteristic did these friends show? What problems did Jesus address in the paralytic? List at least three implications of this passage for you as a helper.
2. Read Matthew 9:10. What did Jesus demonstrate by eating with the tax collectors and "sinners"? In what ways can you show that type of love and concern to others?
3. Read Matthew 14:14; Mark 1:41; 6:32–44; Luke 7:13–15. In each passage Jesus feels something for the people around him and then acts on it. What is this feeling and attitude, and what did it prompt Jesus to do? What does this model for you?
4. Look at the way Jesus confronted the adulterous woman and the Pharisees in John 8. Also read Matthew 7:3–5. What is Jesus' teaching about confrontation? What is His attitude as He confronts? How could you

apply this to yourself as a helper? In what counseling situations could you refer to these passages?

5. Read Luke 10:25–37. In this passage Jesus confronts the lawyer's attitude about himself. What is this attitude? How is it like the rich young ruler's attitude (Luke 18:18–29)? What action did Jesus exhort each to do? How would that change their attitude about themselves?

6. Read Luke 22:24–27. What was the disciples' problem? How did Jesus confront them? What truths did He speak to them?

7. Read Luke 24:13–35. Identify the following: How does Jesus show love and acceptance? What are the disciples' problems that Jesus confronts? How does Jesus encourage the disciples to take action? Identify the changes in the disciples' a) thoughts and beliefs, b) emotions, and c) behavior. Because the disciples did not recognize Jesus at first, they failed to take the help He was offering. When have you failed to see the help that either God or a friend was offering to you? When has someone not seen the help you were trying to offer? How did you feel? What did you do?

8. What might have been some of the obstacles Nicodemus, Martha, and Peter faced as they considered changing?

9. Read John 5:1–15. Why did Jesus ask the lame man if he wanted to get well? What was the significance of picking up his mat? of walking? (Hint: Consider these verses in light of Paul's admonitions in Col. 3:9–10).

For Thought

1. Consider how Jesus showed His concern by getting involved with people. How can you imitate Him? Think particularly of how you can show concern for a non-Christian. How would this be different from loving a believer you know very well?

2. Read the gospel of John and keep a record in your journal of each instance in which Jesus counsels the people around Him. List next to each example which stage of the helping process (confronting, comforting, directing) He is modeling.

3. What are some helping characteristics that you see Jesus model? Write down three that you plan to practice this week. (Examples: not judging others, patience, hopefulness.)
4. How could you use Isaiah 53:3–4 and Hebrews 4:14–16 when helping a friend? In what counseling situations would these passages bring comfort?
5. What are some ways you get to know someone? How do you communicate so that you understand the other person? What could happen if this step were overlooked?
6. Whom do you find particularly hard to feel compassion for? Consider what bothers you about that person and try to think of some new ways that you could reach out to him or her.
7. Are there ways you minimize other people's problems and don't take them seriously? Think of phrases like, "Don't worry. I'm sure God will . . ." or "That wasn't so bad. You should have seen what happened to me yesterday!" In what situations do you respond like this? What could you say instead?
8. How do you usually confront others? Try to think of particular phrases that you commonly use, like, "I can't believe that you . . ." or "You should never . . . ." Read Ephesians 4:15, 25. How could you lovingly confront someone?
9. How do you feel when you don't measure up to your expectations for yourself? Consider your answers to questions 1 and 2 from the For Thought section of chapter 1. How does Jesus provide the answer to your guilt and shame?
10. Write a brief paragraph describing what Jesus' death on the Cross means to you. Be specific.

For Further Reading

1. Read Duncan Buchanan's *The Counseling of Jesus* (Downers Grove, Illinois: InterVarsity Press, 1985) for a survey of the ways in which Jesus met and talked to people.
2. Read Bruce Narramore's *You're Someone Special* (Grand Rapids: Zondervan Publishing House, 1978) for

further discussion of our acceptance through Christ's work on the Cross.

3. Read chapter 5 of William Kirwan's *Biblical Concepts for Christian Counseling* (Grand Rapids: Baker Book House, 1984) for an excellent description of how our relationship to God restores our personal identity.

NOTES

[1] Robert Farrar Capon, *The Youngest Day* (New York: Harper & Row, 1983), quoted in *Eternity* (July/August 1983): 32.

[2] Rebecca Pippert, *Out of the Saltshaker: Evangelism As a Way of Life* (Downers Grove, Illinois: InterVarsity Press), p. 34.

[3] Sinclair Ferguson, *Know Your Christian Life* (Downers Grove, Illinois: InterVarsity Press, 1981), pp. 71–72.

[4] Lawrence Crabb, *Effective Biblical Counseling* (Grand Rapids: Zondervan Publishing House, 1977), pp. 70–71.

[5] Ferguson, *Know Your Christian Life*, p. 100.

[6] David E. Carlson, "Jesus' Style of Relating: The Search for a Biblical View of Counseling," *Psychology and Christianity: Integrative Readings*, ed. J. R. Fleck and J. Carter (Nashville: Abingdon Press, 1981), p. 237.

[7] Ibid., pp. 237–38.

‡

CHAPTER 3

THE HOLY SPIRIT, OUR HELPER

And I will ask the Father, and He will give you another Helper, that He may be with you forever.

—*John 14:16* NASB

"God is timeless, but the Spirit becomes for us the present-tense application of God's nature. . . . In the Spirit we have the indwelling contact point between heaven and earth across which run connections with the sustainer of the universe."[1]

WHO IS THE HOLY SPIRIT?

The Third Person of the Trinity often is not fully appreciated or understood. Yet we shouldn't underestimate His importance. Scripture describes the Holy Spirit as the conveyer of God's power (Acts 1:8; 1 Cor. 2:4–5). As Christian helpers, we need to avail ourselves of this power. To learn how to do that, we'll study the person and work of the Holy Spirit. We'll discover how He "stands alongside" each helper in the body of Christ and how He confronts, comforts, and directs believers toward action and change.

Jesus introduces His disciples to the Holy Spirit (John 14 and 16) by using the Greek name *paraklete* (John 14:16). This word can be translated as "helper," "consoler," "advocate," "comforter," "counselor," "intercessor," or "strengthener."

These names communicate the many ways in which the Holy Spirit helps us.

The Spirit is personally involved with each one of us. He stands alongside each believer—abiding *with* us and living *in* us (John 14:16–17). He enables us to understand *who* God is and *what* He has done for us (1 Cor. 2:10–12). The Holy Spirit's "principal gift to us is to take of the things of Christ and show them unto us."[2] The Spirit makes Jesus, the incarnate Word, alive to us today.

The Holy Spirit also meets four of our basic spiritual needs: He gives new life to the spiritually dead; He brings alienated men and women into fellowship with God; He makes sinners holy; and He fills empty people with power.

The Spirit Makes Us New

John records Jesus' teaching that the Spirit is the one who regenerates us, the one who gives us new life (John 6:63). In this divine act, God changes us at the inner core of our being: "Regeneration is not simply a change of acts, a reformation of life, a renovation of man's thoughts, words and deeds. But in regeneration the Holy Spirit touches the spirit of man, which is itself the root of all these actions. He goes to the heart of the matter—the heart of man, the inner core—which is the central, underlying source of all man's activities."[3]

As we help others, we'll see that their attitudes must be changed before they will desire good and be able to avoid sin. The Holy Spirit accomplishes this by changing people's hearts so that they want to use their intellects, wills, and emotions *for* God instead of *against* Him.

We must remember that renewal is the Holy Spirit's work, not ours (Titus 3:4–6). Simultaneously God holds us responsible to exercise our minds, to believe, and then to act on that belief. Regeneration renews our intellects, emotions, and all of our faculties so that we are free to serve God fully.

Regeneration links us to our Creator, for our renewal is executed *by* Him and acquired *from* Him: "Our true identity is found in accepting our status as creatures of this infinite Creator God and in rooting our sense of identity in his."[4] One of the aspects of being made new is that we receive new identities as members of God's family.

The Spirit Makes Us God's Children

From the moment we first believe, we are "adopted" into an intimate relationship with God the Father. As a result, we are no longer under the authority of sin but under the new authority of God the Father (Rom. 6:1–14).[5]

In a well-known passage in Romans, Paul describes the doctrine of adoption and the role the Holy Spirit plays: "For all who are being led by the Spirit, these are the sons of God. For you have not received a spirit of slavery leading to fear again, but you have received a spirit of adoption as sons by which we cry out, 'Abba! Father!' The Spirit Himself bears witness with our spirit that we are children of God" (Rom. 8:14–16 NASB).

The Holy Spirit reminds us that we are firmly united to God as His sons and daughters even when we fail to live up to His standards. "The Holy Spirit is God's guarantee that once we are adopted sons, we shall always be his sons, never being snatched out of his hands (John 10:28)."[6] The indwelling Holy Spirit is a mark that identifies us as always belonging to our heavenly Father.

Along with our new status as members of God's family, we also receive new privileges and responsibilities. Our privileges include a familiarity that allows us to come boldly to God with our needs and a confidence that allows us to trust Him to work out all things for our good. Our responsibility includes fitting ourselves into God's family by trying to become like our heavenly Father (1 John 3:3; 4:11–12).[7]

As we take on our new identity as children of God, we'll lead transformed lives. Our bondage to sin is over, because the Holy Spirit enables us to live holy lives.

The Spirit Makes Us Holy

We are children by birth and become more like God's children as we mature. Similarly, we are holy by God's election and become holy in the process of sanctification (Col. 3:12). Through the sanctifying work of the Holy Spirit, the believer is purified, is made holy, and is transformed into the likeness of Christ (2 Cor. 3:18).

The first result of sanctification is we achieve victory over sin. Although we still battle with sin, the outcome of the war has been decided.

The second result of sanctification is fruit bearing. In sanctification, we demonstrate the spiritual qualities that flow out of our relationship to Jesus. Thus we receive power from the Spirit to exercise self-control with a fellow church member who is very argumentative or to welcome an ex-prisoner into our congregation. The Holy Spirit's presence is evident in helpers who display the fruit of the Spirit (Gal. 5:22-23).

Recognizing that the Holy Spirit is our power source also provides the proper motivation for our work. Bearing fruit is not a means by which we earn God's stamp of approval. Our work and ministry are an outward demonstration of our relationship to Christ, not blue ribbons to be displayed to win the praise of others. We constantly must remember that our accomplishments are the result of the indwelling Spirit, not the result of our own efforts. Our lives are empty vessels that are best used when filled with the Holy Spirit.

The Spirit Gives Us Power

Just as the Holy Spirit continuously makes us holy, so He also constantly fills us with His power. We receive the Spirit's filling by acknowledging our emptiness and by looking upward to God for His filling. The Spirit's fullness is not a reward for our greatness but power for our weakness. Receiving the Holy Spirit when we are needy strengthens our dependence and trust in God.[8]

The most visible outworking of the Spirit's filling is that we find the full power to do the work that God has given us. By the Spirit's power we'll be able to resist temptation and we'll want to do God's work and follow His Word.

Now that we've seen how the Holy Spirit meets the believer's spiritual needs, let's consider the specific ways that we, as helpers, need Him.

THE HOLY SPIRIT AND US

Without the Holy Spirit's divine power our efforts to help will be incomplete. The Holy Spirit helps us in two specific ways: He is every Christian helper's personal counselor and counseling consultant.

Our Personal Counselor

In the role of counselor, the Holy Spirit confronts and comforts each helper. Each time we are convicted of sin, confess, repent, and receive God's comforting forgiveness, we grow in our ability to communicate the wonder of God's forgiveness to others (Eph. 4:32). Similarly, each time we are comforted during a difficult time, we grow in our ability to comfort our friends. As Paul wrote: "Praise be to the God and Father of our Lord Jesus Christ, the Father of compassion and the God of all comfort, who comforts us in all our troubles *so that we can comfort those in any trouble with the comfort we ourselves have received from God*" (2 Cor. 1:3–4, italics added).

A life that points to God as the one who walked with us through a difficult time stands as an example to a friend who is struggling with similar problems. Sharing how God has changed and helped us also counteracts our friends' assumption that we "have it all together." Furthermore, it keeps us humble. The more we communicate how we have been helped by the Holy Spirit, the more we will make Him known to others.

Our Personal Consultant

We need to remember that we aren't in charge of the helping process—the Holy Spirit is. The Holy Spirit gives the power and wisdom we need in order to be effective helpers (Rom. 15:18–19; 1 Cor. 2:4).

Through prayer, we must seek the power of our divine consultant. We need to think of the Holy Spirit as the invisible counselor who is beside us and our friends. As we counsel, we can send up a silent cry for help, asking for the Spirit's guidance, direction, and wisdom. Like Paul, we must pray in the Spirit with all kinds of prayers and requests on all occasions (Eph. 6:18).

Sometimes when we help a friend, we don't know what to say or do. If you've ever talked with a young man who is ready to give up on his life or if you've tried to comfort a couple who have been childless for twelve years of marriage, then you know the frustrations and limitations of helping. Remember Jesus' promise that the Holy Spirit always stands alongside us and shows us what to say (John 14:25–26; Luke 12:12).

Sometimes we don't even know how to pray. Even then God doesn't leave us without resources. His Word promises that the Holy Spirit is our divine intercessor: "In the same way, the Spirit helps us in our weakness. We do not know what we ought to pray for, but the Spirit himself intercedes for us with groans that words cannot express. And he who searches our hearts knows the mind of the Spirit, because the Spirit intercedes for the saints in accordance with God's will" (Rom. 8:26–27). What a relief to know that our personal counselor and consultant will bring *all* our thoughts to our heavenly Father!

The Holy Spirit, our divine consultant, will give us insight into each person's needs and into how we can apply God's Word. Although each of our friends experiences pain, failure, or discouragement in an individual way, the gospel gives a universal message to all. Our job as helpers will be to make God's Word *relevant* to the bored housewife, the lonely college student, or the worried father. The Scriptures are the voice of the Spirit, speaking to each person in his or her particular problems and situation (Prov. 1:1–6; 2 Tim. 3:16).⁹

As believers, we are comforted and led by the Holy Spirit. Let's look to Him as our model and become "parakletic" helpers, who "inspire others to action, awaken spiritual interest, [and] steady those who are buffeted or faltering."¹⁰ As we yield ourselves to the Spirit, we become available to accomplish His purposes in our friends' lives.

THE HOLY SPIRIT AND OUR FRIENDS

How does the Holy Spirit help our friends? Let's look at three ways that the Holy Spirit comes alongside them.

The Holy Spirit Confronts Our Friends

Jesus called the Holy Spirit the "Spirit of truth" (John 14:17; 15:26). This role is embodied in the Greek word *noutheteo,* which means "to teach," "to admonish," "to warn," "to rebuke," "to reprove," or "to confront." *Noutheteo* suggests the act of calling a person's attention to something important.

What is the truth the Holy Spirit speaks? Jesus summarizes the content of the Spirit's message in John 16:8: "He will convict the world of guilt in regard to sin and righteousness and judgment." In other words, the Holy Spirit shows our friends where they stand in relationship to God and how they need to change. As He works in a person's heart, He is like a prosecuting attorney in a courtroom. In this role He convicts them and declares God's indictment against sinners.[11]

The purpose of conviction of sin is to bring a person to Christ in humility and desire: "It is in proportion to our sense of our need that we are able to grasp the measure of God's grace. The more aware we become of our personal condition, through conviction, the more remarkable does the love of God for us seem to be."[12] Only where there is honest confrontation with guilt and sin will a person receive God's healing forgiveness. Honest confrontation leads us to the comfort of the Cross.

The Holy Spirit Comforts Our Friends

Christ used the word *paraklete* to describe the Holy Spirit. The verb form of that word is *parakaleo,* meaning "to advocate for," "to help," "to exhort," "to cheer on," "to encourage," or "to comfort." This word implies being present and available to someone who needs support and encouragement.

The Holy Spirit provides comfort in three ways. First, the Holy Spirit presents the hope of the gospel: Jesus lived and died so that whoever believes in Him can have new life. Second, the Holy Spirit pleads Jesus' case for our friends. He is like a defense attorney, speaking against Satan, the "accuser." When Satan accuses our believing friends that they are imperfect and worthless, the Holy Spirit reassures them that they are redeemed children of the living God. Third, the Holy Spirit comforts our friends when they are struggling with discouragement, disappointment, or other trials.

The Holy Spirit Encourages Our Friends to Action and Change

The Holy Spirit is also an agent of change. He gives us new life when we are saved and then continues the process of transformation throughout our lives. The Spirit's activity in this context can be summarized in the Greek word, *dunamoo,* which means "to enable" or "to strengthen." This word conveys the idea of empowering someone to change. Jay Adams writes that the Holy Spirit's "activity is everywhere represented as the dynamic and power behind the personality changes in God's people.''[13]

As the author of change, the Spirit uses the Word of God to convince our friends of the changes they need to make in their lives. The Spirit enables them to stand on God's promises and to follow the commands of Scripture. And then, by the same power that raised Christ from the dead, a person is enabled to put off old, destructive habits and put on new, productive ways of living (Col. 3:1–14).

Look at how the Spirit changed the apostle Peter! In just a few weeks he went from a man who denied his Savior to a man who was willing to stand before a great crowd to proclaim the gospel. As our friends submit themselves to the Spirit of change, they'll find the same power to overcome sin in their own lives and to meet any trial.

Summary

In Part I we've seen how God's help toward us demonstrates how we are to help others. Just as He speaks the truth to our hearts, so we must be ready to be lovingly honest. Just as He draws alongside and comforts, so we must also be available to give support and encouragement. Just as He constantly encourages us to action, so we must be able to help others make changes in their lives.

Studying God's Word may make you more aware of your limitations as a helper. This important confrontation will help you increasingly rely on God as your source of wisdom and power.

Your next step in preparing to help your friends is to look inward and to evaluate these limitations. As you examine your strengths and weaknesses, pray that the Holy Spirit will make you honest in assessing yourself.

PERSONAL AND PRACTICAL

For Thought

1. As you read Scripture, perhaps during your daily devotions, consider the person and work of the Holy Spirit. What does He demonstrate about being a helper

and comforter? In what ways can you imitate His example?

2. Review the translations of the word *paraklete*. What does each imply about the person and work of the Holy Spirit?

3. Think about the last time you helped someone and list the ways you relied on the Holy Spirit to aid your counseling.

4. How does the Holy Spirit help you in your everyday life?

5. Review the concept behind the word *noutheteo* by looking up "admonish" and "warn" in a concordance. When might you need to confront a friend?

6. Review the concept behind the word *parakaleo* by looking up the words "comfort" and "encourage" in a concordance. When might you comfort a friend?

7. Review the concept behind the word *dunamoo* by looking up the words "power," "strengthen," and "enable" in a concordance. When have you helped a friend to make changes in his or her life?

8. Read Romans 5:5 and 15:13. What is the common element in these two verses? In what helping situation might you refer to them?

9. Read 1 John 4:13. What type of problem does this verse answer? When might you use it to help a friend?

NOTES

[1] Dr. Paul Brand and Philip Yancey, *In His Image* (Grand Rapids: Zondervan Publishing House, 1984), p. 175.

[2] Roy Hession, *Be Filled Now* (Fort Washington, Pennsylvania: Christian Literature Crusade, 1983), p. 49.

[3] Edwin Palmer, *The Holy Spirit* (Philadelphia: Presbyterian and Reformed Publishing Co., 1964) p. 81. Chapter 7 provides a comprehensive discussion of the work of the Holy Spirit.

[4] Dick Keyes, *Beyond Identity* (Ann Arbor: Servant Books, 1984), p. 76.

[5] Sinclair Ferguson, *Know Your Christian Life* (Downers Grove, Illinois: InterVarsity Press, 1981), pp. 84–85.

[6] Palmer, *The Holy Spirit,* p. 128.

[7] Ferguson, *Know Your Christian Life,* pp. 89–90.

[8] Hession, *Be Filled Now,* pp. 40–41.

[9] For further discussion on the relationship of the Holy Spirit and the Bible in counseling, see Jay Adams, *Competent To Counsel* (Phillipsburg, New Jersey: Presbyterian and Reformed Publishing Co., 1970), pp. 23–24, 61.

[10] Ray Stedman, *Body Life* (Glendale, California: Regal Books, 1972), p. 50.

[11] Ferguson, *Know Your Christian Life,* p. 35.

[12] Ibid., p. 40.

[13] Adams, *Competent To Counsel,* p. 76.

‡

INTRODUCTION TO PART II: LOOKING INWARD

Why do we need to look at ourselves before helping others? Paul suggests that taking an honest look inward keeps us from temptations that would prevent us from effectively helping others (Gal. 6:1).

Honest self-examination also accomplishes several other purposes. It helps us evaluate our relationship to God, assess our helping skills, and determine our strengths and weaknesses. Our introspection also models to our friends a willingness to be open and admit our failures. This in turn helps them to feel comfortable admitting their weaknesses to us.

An important part of this self-examination is making sure that our own lives are in order. Sometimes we become involved in other people's lives in order to avoid the problems in our own. As Jesus taught, we must first look at the log in our own eye before attempting to remove the speck from someone else's (Matt. 7:4–5).

Honest self-confrontation can be painful. We may uncover sins that we previously ignored; we may experience guilt or shame as we acknowledge these sins and weaknesses. These feelings parallel our friends' experiences when they talk to us. Honest self-appraisal reminds us that our sin places us all in the same boat. Then as we take our sins to the Cross and receive the comfort of God's forgiveness, we will be reminded that we, like the people we help, need the Savior.

Jesus said, "Everyone who is fully trained will be like his teacher" (Luke 6:40b). When we listen compassionately and lovingly speak the truth, we show Christ to our friends. When we apply the gospel to our lives, we are a living demonstration of Christianity.

We are about to embark on an adventure of self-discovery. At the same time, we also are adding tools to our helper's tool box. In chapter 4 we'll examine our personal relationship to God, the characteristics of a biblical helper, and the temptations that helpers face. In chapter 5 we'll look at how we handle our own problems, the different ways of responding to our friends' problems, the types of problems we'll be equipped to handle, and an overview of the helping skills we need.

Each skill or characteristic studied in the next two chapters is a skill that our friends need also. Consider the following questions when you are helping your friends: Are they growing in their relationship to God? Do they turn to God for help? Are they able to apply God's Word to their lives? Are they good listeners? Can they express their thoughts and feelings? Can they make changes in their lives? In this way, the yardstick by which we measure ourselves can also be a guide to helping our friends.

CHAPTER 4

A HELPER'S SPIRITUAL INVENTORY

He whose walk is blameless will minister to me.
—Psalm 101:6b

TAKE YOUR SPIRITUAL PULSE

Are You Walking with God?

The strength of your help is your personal relationship to God. You can pass on only what you have learned yourself. Since the help you give communicates your faith, it's important to make sure that your beliefs are biblical.

The author of Hebrews writes: "Anyone who comes to him must believe that he exists" (Heb. 11:6b). In order to identify ourselves as *Christians*, we must recognize that God has revealed Himself through His Son. As Jesus said, "I am the way and the truth and the life. No one comes to the Father, except through me" (John 14:6; see also Matt. 11:27; John 1:1-3, 14; Heb. 1:1-4). Have you confessed your sins and recognized that Jesus is your only hope of salvation? Do you follow His teachings? Affirmative answers to these questions indicate that you are indeed one of His followers.

Are You Showing Fruit of Salvation?

Does your life reflect your beliefs? Is there evidence of God's working in you as you go to work, take care of your family, or talk with your friends? In the parable of the vine, Jesus makes it clear that there should be tangible results of our relationship to Him (John 15:1–11). Is your commitment to Jesus producing the fruits of the Spirit? Helpers especially need to show love, joy, peace, patience, kindness, goodness, faithfulness, gentleness, and self-control (Gal. 5:22).

One way our lives bear fruit is our readiness to confess our faith. Our testimonies are both an encouragement to believers (Philem. 6) and a witness to unbelievers (1 Peter 3:15b). Think about it. When was the last time you encouraged another Christian by sharing your faith? Or when was the last time you talked about the gospel to an unbelieving friend?

What Are Your Helping Talents or Abilities?

In order to evaluate your set of helping talents, write down at least three personal abilities that enable you to be an effective helper. These may include listening attentively, being able to confront without anger, or consistently praying for others. Then compare your list with the ones in 1 Corinthians 12:4–10, 28 and Romans 12:6–8. Are any of your strengths similar to the gifts Paul mentions? Some will be similar and some will be different. For example, generosity is mentioned in Romans 12:8, whereas the ability to be empathic is not, even though both are important helping skills.

Don't despair if you look at these lists and think, "But I don't have any of these gifts!" Paul instructs us to desire earnestly the greater gifts (1 Cor. 12:31). Furthermore, our obedience to Christ demands that all of us be loving, merciful, kind, and encouraging.

BIBLICAL CHARACTERISTICS OF A MATURE CHRISTIAN HELPER

To understand the spiritual qualifications of a Christian helper, let's look at 1 Corinthians 13. Although commonly known as the "love chapter," it also mentions two other qualities that we need to exhibit: faith and hope. Let's see how each of these three virtues should mold and shape us as helpers.

Faith Is Believing

We all know that we are to "have faith," but what does that mean? Dr. Ferguson writes that faith is "related to the idea of leaning on, entrusting oneself to, or having confidence in something. . . . It is trust in God's character and obedience to his living voice expressed in his word."[1] Faith joins us personally to Jesus Christ Himself.

The Old Testament characters listed in Hebrews 11 demonstrate that biblical faith is the ability to replace worry with trust. To have faith is to participate with God in His purposes for us. For the Christian, faith finds its source and focus in the person and promises of God.

Do you integrate your trust of God into your life? Do you grab hold of the lifeline of faith when hard times storm your life? When you are disappointed by unmet expectations or confused by your lack of direction, do you seek God's help? Admittedly, leaning on God isn't always easy. Our feelings tempt us to believe that we may fall headfirst if we let go and trust God. Like so many doubting Thomases, we demand evidence before we confess faith and believe.

But our faith is a guidepost that will direct us to our Lord and His Word. Besides that, as we learn to trust in God's promises, we are able to use those same muscles of faith for our friends. Empathizing with one who is struggling to appropriate God's promises will be easier since we have experienced a similar struggle ourselves.

Hope Is Your Anchor

Paul instructs us that love "always protects, always trusts, always *hopes*, always perseveres" (1 Cor. 13:7). Biblical hope is the confident expectation that God loves us, saves us, keeps His promises to us, and accomplishes His purpose in our lives.

Do you remain hopeful in what appears to be a hopeless situation? Are you optimistic without oversimplifying problems? Can you offer biblical hope to a friend? An honest look inward will enable you to answer these questions.

Our hope has several different dimensions. First, we hope in the new life available to us—a life that joins us intimately and eternally to God (1 Cor. 1:30; 2 Cor. 5:17). Second, we hope in a powerful God who strengthens us, provides for our needs, and gives us ways to handle difficult times (Isa. 40:12–31; Matt. 19:26; 1 Cor. 10:13; Phil. 4:19). Finally, our hope helps us believe in a purpose and a plan behind those difficult times (Ps. 138:8; Jer. 29:11). As Christians, we may not always know the reasons *why* God allows *specific* trials, but we do know that "suffering produces perseverance; perseverance, character; and character, hope" (Rom. 5:3–4).

One of God's universal purposes in allowing His children to suffer is to prepare us to comfort others (2 Cor. 1:4–7). As with faith, exercising the muscle of hope for ourselves gives us the practice we need to use it for our friends. And even if we haven't personally faced the same trauma, our ability to communicate that there is "light at the end of the tunnel" is a very important message of hope.

That tunnel of discouragement and hard times is especially illuminated by the hope of eternal life. God's Word helps us to understand our present pain in light of the life to come. Our present life of suffering is only a preface to the glory that awaits us in eternity (2 Cor. 4:17–18).[2]

Confronting problems head-on can be discouraging. In fact, part of many people's problems is a crippling hopelessness that sighs, "Nothing will ever change." When we first begin to help our friends, we must have a perspective that sees how change is possible. Our friends need hope in the face of their problems and grace (the hope of forgiveness) in order to face their sins.

Hope is also important in situations where, humanly speaking, there appears to be little expectation of change. At that time we must give realistic hope, not false encouragement. The author of Hebrews tells us to "encourage one another daily" (Heb. 3:13; 10:25). This service of hope is an indispensable tool in every helper's tool box.

But the Greatest of These Is Love

Finally, we come to love, the attribute that Paul labels "the greatest of all." He outlines in 1 Corinthians 13 an amazing job description that includes patience and kindness; self-control that avoids jealousy, bragging, or selfishness; the ability to forgive; and the ability to rejoice in truth rather than unrighteousness. In addition, Paul writes that our love should never fail!

The ability to love like this can only come from the person who first loved us. In fact, our sure knowledge of God's love, coupled with thanksgiving for what He has done for us, is the wellspring from which flows our desire to love others (1 John 4:11, 19; John 15:12–17; Eph. 3:17–19). As Martin Luther said, "The love of God and love of neighbor is like a water fountain. God's love flows into us and out to our neighbor."[3]

Practically speaking, what does it mean to love your neighbor as yourself? Our love for others includes two dynamics that parallel God's love for us. In the same way that God both *confronts* our sin and mercifully forgives, accepts, and *comforts* us in spite of that sin, we also love through confrontation and comfort.

Although the primary comfort we offer our friends is forgiveness after they confess their sins, we also offer another type of comfort when we first begin to help them. This welcoming love expresses our love to them and encourages them to open up to us. Both types of comfort are are embodied in the word *parakaleo*. It is a love that is gentle, understanding, patient, and compassionate. Without this love that is both welcoming and forgiving, our friends could experience our counsel as power and control.

For example, Jesus loved Peter in spite of his errors. Although this stubborn disciple often doubted His Savior, Jesus didn't give up on him. This type of love sees sin but accepts the sinner in spite of it. As Paul wrote, "But *because of His great love for us,* God, who is rich in mercy, made us alive with Christ *even when we were dead in transgressions*" (Eph. 2:4–5b, italics added).

Love is hard work. The responsibility to extend ourselves to others isn't always easy. It's particularly difficult when we're asked to love those we find unacceptable. Do you love and accept your teenage daughter even when she voices opinions that differ from yours? Do you welcome your loud, boisterous neighbor into your home? Love is often an act of *will* rather than evidence of *feelings*. Love is a choice; God's love chose us, and we can in turn choose to love others.

It's easy to see how being warm, compassionate, and comforting communicates love, but how does confrontation show love? To answer that question, read Leviticus 19:15–18 and write down all that the Israelites were commanded *not* to do. You've just discovered what love *is not!* Your list may include not slandering, not hating, or not bearing a grudge as well as not being judgmental or revengeful. In contrast, the Israelites were commanded *to reprove* and *to love* their neighbors (Lev. 19:17–18 NASB). From this we can conclude that biblical love includes reproof.

The Hebrew word translated "reprove" means "to correct" or "to bring a person back on track." As we saw in the last chapter, the idea of reproof is summarized in the Greek word *noutheteo*. Scripture directs us to correct our friends with a spirit of gentleness (Gal. 6:1), in order to help them (James 5:19–20) and to encourage them toward fullness in Christ (Col. 1:28).

It's clear that love doesn't *overlook* sin but *confronts* sin and points it out. Just as a loving father disciplines a toddler who pokes her finger into an electrical socket, loving helpers are ready to confront sin that endangers a friend's spiritual well-being.

Paul thanked God for the Thessalonians' "work produced by faith, labor prompted by love, and endurance inspired by hope" (1 Thess. 1:3). As you seek to put on these characteristics of a biblical helper, don't be discouraged when you fail. God is working in you. Just as you need patience with your friends, you also need to be patient with yourself. Recognition of our own shortcomings will keep us leaning on our divine helper—the one who constantly confronts and comforts us.

THE TEMPTATIONS OF HELPING

Our opportunities to help also carry with them possibilities of temptation. As helpers, we have the opportunity to influence someone who is needy, vulnerable, and weak. The feelings of importance and power that come when we tell a friend what to do with his or her life can become addictive. We must be careful to avoid the temptations to manipulate, control, and dominate that person.

The temptations helpers face fall into three categories: the pitfall of pride; the lure of rescuing; and the escape hatch of avoidance. Each of us will experience different snares as we try to help our friends. Pray that God will show you where you are vulnerable. Overcoming these temptations can make the difference between effective helping and destructive helping.

The Pitfall of Pride

One of the most dangerous things about pride is that we rarely see it in ourselves! Without the illumination of God's

Word, we can stumble into this unseen trap. Although pride surfaces in many ways, its root is usually the same—an inner attitude that refuses to kneel in submission before God. Thinking we know it all, we don't look to God for His wisdom and guidance. This stubbornness hurts not only us but also our friends.

Pride hinders our efforts at helping others in five ways. First, pride can lead to an attitude of superiority (Rom. 12:3). Like the Pharisee who thanked God that he wasn't like the sinful tax gatherer, we often project an attitude of superiority toward our friends. A critical tone of voice, a scornful frown, or an appearance of total self-assurance may communicate that you *never* have any struggles yourself. As Job discovered, helpers like this never seem to be stained by the dirt of daily living!

Second, pride can overspiritualize a solution. When you respond to a friend's illness with, "You should just pray and trust God. He is probably disciplining you for your own good," you minimize your friend's experience of discomfort, pain, or fear. This response presumes an inside knowledge of God's will and tries to explain away the other person's problem. Although this may stem from an honest desire to be helpful and to understand the situation, trying to second-guess God's reasons can alienate your friend.

Third, pride also can underspiritualize a friend's problem.[4] If you fail to encourage your friends to turn to God with their problems and instead only encourage them to come to you, you usurp God's place in your friends' lives. Motivated by your pride, your overinvolvement can sabotage the helping process.

Fourth, pride can lead to curiosity. The helper who yields to this temptation often has an unquenchable thirst to know all the intimate details of another person's life. This search for "dirt" frequently feeds the helper's ego at the expense of his or her friend. The helper is built up by finding out just *how bad* the other person is. Frequently such curiosity can lead to gossip, with the "helper" reporting the details to a third person. Members of prayer groups who piously pray for that "poor girl who got herself into so much trouble" need to be aware of their true motivations for Christian "sharing."

Fifth, pride can lead to sexual attraction. Illicit relationships often begin innocently enough with men or women who are "only trying to help" a brother or sister in need. Pride can make us feel so good about being needed that we can become blind to the dangers of sexual attraction.

How can you tell if you are slipping into the pitfall of pride? Prayerfully consider the following questions: How do I feel toward my friends when I am helping them? Do I think I'm better than they are? Do I help them so that I can feel better about myself? Am I just curious, or do I constructively use the facts I gather? If you answer some of these questions in the affirmative, you may have uncovered a pride that needs to be confessed— both to God and to your friend—and turned from.

The Lure of Rescuing

The second category of temptations is the trap of trying to rescue your friends. Imagine this scene. Your friend Maureen calls you up. With panic in her voice she tells you that she blew up at her husband and he decided to leave her. She is stuck with three sick kids, and on top of that, she just found out she is pregnant! You pick up on her urgency, and before you know it, you've agreed to take care of her children so that she can spend a week alone at her mother's house. When you get off the phone, you think, *What have I gotten myself into?* Although your friend may have needed some assistance, your helpfulness has gone too far.

Overinvolved helpers often mistakenly think that their duty is personally to provide the answers to their friends' problems. If you become overinvolved, you easily lose perspective and hear only one side of the story. Then it's a small step to jump to the wrong conclusions and to end up giving help that isn't helpful at all! Maureen, for example, probably needs counseling on how to respond to her husband rather than a week's retreat at her mother's house.

Rescuing also fosters overdependency. We encourage our friends to rely too heavily on us when we subtly communicate, "Don't worry, I'll take care of everything." Unfortunately, we may end up with a string of friends who just don't know what they'd do without us! Friends like this may then act helpless in order to force us into taking responsibility for them. Asking yourself "Am I working harder than they are?" will help you decide if you are solving your friends' problems for them.

If you are overinvolved and if you encourage your friends' dependency, you probably also face two other dilemmas:

unrealistic expectations for yourself and the inability to set limits for others. You may have become so wrapped up in your friends' lives that you can't evaluate whether or not what you are doing is helpful. Following a "more is better" rule, you may continue to offer one solution after another. If you begin to feel frustrated, used, or angry with yourself or with your friends, then your desire to be "helpful" may be outweighing the service you are providing.

If you are overly involved with your friends, you may be motivated by your own desire to be needed, to be loved, or to have a friend. As long as your friend needs help, everything is fine. But when he or she no longer needs assistance, you may feel rejected, unwanted, and unimportant. In fact, you may even try to convince your friends that they are not ready to make decisions on their own. In that case, it is *you* who has become dependent on your friend! Remember, love respects the other person. We don't do our friends or ourselves a favor if we put them in a wheelchair when they need to learn to walk on their own.

In order to guard against the temptation of abusing the helper's role, ask yourself these questions: When I encourage my friend to come to me with every problem, am I satisfying my own desire to be needed? Am I keeping my friend dependent on me? If you answer these questions affirmatively, then you must consider whether you are working to meet your needs or your friend's.

Of course there will be times when we'll feel good that we've helped a friend. Those feelings are a gift, not a payment. We are not rescuers who come to the aid of our friends in order to be paid back some day. If that is the case, our friends will discover that the help they received has a very high price tag indeed!

The Escape Hatch of Avoidance

The third category of temptation includes the various ways we avoid helping people. Have you ever found yourself shying away from someone who is emotionally, spiritually, or physically troubled? Perhaps you excused yourself by thinking that you really don't know what to say to the mentally retarded young man who sits at the end of your pew every Sunday morning. It's easier to choose another way out of church rather than to walk by him and begin a conversation. James reminds us that we need to avoid favoritism, snobbishness, and selfishness (James 2:1–4). It's easy to help those who enjoy intellectual and insightful conversations. But we may be selfishly denying help to others who seem less attractive to us.

We avoid helping people for several reasons. First, we are often uncomfortable or afraid. We may feel afraid to speak to the brassy teenager or a sick relative. We may feel uncomfortable around the shabbily dressed older person or the person from another race or culture. We may not know how to respond to certain problems, like severe marital difficulties, child abuse, or drug addiction. Because of our fear and insecurity, we may resort to giving pat answers and simplistic platitudes. But this is like putting Band-Aids on deep wounds—it fails to heal the true injury.

Second, we avoid helping people because we don't want to feel anxious, sad, or upset. We're afraid that another person's weakness may rub off on us. Similarly, we may avoid giving help because our friend's problems remind us too much of our own.

This avoidance expresses itself in various ways. We may become apathetic and uninvolved. We may become very busy so that we can stay away from a person in need. Perhaps we go off on tangents, exaggerate a problem, or spinoff from our friends' problems to our own—all to keep from helping our friend.

Summary

By this time you are probably feeling as if you won't be able to help a friend because either you're not properly equipped or you're sure to fall into temptation! Don't let these warnings deter you; rather use them to guide you into being a better helper. Remember that, "If a man cleanses himself from these things, he will be a vessel for honor, sanctified, useful to the Master, prepared for every good work" (2 Tim. 2:21 NASB).

Now move on to the Personal and Practical section. In addition to the Scripture study, you will find an evaluation form. You may want to photocopy it first, and then ask a close friend or your spouse to fill it out, evaluating you from his or her perspective. Compare how he or she sees you with how you see yourself. In what areas were your assessments the same? In what areas were they different? Use the results as items for prayer and correction as you proceed in your study.

PERSONAL AND PRACTICAL

Study the Scriptures

1. Read Acts 20:35, Philippians 4:9, and 2 Thessalonians 3:7–9. What does Paul teach about the helper as a model? What do you learn from these passages?
2. Read 1 Thessalonians 5:11, 14–18 and Galatians 6:1–10. List at least ten characteristics of a biblical helper.
3. Read Matthew 5:5 and 1 Peter 3:8. What characteristic do these passages describe? When do you as a helper need to "put off" pride and "put on" humility?
4. Read 1 John 5:4–5. What is the apostle's message to us as helpers? What is our victory? Describe some counseling situations in which you could use this passage.
5. Read Acts 14:22. What is Paul's message to the church? Look at verses 19–20 for the background of this situation. In what situations could you refer to these verses?
6. Read Hebrews 6:18–19 and 3:6. What is the theme of these verses? How do they help you? How could you use them when helping a friend?
7. Read Romans 8:28–29 and 1 Corinthians 10:13. How could you use these passages when helping a friend? What does it mean to be "called according to his purpose"? What does it mean to be conformed to Christ's likeness? What must you be careful of when you give biblical hope?
8. Read Romans 12:12. What does Paul mean by being "joyful in hope, patient in affliction"? Read verse 15 for a clue.
9. Read 2 Thessalonians 3:13. What is the attribute described in this passage? Why is patience a necessary part of a helper's tool box? When do you find yourself growing tired of doing right?
10. Read 1 Corinthians 13:4–8 and Romans 15:7. What are some of the main characteristics of biblical love? Why are they important to you as a helper?
11. Read 1 John 3:18 and 4:18. What relevance do these passages have to helping a friend? When *don't* you love in deed and truth?

12. Read Romans 12:9–12. List at least six aspects of brotherly (and sisterly) love.

For Thought

1. When do you have a hard time being faithful and trusting the Lord?
2. When is it difficult for you to be hopeful?
3. When is it hard for you to be loving?
4. List the temptations you face as a helper. In what situations do you tend to feel proud? When do you try to rescue? What situations are you tempted to avoid? Why? During the next week record in your journal any situations in which you are tempted to become proud, to rescue your friends, or to avoid helping someone. Consider why you responded that way and how else you could have responded.

HELPER'S SPIRITUAL INVENTORY

"Let a man examine himself."

—*1 Cor. 11:28 (NASB)*

Part I. My Relationship to God

Directions: The following statements describe important characteristics of a Christian helper. Prayerfully consider each one and evaluate whether or not the statement accurately reflects your personal relationship to God. Circle the response that best describes you.

1. I am in fellowship with God through faith in Jesus Christ.

    Yes   No

2. Because I rely on Christ's atoning work, I know that God has promised to love me and has forgiven me instead of justly punishing me for my sin.

    Yes   No

3. When I encounter personal problems, I can appropriately apply scriptural principles that help me overcome these problems.

   Always   Usually   Sometimes   Never

4. I generally demonstrate evidence of faith in Christ in my life.

   Always   Usually   Sometimes   Never

5. I turn to God as the ultimate source of help for my life.

   Always   Usually   Sometimes   Never

Part II. Biblical Characteristics of an Effective Helper

Directions: The following statements outline how a Christian helper must demonstrate the attributes of faith, hope, and love. Beneath each statement is a series of numbers. Circle the number that best identifies your present helping response. Use the examples to think of similar situations you have faced.

1. I am able to spontaneously communicate biblical truths.
   Example: "God's Word teaches that abortion is wrong. Scripture also points out that Jesus came to die for all sins. If you are a believer, that includes your abortion."

   Rarely   1 2 3 4 5 6 7 8 9 10   Usually

2. I have helped a person encounter Jesus Christ.
   Example: "I can see that you realize you can't get to heaven based on your own merit. Jesus taught that unless a person is born again, that person will not enter the kingdom of God. Do you know what that means?"

   Rarely   1 2 3 4 5 6 7 8 9 10   Usually

3. I have hope in God's provision for a person in physical, emotional, or psychological pain.
   Example: "I know that the car accident has left you angry and that your life will be very different now. I'm praying that God will show you how He'll provide for you, since He has promised to care for all His children.

   Rarely   1 2 3 4 5 6 7 8 9 10   Usually

4. I can spontaneously communicate eternal hope.
   Example: "You miss your mother very much, but since she was a Christian, you can be comforted by the knowledge that she is at home with the Lord."

   Rarely   1   2   3   4   5   6   7   8   9   10   Usually

5. I try to communicate hope by sharing situations in which God has comforted me.
   Example: "After my son died, I also thought I'd never stop crying. God was faithful to answer my prayers and heal me of that tremendous pain."

   Rarely   1   2   3   4   5   6   7   8   9   10   Usually

6. I show love by confronting a person when it's appropriate.
   Example: "I'm concerned with your attitude toward Mary. I don't think you're fulfilling your role as a loving husband by constantly criticizing her."

   Rarely   1   2   3   4   5   6   7   8   9   10   Usually

7. I show love by accepting other people as they are.
   Example: "I know you've said you're unhappy with the way you look, but that doesn't change the fact that I really enjoy you."

   Rarely   1   2   3   4   5   6   7   8   9   10   Usually

8. I show love by thinking of the other person's needs.
   Example: "While Larry is on his business trip, why don't you and the kids come over for dinner?"

   Rarely   1   2   3   4   5   6   7   8   9   10   Usually

Part III. Temptations of Helping

Directions: Some common problems that helpers face are listed below. Circle the number that best describes your normal response. Note that now "1" is the high score!

1. I feel as if I'm always the best one to help a particular person.

   Rarely   1   2   3   4   5   6   7   8   9   10   Usually

2. I enjoy knowing the intimate details of another person's problems.

   Rarely   1   2   3   4   5   6   7   8   9   10   Usually

3. I think I have the answers to other people's problems.

   Rarely   1   2   3   4   5   6   7   8   9   10   Usually

4. I can't understand why some people continue in bad habits and sin.

   Rarely   1   2   3   4   5   6   7   8   9   10   Usually

5. I only get one side of the story.

   Rarely   1   2   3   4   5   6   7   8   9   10   Usually

6. I enjoy having another person become dependent on me.

   Rarely   1   2   3   4   5   6   7   8   9   10   Usually

7. I fail to encourage the other person's relationship to God.

   Rarely   1   2   3   4   5   6   7   8   9   10   Usually

8. I feel most problems have simple solutions.

   Rarely   1   2   3   4   5   6   7   8   9   10   Usually

9. I help other people so that I will feel better about myself.

   Rarely   1   2   3   4   5   6   7   8   9   10   Usually

10. I try to help people even if I lack the necessary skills.

    Rarely   1   2   3   4   5   6   7   8   9   10   Usually

11. I try to help even when I lack the knowledge about a person's problem.

    Rarely   1   2   3   4   5   6   7   8   9   10   Usually

12. When I help people, I try to make them happy.

    Rarely   1   2   3   4   5   6   7   8   9   10   Usually

13. If I'm not successful at making the other person happy, I feel as if I've failed.

    Rarely   1 2 3 4 5 6 7 8 9 10   Usually

14. If I'm not successful at helping, I feel angry or disappointed with the other person.

    Rarely   1 2 3 4 5 6 7 8 9 10   Usually

15. When I help someone, I expect to be paid back in some way.

    Rarely   1 2 3 4 5 6 7 8 9 10   Usually

NOTE: If many of your scores in Part III were between 7–10, you will have discovered the temptations to which you are prone. These are areas to pray about and be sensitive to.

For Further Reading

1. Read chapter 4 of Jay Adams's *Competent To Counsel* (Phillipsburg, New Jersey: Presbyterian and Reformed Publishing Co., 1970) for another explanation of how biblical love confronts.
2. Read pages 37–43 of Gary Collins' *Effective Counseling* (Carol Stream, Illinois: Creation House, 1972) for another description of the temptations that helpers face.
3. Read chapter 5 of William Kirwan's *Biblical Concepts for Christian Counseling* (Grand Rapids: Baker Book House, 1984) for his description of faith, hope, and love.
4. Read chapters 4 and 5 of Ray Stedman's *Body Life* (Glendale, California: Regal Books, 1972) for further discussion of the discovery and use of your gifts and abilities.

NOTES

[1] Sinclair Ferguson, *Know Your Christian Life* (Downers Grove, Illinois: InterVarsity Press, 1981), p. 56.

[2] For an excellent discussion on suffering, see Edith Schaeffer's *Affliction* (Old Tappan, New Jersey: Fleming H. Revell Company, 1979).

[3] Paul Althaus, *The Ethics of Martin Luther,* translated by Robert Schultz (Philadelphia: Fortress Press, 1972), pp. 14–15.

[4] Gary Collins, *Effective Counseling* (Carol Stream, Illinois: Creation House, 1972), p. 41.

‡

CHAPTER 5

TAKE STOCK OF YOUR HELPING SKILLS

Do not think of yourself more highly than you ought, but rather think of yourself with sober judgment.
—Romans 12:3b

This chapter will help us look in our helper's tool box and determine which helping skills we already have and which we need to acquire. In order to accomplish that, we'll look at how we solve our own problems, the various roles of lay counselors, and the types of problems we'll be equipped to handle. We'll conclude the chapter with a brief overview of each helping skill.

HOW DO YOU SOLVE YOUR OWN PROBLEMS?

A major part of our helping equipment will be the experience of solving our own problems in a biblical way. To determine how you resolve your own problems and conflicts, answer the following questions honestly. As you read through the list, jot down the first answer that comes to you. Then share your answers in your study group, with a close friend, or with your spouse. Don't be surprised if your answers fall on a continuum of "sometimes yes" and "sometimes no." It's common to react to different types of problems in different ways. (For example, it may be easier for you to turn to God when your child is sick than to entrust your financial problems to Him.)

Problem-Solving Checklist

1. How do you respond to your sin? Do you confess it, ask for forgiveness, and then trust that you are forgiven? Or do you dwell on these sins, unable to receive the pardon that God extends to you?
2. Are you able to turn your problems over to God, or do you tend to worry about how things will get resolved?
3. Are you angry with yourself when you fail or make a mistake? Do you give up when you fail, or do you recognize your mistakes and make another attempt at what you are doing?
4. Do you seek other people's opinions and advice when faced with a problem or decision, or do you try to find an answer by yourself?
5. Are you impulsive, or are you a careful planner? Do you make quick and spontaneous decisions, or do you need time to think things through?
6. How have you handled broken relationships, disappointments, or scars in your life? Do they become something that you learn and grow from, or are they sources of bitterness, anger, or fear?
7. Can you receive help when you're in trouble, or do you isolate yourself and take care of things on your own?
8. Do you tend to respond to new situations or problems emotionally or analytically? If emotionally, what feelings usually surface first? If analytically, how do you communicate that to others?
9. How do you handle conflict between yourself and others? Do you avoid it and try to appease the other person, or do you confront it and seek to find a compromise or resolution?
10. What areas in your life need healing?

What did you discover about yourself? How would you evaluate your problem-solving abilities? What areas in your life need your attention?

Do You Impose Your Answers on Your Friends' Problems?

Without realizing it, we sometimes expect friends to adopt our ways of handling situations. Think back on the last few times that you helped your friends. Did you encourage them to solve their problems your way, or did you help them to find a solution using their own resources? Of course you want to encourage your friends to walk in a godly way, but does this mean they must follow your footsteps?

On the other hand, sometimes a friend is stuck and will need your help in discovering new problem-solving techniques. A good helper encourages a friend to think through various possibilities and to evaluate the available choices before arriving at a solution. How can we do that without imposing our own point of view? In other words, what is our role as helpers?

HELPERS ARE SWIMMING COACHES, NOT LIFEGUARDS

Picture the job of a swimming coach. The coach tries to teach each swimmer how to improve his or her stroke, kick, and breathing. The goal of a coach is clear: to help each swimmer swim the best he or she can.

Now picture the job of a lifeguard. The lifeguard protects swimmers and watches out for their safety. Ready and alert, the guard is prepared to rescue someone who may be drowning. The lifeguard's job is different from the coach's: the coach *trains* swimmers; the lifeguard *rescues* them.

What does all this have to do with counseling? As we already saw in the last chapter, it's easy for us to slip into rescuing our friends. In our misguided attempts to help, we try to solve our friends' problems *for* them, instead of *with* them. Let's look at three different helping roles that will keep us working as coaches instead of lifeguards.

You Are a Model

What do you want to model to your friends? First, you'll want to exemplify a life that is grounded in Christ. Your faith in God's promises and your obedience to His commands are powerful demonstrations of genuine Christianity.

Second, you want to model good relationship and communication skills. You do this in the way that you relate to your friend. For example, when you listen patiently and nonjudgmentally to a friend who is frustrated with her teenage son, you show her how she can listen to him. Your friends will discover new ways of relating to the people in their lives by observing your patience, encouragement, and loving confrontation.

Third, you want to model how to handle conflict. Your friends will learn new ways of handling conflicts by observing how you resolve any tensions you may have with them. For instance, as you work with a friend to reconcile differences that you and he have, he may discover a new way of resolving conflicts with his wife.

You Are a Teacher and Guide

I remember the way my father helped me with my math homework in junior high. I hated word problems. I would consistently avoid thinking them through and would guess at the answer instead. My father insisted that I figure out each step of the problem. He wasn't just interested in teaching me math, and he wasn't simply helping me find the right answers. He was showing me that the *way* I solved those problems was important.

As helpers, we want our friends to come up with the right answers. But we need to realize that part of the helping process is for our friends to learn how to solve their problems themselves. Encouraging our friends to look at different components of their problems, to brainstorm about solutions, and to consider the alternatives open to them will encourage them to use their own resources—God's Word, their past experiences, and their God-given intelligence, talents, and abilities.

Similarly, a part of our job will be to guide our friends through their problems. Just as a tour map shows a tourist how to get around in a strange city, we also have a "map" with which to help our friends. Our maps include information about what our friends can expect to find in new situations. Helping one friend consider what it will be like when she attends college or helping another find out about unemployment benefits after he loses his job are both examples of being guides for our friends.

We'll be most effective guides in circumstances that we have been through ourselves. You can help your best friend through the uselessness she feels when her youngest child leaves for school if you've experienced the same "empty nest" feelings yourself.

When we guide our friends through a situation, we give them a map that they can use in the future. This will build their confidence and enable them to face new challenges. When people are constantly rescued by a lifeguard, they learn to think, "I always need someone to help me. I must be pretty dumb or incompetent." But when people are guided to their own solutions, their thinking changes, "What I'm about to go through might not be easy, but I've handled similar situations in the past, and I can apply what I learned then to what I'm going through now."

You Are a Supporter

Finally, good helpers support their friends during difficult times. Never underestimate how important it is just to *be with* a friend. When you volunteer to help your friend clean his basement out after it floods or when you help another pack before her surgery, you are demonstrating your support in concrete, practical ways.

Cheering a friend on is the mark of a good coach and a good helper. Good coaches not only encourage their trainees to practice, but they also recognize what they have accomplished and then congratulate them on a job well done. Our support will encourage our friends to persevere when they feel like giving up.

Assuming our roles of models, teachers, guides, and supporters will keep us from taking on the wrong job. This protects both us and our friends. We'll avoid becoming overinvolved and "burned out" with helping. And our friends will not be smothered by our opinions and advice.

A Time and Place for Lifeguards

By now you've probably resolved never to rescue another friend! But let me add a note of caution. Although most of our friends will not need rescuing, occasionally we'll meet someone who is "drowning." For example, a friend who mentions "ending it all" might be referring to suicide. Similarly, a person who threatens to hurt someone also demands an immediate response. A person who is drowning needs to be rescued; swimming lessons can come later.

Part of your job as a helper is to discern whether someone is actually drowning or whether that person simply doesn't want to swim. Each situation will require a different response. Let's look at the range of problems people face and examine which ones you'll be equipped to help.

WHEN CAN YOU BE HELPFUL?

To be able to understand your sphere of influence as a lay counselor, let's divide all the difficulties that people face into two groups. The first group includes problems that you'll have the skills to help solve. Generally, these encompass the troubles people have in everyday situations. The second group of problems includes troubles that are more severe, such as alcohol abuse, suicide, psychoses, or serious depression.

Keep in mind that the types of problems you end up handling will depend on many factors. The community you live in (urban, suburban, rural), your socioeconomic status, your ethnic group, and your age all help determine the type of people you will encounter. Furthermore, your visibility and availability as a helper also will define who will come to you for help. Whereas some lay counselors may never encounter alcohol abuse, suicide, psychoses, or serious depression, others may come across them more frequently.

The best helpers know their limits and realize that they can't help everyone. When your friend's problems appear to be bigger than you have been trained to help, you need to have a counselor (your pastor, a Christian counselor, psychologist, or psychiatrist) who can answer your questions. (If you are reading this book as a part of a lay counseling training program, use your teacher as this resource person.)

People's problems are complex. Although human difficulties can't be readily compartmentalized, they tend to fall into a continuum. What may be mild anxiety over a job change to one friend will be debilitating fear to another. The extent, duration, and frequency of your friends' problems often will determine how many areas of their life are affected by them and whether or not your help will be sufficient. The deeper your friends' problems have penetrated into their life, the more complicated they will be, and the more your friends will need extra help from their pastor or other professional counselor.

Remember that we live in a fallen world and that all problems are related either directly or indirectly to sin. Some problems are more easily traced to *specific* sins than others. As you read about each problem, consider if it's an expression of one of the problems we listed in chapter 1: hiding; guilt and shame; pride; acceptance; ignorance; evil; sickness; and death.

Times You Can Be Helpful

The most common problems you'll help a friend through are related to normal life stresses. The birth of a first child, a teenager leaving for college, a couple getting married, a person starting a new job or retiring from an old—all produce stress. Feelings of anxiety, sadness, or confusion are common during periods of change and transition. These emotions can be quite unsettling and can last until adjustments have been made to the new situation.

Unexpected events also can produce emotional turmoil. Friends may seek your support when a sudden illness, hospitalization, or death strikes their family. Similarly, the loss of a job, an unexpected transfer, increased marital difficulties, or a teenager who runs away could prompt requests for your help.

Your friends also may share with you their feelings about themselves. Disappointment or dissatisfaction with personal achievements, appearance, or decisions can lead to feelings of worthlessness and frustration. These feelings in turn may affect your friends' ability to function properly on their job or in their relationships.

A friend who is wrestling with spiritual problems may also seek your help. As we've seen, all problems have a spiritual root, but sometimes a person may have a specific difficulty with knowing, trusting, or obeying God. Spiritual problems may include doubting the truth of the gospel, lack of purpose or meaning in life, difficulty in personally appropriating God's love and grace, the inability to believe God's forgiveness, difficulty forgiving others, or anger toward God over specific circumstances in one's life.

You also may be asked to help your friends with their relationships. These can include problems with family members, friends, neighbors, co-workers, or fellow church members. You may be asked to help a friend whose wife always disagrees with him and undermines his authority in the family. Or you may help a teenager in your Sunday school class resolve an argument with his or her parents.

Often you'll help a friend by providing some basic "how-to" information. Helping a shy friend learn how to ask a woman for a date, teaching a young mother how to discipline her two year old, or helping a new Christian to understand the Bible all fall into this category. Remember, you may not have all the answers yourself. Then your job is to help your friend find the proper source of information (e.g., introducing the young mother to another woman who has successfully weathered the "terrible twos").[1]

Times Your Friends May Need Additional Help

When your friends' problems prohibit them from fulfilling their normal responsibilities, they may need the help of a mental health professional. In chapter 13 we'll look more closely at problems that need referral and when professionals can help, but for now, let's consider this overview of more serious problems:
1. Neurosis (the presence of an abnormal amount of anxiety).
2. Depression that is marked by a prolonged sadness not caused by a specific loss, such as death, divorce, the loss of home or property, or the loss of physical abilities through an accident or illness.
3. Marriage, family, or sexual problems.
4. *Ongoing* difficulties with a child (truancy, stealing, constant lying).
5. Drug or alcohol problems.
6. Physical abuse or threats of physical violence (including child or spouse abuse, incest, or rape).
7. Threats of injury to oneself.
8. Psychosis (recognized by a person's jumbled thoughts, speech, and bizarre behavior).

We need to encourage friends with these types of problems to seek help from their pastor, who may then refer them to a qualified Christian professional. Finding extra help is often the most important way we can help our friends.

WHAT'S IN YOUR TOOL BOX?

Good helping skills basically are good relationship skills. What do these relationship skills involve? First of all, you must be a person who can get close to others. Then, you need to be able to translate this willingness to be involved into helpful interventions. In order to do this, you need the tools of the trade—good helping skills.

Your helper's tool box holds a variety of equipment. The skills of listening well, speaking clearly and honestly, and directing someone toward change and action are your basic helping tools. Read the brief overview of each skill given below. Then determine your present level of proficiency by filling out the evaluation forms found in the Personal and Practical section. Remember, you aren't expected to be an expert helper now. We'll be studying each of these skills in Part III.

Do I Listen Well?

Good listening is a prerequisite to good counseling for several reasons. First, accurate listening enables you to gain the necessary information you need. Second, good listening communicates love and concern. Third, it shows that you value your friends enough to hear them out. We model our divine counselor, Jesus, when we listen well.

Listening is more complicated than you may think. We each have a set of filters that prevent us from receiving our friends' messages *exactly* as they are sent. These filters include our opinions, prejudices, emotions, and past experiences. It takes a great deal of concentration to focus on our friend's message at the same time that we set aside our own preconceived ideas. This doesn't mean that we *never* apply our own experiences to the problems that our friends share. But we must be careful not to assume that our friends will react or feel exactly as we did.

Listening is one of the first gifts we give our friends. By sensitively hearing their problems, pain, joys, and victories, we become involved in their lives. Sensitive and careful listening will show that we take our friends and their problems seriously. Furthermore, we give them the freedom to *express* themselves and to *be* themselves. This atmosphere of acceptance paves the way for speaking the truth in love, the next tool you'll add to your collection.

Do I Speak the Truth?

God's Word challenges us to be truth speakers (Eph. 4:15). Dr. Sinclair Ferguson explains that even beyond "speaking the truth in love," we are called literally to "truth it to one another . . . living truthfully, openly and honestly with one another."[2] What does it mean not only to *speak* the truth but also to *live* the truth?

First of all, we must be willing to speak the truth about ourselves, admitting our own sin, failures, and weaknesses. Second, we must be willing to speak the truth to our friends. We must be prepared to be honest and clear communicators. This includes not being afraid to discuss subjects or feelings that make us feel uncomfortable.

Truth speaking has the same two components that are present in biblical love: *comfort* and *confrontation*. Affirmation, support, encouragement, and words of affection all express welcoming comfort to our friends. We must be able to recognize our friends' strengths, to compliment their successes, and to express our care for them. Without the ability to express this type of comfort, we would be like merciless judges, trapping our friends in a prison of condemnation.

Confrontation, the second component of truth speaking, involves giving feedback. We don't ignore our friends' sins, problems, or difficulties. Instead, we help by giving feedback and pointing out these difficulties. We have to be honest even when our friends may not like what we have to say! Without the ability to confront, we would be powerless, passively agreeing with every complaint or conclusion we hear.

COMMUNICATION FILTERS[4]

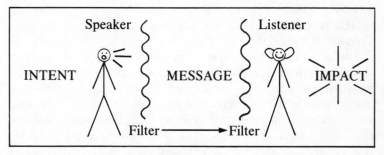

But we must be aware of not only *what* we say but also *how* we say it. Research has shown that the words we use make up only seven percent of the impression we give others. Our voice quality (soothing, critical, irritated) makes up another thirty-eight percent of our message. Facial expressions and body movements comprise approximately fifty-three percent of our communication.[3] We must always consider, "What is my tone of voice conveying? What are my eyes and body language communicating?'' Remember, our friends also will respond to the messages we send between the lines.

Our goal in speaking the truth to our friends is to ensure that the *intent* of our message equals the *impact* on them. Just as listening filters can interfere with receiving a message, speaking filters such as a sarcastic tone of voice or unfamiliar vocabulary also can prevent good communication.

Do I Direct Toward Action?

In chapter 3 we discovered that *dunamoo* means "to enable" or "to strengthen." For helpers, this translates into the ability to encourage another person toward the changes that need to be made; to go from *talking* to *doing*. Help that ends without a friend taking action is incomplete, for then change will be limited, if it occurs at all.

What skills do you need at this stage of the helping process? In addition to your listening and speaking skills, you must be able to help your friends take the information that they have gained and use it to make specific and concrete changes.

Change can occur in three different areas: attitudes, emotions, or behavior. Changes in attitude or understanding usually precede changes in emotions and behavior.

One important way we enable our friends to act is to apply scriptural principles to their problem. Referring to specific biblical promises or commands points our friends in the right direction for change.

It's common for helpers and their friends to face many obstacles at this stage of the helping process. You may feel that a friend isn't changing fast enough. Your friend feels unready to change. Be careful that you don't push your timetable unto your friends or want them to change more than they want to. Once again, awareness of your own responses will keep you working as a coach instead of as a lifeguard.

Keep in mind that the *way* you direct and advise your friends will affect how they receive your counsel. Just as you filter what you hear, your friend also filters what you are saying. For example, threatening your friend to hurry up and do what you have suggested will guarantee to turn your friend off. Your "help" will be effectively screened out. A more helpful response includes communicating your support, respect, and willingness to work with your friend while he or she changes.

PERSONAL AND PRACTICAL

Now that we have studied each of the basic helping skills, it's time to figure out which tools you have and which you need to obtain. Use the same procedure you followed in chapter 4. First, photocopy the evaluation forms. Fill out one yourself and then ask someone who knows you well to fill one out, evaluating you from his or her perspective. (Make extra copies of each form so that you can evaluate yourself again at the end of the study. Then compare the evaluations, noting the differences in how you responded before and after learning these helping skills.) Compare your evaluation with your friend's evaluation of you. Did he or she notice things you aren't aware of? Did you realize some new strengths or weaknesses? Don't get upset if you don't score as well as you expect. You're reading this book because you want to *learn* to be a lay counselor, not because you *already have* each helping tool. If you have identified sin, be sure to confess and repent. Once again, your experience of properly taking care of your sin will enable you to help your friends do the same.

Use all the results to identify areas in which you need strengthening or correction. In particular, notice the Part II scores that fall between 7–10. These are weak areas that you need to guard against prayerfully and to work toward changing. Your experience of honest self-confrontation will help you to begin with your most important helping tool of all—humility.

EVALUATE YOUR LISTENING SKILLS

Part I. Characteristics of a Good Listener

Directions: The following statements describe the characteristics of a good listener. Beneath each statement is a series of numbers. Circle the number that best identifies where you fall on the scale.

1. I let people finish their sentences before I respond to them.

   Rarely   1 2 3 4 5 6 7 8 9 10   Usually

2. Others often tell me that they feel I understand their point of view.

   Rarely   1 2 3 4 5 6 7 8 9 10   Usually

3. Others have responded to me by saying, "That's exactly what I'm feeling."

Rarely   1 2 3 4 5 6 7 8 9 10   Usually

4. I'm interested in hearing the speaker's entire message.

Rarely   1 2 3 4 5 6 7 8 9 10   Usually

5. I stop what I'm doing to listen.

Rarely   1 2 3 4 5 6 7 8 9 10   Usually

6. I'm comfortable with silence.

Rarely   1 2 3 4 5 6 7 8 9 10   Usually

7. I don't try to control the conversation.

Rarely   1 2 3 4 5 6 7 8 9 10   Usually

8. I'm not easily distracted.

Rarely   1 2 3 4 5 6 7 8 9 10   Usually

9. I can listen to feelings of anger or resentment.

Rarely   1 2 3 4 5 6 7 8 9 10   Usually

10. Listening to feelings of despair, pain, or grief doesn't overwhelm me.

Rarely   1 2 3 4 5 6 7 8 9 10   Usually

11. I can listen to feelings of fear or anxiety.

Rarely   1 2 3 4 5 6 7 8 9 10   Usually

12. A person's feelings of depression or thoughts of suicide don't frighten me.

Rarely   1 2 3 4 5 6 7 8 9 10   Usually

13. I can listen to values different from my own.

Rarely   1 2 3 4 5 6 7 8 9 10   Usually

14. I can listen to someone talk about sexuality.

    Rarely   1 2 3 4 5 6 7 8 9 10   Usually

15. I am comfortable listening to someone whose socioeconomic background is different from mine.

    Rarely   1 2 3 4 5 6 7 8 9 10   Usually

Part II. Obstacles to Good Listening

Directions: The following statements describe common filters that create obstacles to good listening. Again, circle the number under the statement that best identifies where you fall on the scale. (Note that the high score is 1.)

1. I tune out a person who uses offensive language.

    Rarely   1 2 3 4 5 6 7 8 9 10   Usually

2. I don't listen to a person's problems if they remind me of my own.

    Rarely   1 2 3 4 5 6 7 8 9 10   Usually

3. I tune out a person who criticizes or verbally attacks me.

    Rarely   1 2 3 4 5 6 7 8 9 10   Usually

4. My listening stops when I think I know the subject better than the speaker does.

    Rarely   1 2 3 4 5 6 7 8 9 10   Usually

5. I stop listening when I think I know what the other person is going to say next.

    Rarely   1 2 3 4 5 6 7 8 9 10   Usually

6. I stop listening when I've decided the answer to the person's problem.

    Rarely   1 2 3 4 5 6 7 8 9 10   Usually

7. My listening stops when I get bored.

   Rarely   1 2 3 4 5 6 7 8 9 10   Usually

8. My listening is interrupted because I'm rehearsing my response.

   Rarely   1 2 3 4 5 6 7 8 9 10   Usually

9. I stop listening when I decide the speaker has nothing worthwhile to say.

   Rarely   1 2 3 4 5 6 7 8 9 10   Usually

10. My listening gets interrupted by my own worries.

    Rarely   1 2 3 4 5 6 7 8 9 10   Usually

11. I stop listening because I'm busy evaluating the speaker and his or her style.

    Rarely   1 2 3 4 5 6 7 8 9 10   Usually

EVALUATE YOUR SPEAKING SKILLS

PART I. Characteristics of a Good Speaker

Directions: The following statements describe the characteristics of a good speaker. Beneath each statement is a series of numbers. Circle the number that best identifies where you fall on the scale.

1. I can keep something confidential.

   Rarely   1 2 3 4 5 6 7 8 9 10   Usually

2. I try not to criticize other people.

   Rarely   1 2 3 4 5 6 7 8 9 10   Usually

3. I don't overuse questions to get the other person to talk.

   Rarely   1 2 3 4 5 6 7 8 9 10   Usually

4. I don't interrupt when another person is talking.

   Rarely   1 2 3 4 5 6 7 8 9 10   Usually

5. I'm able to keep to the speaker's topic.

Rarely   1 2 3 4 5 6 7 8 9 10   Usually

6. I use language that the other person will understand.

Rarely   1 2 3 4 5 6 7 8 9 10   Usually

7. I can share my own experience if it is appropriate.

Rarely   1 2 3 4 5 6 7 8 9 10   Usually

8. I don't give quick reassurance or easy answers to problems.

Rarely   1 2 3 4 5 6 7 8 9 10   Usually

9. I'm not afraid to give feedback to another person.

Rarely   1 2 3 4 5 6 7 8 9 10   Usually

10. I can receive confrontation without responding defensively.

Rarely   1 2 3 4 5 6 7 8 9 10   Usually

11. I can encourage another person.

Rarely   1 2 3 4 5 6 7 8 9 10   Usually

12. I can affirm growth and change in another person.

Rarely   1 2 3 4 5 6 7 8 9 10   Usually

PART II. Obstacles to Good Speaking

Directions: The following statements describe common speaking problems that often alienate the other person. Beneath each statement is a series of numbers. Circle the number that best identifies where you are on the scale. (Again, a high score is a 1.)

1. I tend to minimize another person's problem.

Rarely   1 2 3 4 5 6 7 8 9 10   Usually

2. I often argue and insist on my point of view.

   Rarely   1   2   3   4   5   6   7   8   9   10   Usually

3. I say one thing, but my tone of voice contradicts what I'm saying.

   Rarely   1   2   3   4   5   6   7   8   9   10   Usually

4. I tend to give advice.

   Rarely   1   2   3   4   5   6   7   8   9   10   Usually

5. I often tell other people what to do.

   Rarely   1   2   3   4   5   6   7   8   9   10   Usually

6. I often blame and evaluate the other person.

   Rarely   1   2   3   4   5   6   7   8   9   10   Usually

7. I shame or embarrass the other person.

   Rarely   1   2   3   4   5   6   7   8   9   10   Usually

8. I can be threatening.

   Rarely   1   2   3   4   5   6   7   8   9   10   Usually

9. I cross-examine the other person.

   Rarely   1   2   3   4   5   6   7   8   9   10   Usually

10. I cut off the other person when he or she expresses an emotion with which I'm uncomfortable.

    Rarely   1   2   3   4   5   6   7   8   9   10   Usually

EVALUATE YOUR ACTION SKILLS

Part I. Characteristics of One Who Encourages to Action

Directions: The following statements describe the characteristics of a person who can help someone change. Beneath each statement is a series of numbers. Circle the number that best identifies where you are on the scale.

1. I am able to lead a person to confession and repentance if he or she has sinned.

   Rarely   1 2 3 4 5 6 7 8 9 10   Usually

2. I have helped a person develop a new attitude and perspective on a difficult situation.

   Rarely   1 2 3 4 5 6 7 8 9 10   Usually

3. I can help a person identify and prioritize problems.

   Rarely   1 2 3 4 5 6 7 8 9 10   Usually

4. I can lead a person toward acceptance of an unchangeable situation.

   Rarely   1 2 3 4 5 6 7 8 9 10   Usually

5. I can help a person make clear goals.

   Rarely   1 2 3 4 5 6 7 8 9 10   Usually

6. I remember the person's goals as I talk to him or her.

   Rarely   1 2 3 4 5 6 7 8 9 10   Usually

7. I can help evaluate the person's resources.

   Rarely   1 2 3 4 5 6 7 8 9 10   Usually

8. I can brainstorm about alternatives and help evaluate the pros and cons to various solutions.

   Rarely   1 2 3 4 5 6 7 8 9 10   Usually

9. I can identify if the other person needs to learn a new skill.

   Rarely   1 2 3 4 5 6 7 8 9 10   Usually

10. I can assign suitable homework.

   Rarely   1 2 3 4 5 6 7 8 9 10   Usually

11. I follow up on the other person.

    Rarely   1   2   3   4   5   6   7   8   9   10   Usually

12. I am patient, encouraging, and hopeful as the person changes.

    Rarely   1   2   3   4   5   6   7   8   9   10   Usually

PART II. Obstacles to Taking Action

Directions: The following statements describe common problems that occur in the taking-action stage. Circle the number beneath each statement that best identifies where you are on the scale. (Again, a high score is a 1.)

1. I make action plans that are too difficult for the other person to accomplish, or I expect change they aren't prepared for.

   Rarely   1   2   3   4   5   6   7   8   9   10   Usually

2. I accept vague and unmeasurable goals.

   Rarely   1   2   3   4   5   6   7   8   9   10   Usually

3. I overlook repeated but superficial attempts at confession and repentance.

   Rarely   1   2   3   4   5   6   7   8   9   10   Usually

4. I overlook a person's reluctance to make Jesus the Lord of his/her life.

   Rarely   1   2   3   4   5   6   7   8   9   10   Usually

5. I accept fear of change as a reason not to carry out a plan of action.

   Rarely   1   2   3   4   5   6   7   8   9   10   Usually

6. I overlook "Yes, buts" and "I can'ts."

   Rarely   1   2   3   4   5   6   7   8   9   10   Usually

7. I accept inappropriate expectations of change.

   Rarely   1   2   3   4   5   6   7   8   9   10   Usually

8. I get tired of the other person's problem and the lack of change in his/her life.

   Rarely   1 2 3 4 5 6 7 8 9 10   Usually

9. I get frustrated when a person doesn't take my help or advice.

   Rarely   1 2 3 4 5 6 7 8 9 10   Usually

10. I'm afraid to let the person try things on his or her own.

   Rarely   1 2 3 4 5 6 7 8 9 10   Usually

For Thought

1. Ask a close family member or friend to evaluate how you handle your problems by responding to the problem-solving checklist in this chapter. Do they see you in the same ways that you see yourself? Discuss your findings in the group.

2. In what situations do you act as a rescuer? Try to discover why you respond like that. What other helping response could you give instead of rescuing?

3. Consider the different helping roles discussed in this chapter. Think about times when you helped a friend by assuming one of these roles. What was the outcome of your assistance?

4. Think about the three goals that you set for yourself in chapter 1. Based on what you have just studied, are there other areas in which you need to work? You may decide to rework your goals after completing the self-evaluation forms. Consider specifically whether you want to improve your listening, speaking, or directing to action skills.

5. Now look at your goals and ask yourself if they are realistic. How will you know when you have reached them? What will you be doing differently at that time? Pick a close friend or someone in your study group or in your family with whom you can practice your skills. Ask them to give you honest feedback and to hold you accountable to your goals.

6. What types of problems do you think you will be called upon to help solve? Which ones may you find difficult to respond to either because of your lack of experience or because of your own prejudices?

7. Keep a written record (or journal) of the times you use any one of the helping skills. Keep track of any problems you have as a helper as well as when your help is on target. You also can use this journal to record what God is teaching you about yourself and about Him during this study.

For Further Reading

1. Read chapters 3 and 4 of Everett Worthington's *When Someone Asks for Help* (Downers Grove, Illinois: InterVarsity Press, 1982) for his description of what causes problems and how people solve them.
2. Read Everett Worthington's *How To Help the Hurting* (Downers Grove, Illinois: InterVarsity Press, 1985) for his discussion of situations in which a lay counselor can be helpful.

NOTES

[1] For more information about times you can be helpful, see Gary Collins, *Effective Counseling* (Carol Stream, Illinois: Creation House, 1972), pp. 50–54.

[2] Sinclair Ferguson, *Know Your Christian Life* (Downers Grove, Illinois: InterVarsity Press, 1981), p. 145.

[3] Albert Mehrabian, *Tactics of Social Influence* (Englewood Cliffs, New Jersey: Prentice Hall, 1970), quoted in Everett Worthington, *When Someone Asks for Help* (Downers Grove, Illinois: InterVarsity Press, 1982), p. 62.

[4] John Gottman, Cliff Notarius, Jonni Gonso, and Howard Markman, "A Couple's Guide to Communication" (Champaign, Ill.: Research Press, 1976), p. 1.

‡

INTRODUCTION TO PART III: LOOKING OUTWARD

We have looked *upward* and have seen how God models and directs how we are to help our friends: He absolutely confronts sin and mercifully comforts with forgiveness. Then we saw how important it was to follow this same blueprint when we looked *inward* and evaluated ourselves as helpers. Now it is time to turn our attention *outward* and learn how to both confront and comfort our friends.

Since we first must have a relationship established before we confront our friends, we will begin the helping process by providing a type of comfort first. We will welcome our friends by creating an atmosphere of understanding, trust, and acceptance (chapter 6). Chapter 7 discusses the next level of the helping process: listening. Biblical acceptance and sensitive listening communicate welcoming comfort to our friends.

In chapters 8 and 9 we'll learn the second type of helping response: truth speaking. The skills we'll learn in these two chapters will help us *confront* our friends and give them another perspective on their situation. We'll also look at forgiveness, the type of comfort that follows confrontation. Chapter 10 describes the final step in the helping process—how to direct our friends toward action.

Finally, in chapters 11–13 we'll learn how to apply these helping skills to a variety of situations: how to initiate giving help, how to help in a crisis, how to help a non-Christian, how to help someone from another culture, how to involve other helpers, and how to prevent problems.

Although the helping process, like a house, is built in stages, we'll frequently use all our different helping tools in helping our friends. The more we become proficient in using these tools, the more they'll become a part of our interactions with our friends whom we are called alongside to help. We can visualize the helping process to look like this:

THE HELPING PROCESS

action
confrontation
speaking and feedback
questioning and listening
acceptance, love, caring, welcome

CHAPTER 6

LOVE AND WELCOME: THE FOUNDATION FOR HELPING

Accept one another, then, just as Christ accepted you, in order to bring praise to God.

—*Romans 15:7*

BIBLICAL PRINCIPLES

Put Out the Welcome Mat

The New Testament frequently commands us to love one another. If we are to love each other, we must learn to accept and welcome each other. What is a Christian view of acceptance, and what makes it different from a secular psychologist's approach?

The confrontation-comfort model that we have established so far contrasts greatly with the "unconditional positive regard" that Carl Rogers, a noted secular psychologist, defines as "an outgoing positive feeling without reservations [or] evaluations."[1] Although Rogers rightly emphasizes our need to value one another, his definition of acceptance is incomplete. He ignores the existence of sin and thereby implies that all standards of right and wrong should be eliminated in favor of "accepting" a person. As a result, permissiveness is often misconstrued as acceptance. This attitude lacks the power of honest biblical love.[2]

The parable of the Prodigal Son in Luke 15 is an example of

true unconditional acceptance. Here we see how we don't need to give up absolute standards in order to give absolute love. In this story a rich man's son leaves his father's house, squanders his money on loose living, and ends up hungry, poor, and drastically underemployed—feeding pigs! Finally the son comes to his senses, realizes his sin, and returns home to ask his father's forgiveness. Look at the surprise greeting he receives: "But while he was still a long way off, his father saw him, and was filled with compassion for him; he ran to his son, threw his arms around him and kissed him" (Luke 15:20b). With an acceptance that extended beyond forgiveness, the father received his sinful son back into the family.

This is a wonderful parable of God's love for His people who have gone off on their own. Beyond that, this parable pictures how we are to accept our brothers and sisters. Just as God embraces each sinner who "returns home" to Him, so we are instructed to receive and welcome our friends. Paul instructs us to "receive ye one another, as Christ also received us to the glory of God" (Rom. 15:7 KJV). As we accept our friends, they'll feel safe to open up and share their problems, failures, and weaknesses with us.

Walk Alongside—It's Good Exercise

The Greek word *parakaleo* helps us to understand further the meaning of biblical acceptance. As we saw in chapter 3, *parakaleo* can mean "to advocate for," "to help," "to comfort," "to encourage" "to exhort, " and "to cheer on." Parakletic helpers are like advocates in a courtroom or like nurses in a hospital, standing beside their patients with encouragement and support. We demonstrate our love and acceptance for our friends when we walk alongside them during their time of need.

In order to understand what it means to walk alongside our friends, picture a track meet where Tom is about to enter his first race. His brother Bill has been coaching and training him for months. As the race begins, Tom is out front. Seeing a chance to shoot into the lead, he pulls to the inside, glancing over his shoulder at the competition. Suddenly, he loses his balance and falls. Dazed but unhurt, he sits on the track, defeated.

To the crowd's amazement Bill jumps up, runs to him, and holds out his hand. Tom looks up and realizes that his brother is encouraging him to continue. Taking the outstretched hand, Tom pulls himself up. Then side by side, the brothers run the last lap together. As Bill runs alongside, he doesn't say a word. With every stride he silently communicates, "I know you're disappointed that you haven't won, but come on, we'll finish together." Bill's presence and support convince Tom that although he stumbled and fell, he can still complete the race.

Our friends are often like Tom, first needing that uncritical love and encouragement that communicate, "I know you're hurting, but I'm right here alongside you." Bill didn't stand back and criticize ("How could Tom be so careless."). He didn't just resign himself to what happened ("It's too bad Tom fell."). Bill's love was strong enough to join in and help.

Unfortunately, this is the place where potential helpers often stumble themselves. We avoid a person in pain by becoming overwhelmed by our own feelings of helplessness, fear, or discomfort.

Welcoming and walking alongside our friends are not easy jobs. They demand love, courage, and patience. But as a result, our friends will trust us with the privilege of helping them. Welcoming and walking alongside form a helping relationship that is fundamental to the entire helping process.

Build a Bridge

As we accept our friends by welcoming them and walking alongside them, we show that they are important to us. By investing our time, interest, and energy, we build a loving, committed relationship. This relationship is a bridge between us and our friends.

The strength of the helping relationship will determine whether our help is received or rejected. When we help our friends, our friendship is temporarily changed because we focus on their problems. After the problem has been solved or the crisis is over, the relationship needs to return to a mutual basis. Often a deeper level of commitment has been formed since we shared our friends' struggles and pain.

HOW CAN WE HELP?

How do we welcome our friends? How do we walk alongside them? Each person you help will be different. What helps one won't work with another. In addition, some of the ways of showing love and acceptance will be easier for you than other ways. As you consider the following ways you can help, pray that God will prepare you to help the different people you meet.

Pray—A Third Person Is Ready To Help

One of the best ways to initiate the helping process is with prayer. When we ask God to be present with us as we help our friends, we acknowledge our need for His wisdom and power. Furthermore, when we recognize God as the one who provides the solutions to our friends' problems, our pride dissolves.

As you meet with your friends or talk with them over the phone, begin by asking God for His direction. Pray that the Holy Spirit will give you wisdom and that God will provide the healing, answers, and guidance that your friend needs. If your friend feels unable to pray, pray for him or her.

Continue to pray throughout the entire helping process. We can pray when our friends become aware of some sin that needs confessing or when they share a problem. We also can seal our conversations with prayer. And don't forget to thank God for answered prayer! It may be encouraging for your friends to keep a prayer journal that records prayers and answers, reminding them of God's faithfulness.

When you pray, make sure that you speak your friend's language. For example, don't use "Thee" and "Thou" when praying with a teenager. When you pray with a nonbeliever, choose your words carefully. Avoid Christian jargon like "redeemed by the blood," "sanctified by the Spirit," or "debtor to grace."

We communicate our care and concern by promising to pray for our friends when we're apart. We build trust and cement the relationship, because our prayers communicate that our friends' problems matter to us. Prayer gets us involved.

Join In—You're in This Together

Jesus joined the disciples on the road to Emmaus by drawing near to them. Bill joined his brother Tom by running alongside of him. Similarly, we bridge the gap between ourselves and our friends every time we join them in their struggles. As we get on their side, our friends become open to our help.

The first way we join our friends is simply by paying attention to them. In your next conversation with someone, position yourself so that you face him or her, lean forward slightly in your chair, and maintain eye contact. Sit in a relaxed posture and keep your arms and legs uncrossed. If at all possible, arrange to talk in a room where the two of you won't be disturbed and where you both are comfortable. All of these will communicate that the other person's concerns are important to you.

Second, we join our friends when we go to be with them. Just as Jesus went to Bethany after He heard that His friend Lazarus was sick (John 11), we too can provide the comfort of our physical presence. This is especially important during times of illness or grief, when often the only thing that we can do is *be with* the person who is hurting. Sitting with your friend in the hospital waiting room as his wife undergoes surgery or visiting your friend after the death of a relative are practical demonstrations of love and concern that communicate, "You aren't alone. I care about what you are going through."

Third, we join our friends by adopting their style. Wendy, a sixteen year old with a mind of her own, taught me this lesson when she began her counseling session with the announcement, "I'm sitting on the floor!" and plopped herself down on the rug in my office. Wanting to demonstrate my acceptance, I plopped myself right down beside her! Any soreness I received from spending an hour a week on the floor was well worth the price of communicating to Wendy that I accepted her on her terms.

Fortunately, we're not usually called to demonstrate acceptance by sitting on the floor with our friends! But joining may mean giving up our normal way of doing things. For instance, it could mean modifying our vocabulary so that a younger or less-educated person can understand what we are saying. Similarly we wouldn't want to chatter incessantly with a friend who was depressed. Like a chameleon, you want to match yourself to your friends' style, tone of voice, pace of talking, and mood. By joining them, you communicate that you are *with* them.

Put Your Judgments on Hold

It's an honor to be chosen to hear our friends' problems, disappointments, or struggles. We destroy this privilege when we prematurely rush in with criticism, quick judgments, or advice. Sometimes a husband wonders why his wife never shares anything with him, never realizing that when she does, he quickly overrules her views with his own (or vice versa). In the same way, our friends learn to keep quiet if their thoughts and feelings are constantly criticized.

In order to be good helpers, we must temporarily suspend our own opinions, learn to listen to things with which we may disagree, and seek to understand our friends' point of view. As Jesus taught, we must be very careful about judging each other (Luke 6:37). Evaluating our friends' behavior before we have all the facts, judging their personality, or dogmatically asserting our point of view too quickly will prevent our friends from opening up to us.

Let's take the example of Phillip, one of your single friends who wants to quit his job because he is bored. You think he's making a poor decision, and you think it's your job to tell him that before it's too late. But if you give premature advice ("But Phillip, you just *can't* quit without first finding another job!") or pose emotion-laden questions ("Don't you think that quitting your job is stupid?"), you'll judge Phillip inappropriately and destroy an opportunity to help him. We often give hasty, opinionated responses when our friend's problem arouses strong emotions or deep biblical convictions in us.

How do you suspend your judgments when you are convinced the person you are talking to is making a wrong decision? Even though Phillip may not be thinking too clearly, your first job is not to advise but to communicate biblical acceptance that will invite him to "show and tell" you about himself. As a result of your welcoming attitude, Phillip will then be free to express the frustration or confusion he is feeling. Helping Phillip get his *whole* story out also may help him see his situation more clearly.

Second, you must respect your friends' freedom to think and feel differently from you. As you listen quietly, you show there is room for your friend's personal choices, responses, and actions. You must be willing to let your friends choose paths with which you might not agree. The decision and consequences are theirs, not yours.

This is not to say that we should never confront sin—we must! As we'll see later, confrontation is an important part of the helping process. But, generally it comes after we have established a relationship with the person whom we are helping. As a result, when we do confront, we will confront with knowledge and without condemnation. Furthermore, our friends will not be defensive, which will make them more receptive to what we have to say.

Putting our own opinions on hold is vital to the helping process. As helpers, we can either open the door to personal disclosure by suspending our judgments or shut it with condemning words and opinions. *That* decision and responsibility is ours.

Climb Into Your Friend's Skin

Can we ever see a situation from our friends' point of view? Fortunately, we don't have to personally go through each experience in order to help our friends. Instead, we can develop empathy, the skill of seeing and feeling life from their perspective. Psychologists have found that empathy and acceptance help initiate any counseling process.[3]

God instructed the Israelites to be empathic when He commanded them not to oppress strangers in their midst. He reminded them that they knew how it felt to be aliens since they also had been strangers in Egypt (Exod. 23:9). Similarly, God has given us two tools that enable us to be empathic: our eyes and ears. As we observe our friends' body language, facial expressions, and tone of voice, we catch glimpses of the emotions and conflicts that lie inside our friends.

Let's take another look at Phillip. Although he says he is bored, what message does his body communicate? When you begin talking, you notice how he fidgets and paces restlessly—possible signs of fear or worry. His clenched fists indicate he may be feeling angry. Occasionally he throws his arms up in a gesture of helplessness. His eyes seem alternately angry or sad; his voice sounds defeated.[4]

Consider the difference between what Phillip has told you and what you have observed. He is obviously more than just bored. His nonverbal behavior indicates that he also. may be feeling frustrated, angry, worried, and defeated. Our friends may be unaware of their deeper feelings; our accurate feedback will help them become more aware of all that is going on inside them. (In chapter 8 we'll learn how to incorporate these observations into our helping responses.)

"Listening" with our eyes as well as with our ears helps us to see the situation from the other person's point of view. As a result, we'll be more likely to respond with love, understanding, and empathy.

Reach Out and Touch Someone

Love is also communicated through touch. Perhaps you've been with your best friends just after they learned that their son has leukemia, and you tried to comfort them. Words often can't communicate the reassurance and love that touch can express. A hug, an arm around the shoulders, or even just a touch on the arm show that you care *for* them and that you feel their pain *with* them.

Physical contact is also important to those who lack intimate relationships. The elderly person in a nursing home, the homesick college student, the single person living alone—all share a need to be loved and comforted through touch. Dr. Paul Brand, a pioneer in leprosy research, has termed physical contact "tactile Christian love." Brand asserts that touching is part of the Christian's responsibility: "The skin of the Body of Christ is an organ of communication: [it is] our vehicle for expressing love."[5]

Since touch is an intimate form of contact, it also can be misunderstood either by the friend or by the helper. A woman who offers sympathy to a distraught father by placing her hand on his arm may alarm other family members. Likewise, a pastor's comforting hug offered to a bereaved woman could be misconstrued as a sexual advance. Avoid misunderstanding by considering the appropriate behavior within the social context and by thinking about what your touch will mean to the other person.

We can get an idea of how our touch will be received by considering how well we know the other person. Often we can determine if our friends are comfortable with physical contact by observing them. If a friend draws back from a pat on the arm, he or she probably feels uneasy. A person who is not used to being hugged may appear stiff and uncomfortable, although inside he or she longs for physical contact. If you aren't sure, ask your friends how they feel about being touched.

Finally, we also must be aware of our own feelings. We can feel very important and needed as our friends literally lean on us for support. Romance can be encouraged by hugs that begin as innocent exchanges between friends but then switch to expressions of sexual attraction. These warnings shouldn't stop us from touching our friends, but they should make us aware that touching must be done with care and sensitivity.

Do Something Helpful—Small Gestures Say a Lot

We also help our friends by serving them. Paul reminds us, "Therefore, as we have opportunity, let us do good to all people, especially to those who belong to the family of believers" (Gal. 6:10). Bringing a meal to a family where the mother is sick or providing baby-sitting for new parents are concrete demonstrations of our Christian love and commitment.

We need to be creative in the services that we offer, thinking first of our friends' needs. Perhaps you have a neighbor who is so depressed that she is unable to complete her housework. Offer to clean *with* her. As you work by her side, you not only let her know that she isn't alone, but you also help her complete her work! Then as you work, she may begin to pour out how sad she feels since her last child left for college. Your gift of service builds trust that enables her to share her loneliness.

Be specific in offering help. Although "Call me if you need me" may be a sincere offer, most people hesitate to bother their friends with requests. Instead, put yourself in your friends' place and sensitively consider their needs. For example, what would you need if you just had a heart attack and were now at home recuperating? Among other things you might be worried about who would take care of your house, do the yard work, fix the leaky shower, or put up the storm windows. A friend who would spend a Saturday taking care of odd jobs around your house would be communicating his or her love without saying a word.

Make sure to check your plans with your friends. They may not need one more tuna casserole! In addition, be sure to respect a person's pride. Your friend may not be accustomed to receiving help. Suggesting several things that you are willing to do enables your friend to take what he or she needs.

Similarly, you can allow your friend to reciprocate by helping you. Providing a service for you will build your friend's self-respect and dignity. This also keeps the helping relationship mutual and avoids some of the temptations we studied in chapter 4.

Forgive and Forbear

Sometimes we'll find that the person who comes to us for help will be someone who has wronged us. Before we can even begin to help, we first need to forgive that person (unless that has already been done). That may mean swallowing our pride, putting aside our desire to get even, and releasing our grudges against that person.

Paul teaches that we should forgive others as God has forgiven us (Eph. 4:32; Col. 3:12–13). We must remember that it will cost us to forgive; it's rarely an easy task. A forgiving spirit doesn't bring up the wrong that has been done once forgiveness has been genuinely granted.

In practical terms this means that when it's time to help someone who has slighted you, do the following: meditate on what Jesus has done for you; listen without replaying the other person's offenses to yourself; focus your attention on their problems and how you can help; and finally, pray for them and whenever you can, speak well of them.[6] Ultimately forgiveness is a choice to put off bitterness and past grievances and to put on love and reconciliation. Forgiveness, like love, is hard work.

Even when we haven't been sinned against, it's still sometimes difficult to love certain people. Perhaps we're turned off by their personal habits or mannerisms. Their shrill tone of voice, offensive language, constant interruptions, or overbearing manner can be irritating to the point that we even dread talking to them. How can we help someone that we find unappealing?

We can do two things to help us deal with a person who irritates us. First, we can prayerfully look at the other person as a fellow sinner who needs God's mercy just as much as we do. Second, we can ask God to enable us to put off our prejudices and to put on patience and compassion.

You must consider also that whatever offends you (someone's overbearing manner, for example) may also offend others. At some point in the helping process, you may be able to confront the person about this personal habit. Your help would fall short if you ignored the fact that your friend's mannerisms drive people away from him or her.

As we've already noted, biblical love both confronts and comforts; one without the other is incomplete. Peter's admonition that "love covers over a multitude of sins" (1 Peter 4:8) should be our umbrella passage as we forgive and forbear with our friends (see also Prov. 17:9). As we walk alongside our friends and bear with these irritants, we'll earn the right to confront them.

Walk the Two-Way Street of Trust

The helping relationship is cemented by the trust that our friends place in us. As we have been dependable, followed through on our promises to help, walked alongside, placed our own opinions on hold, and understood their perspective, we have demonstrated that we are trustworthy. In addition, we need to reassure our friends that what they tell us will remain confidential. Nothing destroys a helping relationship faster than the wagging tongue of gossip (Prov. 11:13; 16:28; James 3:5).

As with most rules, there are a few exceptions. If your friends give you information that suggests they are dangerous to themselves (suicidal, abusing drugs) or others (violent, homicidal), you may need to contact the appropriate authorities and relay this information. Similarly, if you confront a friend about sin and if your friend refuses to listen, Scripture commands us to take certain steps that may break confidentiality (Matt. 18:15– 17).[7] As a rule, other helpers should be brought in only if they are needed to help solve the problem. (When and how to bring in other helpers will be discussed further in chapters 11 and 13.)

In less extreme situations, friends may tell you about marriage problems that need to be discussed with a spouse. Or they may complain about church difficulties that should be shared with the pastor. The inability or fear of confronting someone can end up increasing our friend's difficulties. We should encourage our friends to talk to the person with whom they have conflict, but if they refuse, ask permission to share the information yourself. Only in emergency situations such as mentioned above should you talk to a third person without your friends' permission.

But trust works both ways. When you help your friends by joining them, praying for them, and assisting them in all the ways listed above, you also place your trust in them. To hope for another person and to be their helper is an act of trust. In this way God is also helping you grow as a worker in His kingdom.

You have now prepared the foundation of helping by equipping yourself with love and acceptance. As you move on to the first level of helping, remember that it is God's wisdom and power that will ultimately make you an effective helper.

PERSONAL AND PRACTICAL

Study the Scriptures

1. Read Mark 9:37. What does Jesus teach about how we are to welcome and receive our friends? Consider Abraham's example in Genesis 18:1–8. In what ways did Abraham demonstrate a welcoming love? How can you apply this to helping your friends?
2. Read Hebrews 4:15. How does Jesus show that He understands us? What does this passage teach you about being empathic? How could you use it when helping a friend?
3. Read Colossians 1:9–12. What five things did Paul ask God to give to the Colossian church? Use Paul's guidelines to pray for a friend.
4. Read Matthew 9:9–13. How did Jesus "join" the tax gatherers and sinners? How do you think you could apply this passage in helping someone? Think of a friend whom you'd like to join this week and develop a plan for how you'll do it. Read 1 Corinthians 9:22. How does Paul's example apply to us?
5. Read Matthew 7:1–5 and Luke 6:37. What is Jesus' message about those who judge others? What types of people do you tend to judge? What steps can you take to put your judgments on hold?
6. Read Matthew 8:2–4 and Mark 1:40–42. What is your response to Jesus touching the leper? How would you feel touching a leper? How would you feel if you were the leper? Think of someone in your family, church, or neighborhood who needs to be touched and decide how you'll reach out to him or her.
7. Read Mark 10:43–45. What does Jesus teach about serving one another? Read 2 Corinthians 8:2, 9, and 14.

What is Paul's main point in these verses? Consider the two passages together. How does God expect you to serve Him? Think of the talents, abilities, and material wealth He has given you. How could you share these with someone in need? Plan to do something helpful for someone in your church, school, or neighborhood.

8. Read Matthew 18:21–35. What does Jesus teach about forgiveness? What people do you have a hard time forgiving and loving? When is it hard for you to forbear with someone? What will you do about this?

9. Read Proverbs 11:13; 25:9–10; Matthew 18:15 and 1 Peter 2:1. What do these passages teach us about trust? Think of at least three specific ways you can demonstrate that you are a trustworthy friend.

For Further Reading

1. Read chapters 1 and 2 of David Augsburger's *Caring Enough To Hear* (Ventura, California: Regal Books, 1982) for more information on listening and attending skills.

2. Read David Augsburger's short paperback *The Freedom of Forgiveness* (Chicago: Moody Press, 1970).

3. Read chapter 2 of Gary Collins' *How To Be a People Helper* (Santa Ana, California: Vision House, 1976). Complete chapters 4 and 5 in the *People Helper Growthbook* for more background information on people helping.

4. Read chapter 3 of Gerard Egan's *The Skilled Helper: Model Skills and Methods for Effective Helping* (Monterey, California: Brooks-Cole Publishing Co., 1975) for information on prehelping skills and read chapter 4 for help in developing empathy.

5. Read Dan Hamilton's pamphlet *Forgiveness* (Downers Grove, Illinois: InterVarsity Press, 1980).

6. Read Lewis Smedes' *Forgive and Forget* (San Francisco: Harper & Row, 1984) for his discussion of forgiveness.

7. Read chapters 6 and 8 of Everett Worthington's *When Someone Asks for Help* (Downers Grove, Illinois: InterVarsity Press, 1985) for help to develop your understanding of people's emotions and problems.

NOTES

[1] Carl Rogers, *On Becoming a Person* (Boston: Houghton Mifflin Company, 1961), p. 62.

[2] Barry Seagran, "Who Is God?", *What in the World Is Real?* (Champaign, Illinois: Communication Institute, 1982), p. 301.

[3] Gerard Egan, *The Skilled Helper: Model Skills and Methods for Effective Helping* (Monterey, California: Brooks-Cole Publishing Co., 1975), p. 75.

[4] For more information on body language see William Hinds, "Emotions in Psychotherapy," quoted in Everett Worthington, *When Someone Asks for Help* (Downers Grove, Illinois: InterVarsity Press, 1982), p. 79.

[5] Paul Brand and Philip Yancey, *Fearfully and Wonderfully Made* (Grand Rapids: Zondervan Publishing House, 1980), p. 139.

[6] These suggestions were made by Jay Adams (*The Christian Counselor's Manual* [Phillipsburg, New Jersey: Presbyterian and Reformed Publishing Co., 1973], p. 66) and by James Kennedy (sermon about forgiveness, delivered June 19, 1979, at the Coral Ridge Presbyterian Church, Fort Lauderdale, Florida).

[7] The issue of bringing in the elders of the church is discussed in chapter 9.

‡

CHAPTER 7

LEARN TO LISTEN: THE FIRST LEVEL OF HELPING

He who answers before listening—that is his folly and his shame.

—Proverbs 18:13

LISTENING PRINCIPLES

One of our primary skills as helpers is our ability to listen. We communicate love and acceptance when we listen to our friends' anger, fears, despair, or desires. Whether it's hearing the fears of an older person, taking a child's doubts seriously, or sitting with a friend who bitterly mourns her child's death, our listening is helpful.

Often our friends will experience tremendous relief just knowing they can talk about something that is bothering them. They may feel that no one cares enough to listen or that people would reject them if they shared their *real* feelings and thoughts. Listening recognizes and affirms our friends' experiences.

Some people may be afraid of our willingness to listen, for listening is an invitation to growth as well as a call to accountability. Friends who aren't used to being open and honest will fear what they might divulge to you as well as what they might discover about themselves. Again, your attitude of acceptance will facilitate this process.

Our attentive listening serves several purposes. First, careful listening gives us information about our friends' problems, needs, thoughts, hopes, and feelings. Second, empathic listening builds trust that communicates our care and our willingness to become involved in their struggles. Third, attentive listening also discovers the meaning our friends attribute to what they are experiencing. Fourth, careful listening helps us understand how our friends are fitting together the pieces of their lives. Finally, good listening also keeps us from the helping temptations that we studied in chapter 4. If we are intent on serving our friends by listening to them, we'll be less likely to jump to conclusions, interrupt with our opinions, judge the situation prematurely, let our minds wander, or criticize them while they are talking.

The Bible teaches us about the importance of listening. In the Old Testament, God is the one who listens to our voices and requests each morning (Ps. 5:3; see also Ps. 102:2b, 14–20). In the New Testament, we see Jesus carefully listening to the problems and requests brought to Him. James 1:19 instructs us how we can follow Christ's pattern: We "should be quick to listen, slow to speak and slow to become angry."

Careful listening prevents us from giving quick solutions that may miss the mark. It also helps us understand the other person so that we can give good responses (Prov. 15:28; 17:27). Ultimately, listening carefully will prepare us to be truth speakers with "apt answers" for our friends (Prov. 15:23).

GETTING TO KNOW YOU

One of the first things we need to do when helping our friends is find out what's going on in their lives. What are the problems, stresses, or conflicts they face? What are their strengths, joys, and victories? We must try to understand how they view themselves, their lives, and the other people around them.

We can gather this information in two ways: by asking good questions and by listening carefully to the answers. Don't forget—you will risk turning your friend off if you forget his or her answers and wind up repeating your questions.

Ask the Right Kind of Questions

Precise questions serve two purposes: they give us information about our friend's experience and they help our friends focus on how they need to change.

A warning is appropriate here: don't ask questions to satisfy your own curiosity. A friend can detect your true motivation through your tone of voice and facial expressions. For example, let's say that your friend Lisa's husband recently left her. Consider the difference between inquiring with a shocked look on your face, "What happened between you and Jonathan?" or saying "I heard Jonathan just left, and I'm concerned for you and the kids" with sympathy in your voice and concern in your eyes.

Helpful questions are generally open-ended; they can't be answered with a simple yes or no. Instead, they encourage your friend to think through his or her response, and they invite discussion. For instance, if you ask Lisa whether she's been depressed since Jonathan left, you are assuming how she is feeling and limiting her response. She may be feeling angry, worried, guilty, or relieved. "How are you feeling?" is an open-ended question that would give Lisa the freedom to choose her own response.

"Either-or" questions are also restrictive. Asking Lisa, "Did you feel helpless or frustrated after Jonathan left?" will lock her into your choices rather than help her come up with her own. Using the nonverbal data that you observe, encourage your friends to express their own personal combination of thoughts and feelings. For example, if you see that Lisa is close to tears, ask an open-ended question like, "You look as if you're feeling really hurt. How has it been for you since Jonathan left?" Questions like these invite Lisa to share her experience with you.

Don't use questions as an opportunity to grill a friend. Your job is to open up a conversation, not to cross-examine or interrogate your friend. Consider what your friend is experiencing and pace your questions accordingly. Hitting Lisa with a barrage of "What do you think will happen to your marriage?" and "When will you see him again?" and "Where is he living?" and "How are you ever going to get along without him?" will probably overwhelm Lisa. A series of questions also can be very confusing—Lisa won't know which to answer first.

Helpful questions explore a situation without putting the other person on the defensive. If you're trying to help Lisa think about why Jonathan left, avoid saying, "Don't you think that Jonathan walked out because of how you nag him all the time?" That probably will eliminate all further discussion! Eventually you may be in a position to say, "Have you ever thought about how you tried to get Jonathan to help around the house? I wonder if he started to resent the way you asked him to do things." This combination of question and personal statement is less threatening and will be easier for Lisa to hear. In addition, your tone of voice and choice of words can convey either criticism or a genuine desire to help. Thinking about how you like questions asked of you will give you clues about how to ask questions of others.

Avoid asking questions that camouflage your personal opinions. "Do you really think that the argument between the two of you was just Jonathan's fault?" or "Don't you think you should be the one to call and apologize first?" are questions that answer themselves and predetermine Lisa's response. Instead, exploratory questions encourage the other person to think. Asking, "How do you think you should respond to Jonathan now?" will challenge Lisa to honestly examine herself. Then use her response and probe further by asking, "What do you think will happen if you say or do that?" Questions like these help Lisa decide what she will do next.

Specific questions will encourage your friend to talk more. "When did the arguments with Jonathan begin?" will help Lisa open up about the tension at home. If Lisa responds, "About two months ago," follow up by asking, "Did anything unusual or different happen around that time?" Careful questioning will help you assess the situation and help Lisa gain perspective on her present situation.

In general, avoid excessive use of "why" questions. Like the four-year-old boy who pesters his mother by asking why all the time, helpers also can lean too heavily on this word. Use why only to get more information or to help a person understand his or her motivation. For instance, you can ask, "Do you know why you were arguing that night?" or "Do you know why Jonathan left?" But don't use why questions to delve into a person's past. "Do you know why you nag Jonathan? Is it because that's how your mother treated your father?" are questions that provide a person with excuses for not changing. Similarly, beware of beginning a question with why. "Why can't you just learn to be a more loving wife?" communicates judgment and criticism.

Often a person will pour out a load of troubles all at once. Careful questioning can help your friend focus on the most pressing problem. Questions that define the problem help a friend distinguish side issues from those that are more important. For example, Lisa may feel overwhelmed as she considers that besides Jonathan's leaving, her car isn't running, the cat is sick, her son has a dentist appointment, and Jonathan took the checkbook. She doesn't know how she'll get to the dentist or the vet or how she'll pay their bills. Helping Lisa to think through her priorities and resources ("Can the dentist appointment wait?" "How sick is the cat?" "Can you borrow a friend's car?" "Do you have another way of getting cash?") will help her decide what to do first.

You can use a variety of questions to gather information. Consult chart #1, "Questions That Probe," for some examples. Keep track of the questions that you ask family members and friends. Observe which questions open up conversations and which shut them down. Jot down in your journal questions you have used to encourage friends to talk about themselves more.

CHART #1: QUESTIONS THAT PROBE

1. What do you think you need? What are you looking for? What do you feel you're missing in your life (school, relationships, job)?

2. What would you like to see happen or change in your life? By when?

3. What have you already done to solve this problem?

4. Who else have you talked to about this? How have they helped you? What wasn't helpful?

5. How often does this happen (frequency of problem)?

6. How much is it affecting the rest of your life (intensity of problem)?

7. How long have you been experiencing this problem (duration of problem)?

8. When do you experience this problem?

9. What is your relationship to the Lord at this time?

10. What is bothering you the most right now?

11. Do you really want to change? What will you gain or lose by changing? (This helps to find out a person's *real* reason and motivation for changing.)

12. What do you hope to feel/think/do differently?

13. Has anything unusual happened in the last six months?

14. If you could change one thing in your life, what would that be?

15. What do you hope I can do for you?

LEARN WHAT TO LISTEN FOR

How do you know what to listen for? Beginning helpers often feel overwhelmed with all the details of their friends' stories. What is important to discover and what can be screened out?

Imagine that you're talking to Peter, a man with whom you've worked for four years. Peter frequently complains that he gets passed over when it's time for promotions. For the last two years he hasn't advanced at all in the company. He's worried that he'll never reach his goal of division manager. He feels that his efforts are never recognized, although he works very hard. When he asks you why everybody else gets treated better than he does, you wonder how to respond.

In order to help Peter, you first need a complete and accurate assessment of his situation. Preconceived ideas about him ("Peter is such a complainer") or his problems ("His worries aren't really important") will distort your perception of him. Don't jump to conclusions or make unfounded assumptions. As you listen, pay attention to several things.

Listen for requests for help. For instance, if Peter says, "I don't know what to do. I seem to be the only one who never gets a promotion around here," he's saying a great deal. Not only does he feel alone and frustrated, but he doesn't know how to respond to his situation. This is an indirect request for help.

Peter might begin by talking about a related topic. He may let you know that he's discouraged or disappointed by saying, "I'm really tired of trying to please the boss. Even when I put in overtime, he doesn't notice me. Working here just doesn't pay off." Probing him a little, you may discover that at Peter's recent review, only passing mention was given to the extra work he's done for the company. Listen well and you'll hear that Peter is considering finding a different job since he's not achieving his career goals.

If Peter is a Christian, his comments may be expressed in terms of his relationship to God. He might begin by saying something like, "I'm really confused about whether God wants me to stay in this job. I pray about it, but I still don't get any clear direction." Sometimes Christians overspiritualize their problems and don't say what they're really thinking or feeling. You can help Peter by encouraging him to express the real issues—his underlying confusion and frustration.

Requests for help also can be expressed directly. If Peter asks, "What would you do if you were in my situation?" he is openly soliciting your advice. But if you give him advice or tell him what you'd do, you probably will prevent him from going through the problem-solving process himself. Remember, you're a coach, not a lifeguard.

Listen for why your friend wants help now. As a person begins to open up to you, listen for the reasons that he or she is talking to you *now*. Sometimes the problem has been around for a while, and your friend is just now feeling unable to cope with the situation. Other times a specific event (like Peter's recent unsatisfactory review) triggers a conversation. As you gather data, you begin to understand what led up to your friend's decision to confide in you at this time.

Asking open-ended questions will help you gather information. Find out how Peter has tried to secure a promotion and how long he has tried this particular tactic. If you discover that Peter has only been working overtime for two weeks and before that he spent two weeks buying his boss coffee and donuts, you may find out that *the way* Peter tries to secure a promotion is part of his problem! Besides, if you've overheard Peter complain about every new assignment that his boss gives him, then you'll have heard more of the *real* reason that he hasn't been promoted.

Listen for background events. It's important to find out what else is going on in Peter's life right now. If you ask Peter for the reasons he had a mediocre job review, you may find out that his attitude was rated poor. As you explore what else he's been experiencing lately, you may find out that his wife just quit her job to stay home and take care of her sick mother. On top of it all, her brother just received a hefty promotion on his job. Peter's loss of income, his mother-in-law's health, and his brother-in-law's success will have an impact on him. Unusual events, crises, or stressful situations can affect a person in many ways. Look at chart #2, "Is Your Friend Under Stress?," to see how different types of events can add considerable stress to a person's life.

CHART #2: IS YOUR FRIEND UNDER STRESS?[1]

The following list of "life stress" events was developed by social scientists to measure the amount of cumulative stress to which a person has been exposed. Of persons scoring higher than 300 on this list, about eighty percent developed serious illness in the next two years! If a person scores 200 or more and isn't feeling well, he or she should probably get a medical checkup. A score of 150 or more suggests that a person should start reducing the stress in his or her life. To measure how much stress your friend is facing, check off the events he or she has experienced in the last year and then add up the numerical values assigned to each. (Note how many of these stresses are common to ordinary life.)

Events	Scale of Impact
Death of Spouse	100
Divorce	73
Marital separation	65
Jailing or institutionalization	63
Death of close family member	63
Major injury or illness	53
Marriage	50
Fired from job	47
Marital reconciliation	45

Retirement	45
Change in health of family member	44
Pregnancy	40
Sex difficulties	39
Gain of new family member	39
Major business change	39
Major change in financial state	38
Death of close friend	37
Change to different line of work	36
Change in frequency of arguments with spouse	35
Mortgage or loan for major purchase	31
Foreclosure of mortgage or loan	30
Change in responsibility at work	29
Son or daughter leaving home	29
Outstanding personal achievement	28
Wife begins or stops work	26
Begin or end school	26
Major change in living situations	25
Revision of personal habits	24
Trouble with boss	23
Change in work hours	20
Change in residence	20
Change in schools	20
Change in recreation	19
Change in church activities	19

Change in social activities	18
Small mortgage or loan	17
Change in sleeping habits	15
Change in number of family gatherings	15
Change in eating habits	15
Vacation	13
Christmas	12
Minor law violations	11

As you talk to Peter, consider what stage of life he's in right now. Depending on a person's age, different life events have different meanings.[2] If Peter is thirty-two and just beginning his career, then he has time to consider how he can climb the corporate ladder. His fears can be relieved with good career planning. But if Peter is fifty-seven and thinking of retiring in a few years, the picture changes considerably. Then he's facing disappointment and shame over unmet dreams and goals.

Listen for religious beliefs. A person's religion and life philosophy will affect how that person responds to his or her circumstances. It's important to listen for the particular value system and frame of reference that gives meaning to your friend's life. Christians and non-Christians will interpret life experiences differently. If Peter is not a Christian, a philosophy of "I've got to look out for #1" may dominate his thinking and direct his behavior.

If Peter is a Christian, then you want to evaluate how his relationship to the Lord influences his thoughts and behavior. Peter's answers to, "What does God's Word say about how we are to relate to our employers?" and "What attitude are we commanded to have as we work?" will help you determine if Peter is able to integrate his Christian faith into the everyday events of his life.

You also need to listen for any sin of which Peter might not be aware. Is his grumbling and complaining affecting his work? Is his attitude causing dissatisfaction among his co-workers? Or perhaps he's so focused on reaching a certain level of management that he neglects his family or his responsibilities at church. Listening intently not only will help you consider how Peter's work problems fit into his entire life but it also will help you determine what you say to him.

Listen for how your friend talks about himself or herself. You also need to listen for any patterns in how your friend speaks about his or her problems. Listen not only for what your friend talks about but also the words and expressions that he or she uses.

Does Peter, for instance, report about himself or the events that happen to him in the third person? Does he say, "Some people are getting mad that they don't get promoted" or does he say, "I'm frustrated that I haven't been promoted." People who have difficulty revealing how they really think or feel may hide their opinions behind the general description of "they" or "other people."

Listen to whether Peter describes situations in terms of what other people do to him ("My boss doesn't treat me fairly.") or in terms of his own responsibility ("I wonder what I'm doing wrong that I haven't received a promotion."). In the first example, Peter is blaming his boss; in the second he is taking responsibility for himself. Peter will feel helpless and will not see what he can do to change the situation as long as he thinks that it's his boss's problem and not his.

Listen to determine if Peter is facing the full impact of his problem. You may find that Peter starts talking about his jealousy over his brother-in-law's promotion, but then switches to last night's basketball game. Talking in the third person, switching subjects, or sticking to less threatening topics are indications that Peter is trying to maintain distance between himself and his problems.

Listen to your friend's questions. You also want to listen for any pattern to Peter's questions. Do his questions have answers hidden inside them? For instance, "Don't you think I should ask for a promotion?" tells you that Peter has already decided what he is going to do and is simply looking for your stamp of approval.

Listen to your friend's answers. Similarly, notice if Peter consistently asks for your opinion but then ignores your answers. If so, he might be seeking attention rather than real solutions. Does he frequently respond with "yes, but" and a list of excuses after you've made a suggestion? Then you may be caught up in a rescuing game that will leave you angry and frustrated.[3] Responding to Peter's request for advice with,

"How would you handle the situation?" will help him discover his choices rather than solve his problems for him.

Listen for underlying assumptions and expectations. Peter's comment, "Employers should appreciate extra work and recognize it by giving promotions" summarizes his ideas about how work should be rewarded. A person's tone of voice also communicates what he or she believes should happen. Expectations also can hide in sentences beginning with "if only" or "I wish." When Peter says, "If only I had a more appreciative boss, then my life would be so much easier," he is telling you who he wishes would change! Listen to whether or not your friend's expectations are realistic and appropriate. In the same way, listen for what he or she may expect from you as a friend. People often become disappointed or angry when their expectations aren't met.

Listen for generalities and exaggerations. Broad statements tend to paint a distorted picture of reality. You may well doubt Peter's accuracy and honesty if he says, "I *always* try my hardest, but no one *ever* notices me." Statements aimed at getting your attention and sympathy can have the opposite effect! Similarly, listen for Peter's conclusions. "I never thought I could make it as a manager. Everything I try always fails." Peter's preconceived attitude and conclusions may be keeping him from reaching his goals.

Listen for repeated words and phrases. Does Peter often say "I can't," "I should," "Things never work out right," or "Nobody understands"? As you carefully listen, you'll find that such words are windows into that person's self-perception as well as into his or her view of life.

In the same way listen to whether *what* Peter says matches *how* he says it. He may pretend nothing is bothering him, but his cynical digs about the boss and the company tell you a different story. It may be easier for Peter to sound tough and sarcastic than to admit his sense of shame and failure.

Listen for themes. Does Peter always bring up the same topics or does he frequently express the same emotions? His failure to be successful at work may run parallel to his experience of not measuring up to his wife's expectations. Similarly, the way he responds to his boss ("I'm going to stop trying to please him. He never appreciates what I do anyway.") may be similar to how he reacts to his wife ("All she does is complain that I'm not as good as her brother. She never notices what I do for her. Why bother trying?'').

LISTENING IS AN ACTIVE EXPERIENCE

Now that we know *what* to listen for, we'll examine *how* we can listen more effectively. We'll learn to use what counselors call "active listening." Although it's never a substitute for genuinely getting to know the other person, active listening will *show* our friends that we understand what they are telling us.

Active listening focuses our attention on our friends' entire message: both the overt meaning of their statements and the subtle nuances of meaning that compose the background. It's like listening to a piano concerto. While it's easy to hear the melody the pianist is playing, it takes a little more effort to hear each of the instruments in the background. Yet the piano melody is incomplete without the violins, cellos, and clarinets that accompany it. In a similar way, the content of a person's statement is best understood within the context of his or her entire message.

How can you hear both the "melody" of a person's words as well as all the "music" playing in the background? We must empathically listen for three distinct elements of our friends' message: the *content, feelings,* and *implication.*

Each Message Is a Trio

Content. Since we're used to figuring out *what* a person is telling us, it's pretty easy to hear content. Like a news reporter, we listen for the facts and information that make up a person's story. This content includes the specific details of who, what, where, and when. As you listen for content, think about what the person is telling you. Listen for what is important to him or her at that moment.

Let's take Peter as an example. What was the content of his message? Basically, he was troubled that he hadn't received a promotion in two years. He also was concerned that his efforts to reach his goal of division manager would not pay off.

Feelings. Unless Peter comes right out and says "I'm worried" or "I'm depressed," it can be more difficult to determine *how* he's feeling than *what* he's saying. You'll need to observe what emotions he conveys in his tone of voice, body language, and eyes.

With Peter, you may hear a background of bitterness and defeat when he talks. At first his complaining voice may sound sullen and cynical. But then notice how his shoulders sag and how he looks tired and worn out. Observe the hurt reflected in his eyes when he recounts how his wife compares him to his brother-in-law. All in all, Peter looks and sounds like a man who feels frustrated, discouraged, and defeated.

Implication. Third, listen for the possible implications of your friend's message. Implications fall into two different categories: our friends' *interpretation* of the situation and our friends' *intention* (what they plan to do) about the situation.

Like the listening filters that screen all incoming information (see chapter 5), we also have filters which screen and interpret our experiences. For instance, how does Peter interpret the fact that he hasn't received a promotion? His grumbling indicates his dissatisfaction with his boss, with the company, and with himself. His filters say: "No one appreciates the work I do. Everybody else gets what they want around here, except me. I can't do anything right!" His filters also could determine how he perceives God: "God sure doesn't seem to care about my prayers!"

Next listen for how Peter is planning to respond to not receiving a promotion. Ask yourself, "What is he deciding now? What will be the long-term consequences of these decisions?" As you listen, you'll be able to discern the direction in which your friend is headed.

In Peter's case, his defeatist attitude indicates that he is concluding, "Why should I bother trying? Nothing I do ever pays off. I may as well give up and learn to live with the way things are. I probably wouldn't be a very good manager anyway." This superficial acceptance may later lead to even greater personal dissatisfaction when Peter still hasn't met his goals.

Obviously, we won't be able to respond to *everything* our friends say. We must pray that God will help us discern what the most important thing is to which we need to respond.

The Active-Listening Response

After we have listened carefully to our friends, we'll be able to respond by reflecting or mirroring the content, feelings, and implications of their message. This chart explains the active-listening response.[4]

CHART #3 THE ACTIVE-LISTENING RESPONSE

CONTENT + FEELING + IMPLICATIONS = ACTIVE-LISTENING RESPONSE

An active-listening response to Peter would sound like this: "I understand that you're really disappointed and frustrated that you haven't been promoted. It sounds as if you're ready to give up on your goal of manager. It also sounds as if you're confused because God does not seem to be answering your prayers." This summarizes what Peter has been saying, how he's feeling, and what he's concluding. You know that you have listened well if you can accurately articulate your friends' point of view and if they respond to you by saying "Yes, that's how I feel," or if they continue their story.

Using the Active-Listening Response

Our ability to listen attentively will come in handy in many situations. Let's look at some examples.

First of all, we'll use our active-listening skills when our friends first open up to us. Our attentive listening while our friends let off steam will encourage them to express their thoughts and feelings and will give us the opportunity to gather information. Then together we'll be able to explore the various aspects of their situation. Listening to Lisa's fears or hearing Peter's frustrations are both good opportunities to use active listening.

Throughout the helping process, active listening shows that we empathize with what our friends are facing. If we first show that we understand, our friends will be more likely to hear us when we confront them. For instance, first saying to Peter, "I can see that you're really angry because your efforts haven't produced what you expected" communicates your understanding. Then you could add, "I wonder if the fact that you don't always do what your boss asks might be part of the reason why you're not getting promoted." (The speaking skills of feedback and confrontation will be studied in detail in chapters 8 and 9.) Helpful responses combine both listening and speaking skills.

The active-listening response is a skill you'll want to take with you wherever you go and is not limited just to solving people's problems. Responding to your daughter's feeling of pride when she passes her driver's test by saying, "You're really pleased with yourself that you got your license" shows her that you know how proud she is of her accomplishment. You'll find active listening is a good communication tool in your family, on the job, and in everyday conversation.

Active listening is also a good tool when two people disagree. Taking the time to really listen and understand the other person's point of view will minimize argumentative responses. Next time you're about to hotly defend your opinion, first reflect on what the other person has said to you. You'll find that your friend (spouse, child, or co-worker) will appreciate that you've listened to his or her side of the story. And besides that, your response may change! Dialogue is facilitated when people care enough to listen fully to one another.

Helpers are often uncomfortable with silence. You can "listen" to a friend's silence by reflecting to him or her the nonverbal cues that you observe. "You look bothered by what we've been talking about. I can see you're really thinking it over" lets your friend know that you respect his or her silence.

Finally, when you don't know how else to respond, you can always fall back on an active-listening response. When you're not sure what to say next, reflecting what you've heard will help review a conversation. This is also a way to clarify the issues and helps you and your friend decide what to discuss next.

Listening Liabilities

Listening, however, also has its pitfalls. Let's look at five obstacles to avoid as we respond to what we hear.

Caution #1: Don't trivialize your friend's problem. Helpers who feel overwhelmed with a friend's problem can react by minimizing the situation. Sympathetic pat responses of "Things will be better soon" more often ease the helper's discomfort than help the friend. We may unwittingly deny the other person's full range of emotions by what we say. Saying to Lisa, "It must have been disappointing to have Jonathan leave" doesn't accurately reflect her stronger feelings of anger or panic. Awareness of your own discomfort will help keep you from screening out the full impact of your friend's message.

Caution #2: Don't deny your friend's problem. In a misdirected attempt to help, sometimes helpers end up denying a friend's problem altogether. When Peter says to you "I'm a total failure" and you respond with "That's not true," you are missing what he's telling you. Similarly, if you ask him how he's doing, don't argue with his answer! After pouring out his feelings, he doesn't want to hear, "Well, that's not really so bad. Things could be a lot worse, you know." Arguing with his self-perceptions will keep him from trusting you and will break off further communication.

Caution #3: Don't be a parrot. Instead of paraphrasing a friend's message in his or her own words, some helpers repeat verbatim what they've just heard. Eager to get the message right, these helpers end up sounding like parrots! If Lisa says, "I feel so lonely," you need to respond with more than just "You're feeling really lonely, aren't you?" Try to imagine what Lisa's life is like and form an empathic response. You could say, "I imagine that your life seems really empty now without Jonathan."

Caution #4: Don't overinterpret. It's important not to project your own feelings onto your friend. As much as possible, listen accurately and avoid reading in your own ideas. Responding to Lisa with, "You must feel abandoned" is really adding more than what she has said so far. Stay with your friend; don't get ahead of what he or she is saying.

Caution #5: Don't overuse active listening. There are times when it's not helpful to use an active-listening response. For example, if Peter continues to complain about how his boss is unfair but never talks about what he can do to change the situation, then it's time for more than just another, "You really think your boss doesn't treat you right." At this point, Peter sounds like a broken record and needs his friend to help him see his part of the problem.

Active listening is also inappropriate if a friend is seeking specific information. When Peter asks, "Do you know why I haven't been promoted?" is no time to say, "You'd like to find out why you haven't received a promotion." If you know why Peter was not promoted, give Peter feedback on the behavior you've observed in the office. If you don't know the reasons behind the boss's decision, then your next step would be to help Peter figure out how he can get the information himself.

If your friend is in a crisis or needs immediate action, you'll use the active-listening skills for only a short period of time. Listening will help you to assess the situation so that you and your friend can take quick action. Similarly, if you are talking to someone who is suicidal, homicidal, violent, under the influence of drugs or alcohol, or in some way not in touch with reality, active listening is also an insufficient response.

SET CLEAR GOALS

The final aspect of this level of the helping process is to help our friends translate vague, general wishes into observable behavior by helping them establish measurable goals. Like a runner's finish line, goals help a person focus on where he or she is heading. As they think about what changes they'd like to see in their lives, our friends need to consider what they are willing *to do* to achieve that change. Setting goals is also like drawing up a blueprint. It provides an outline of what a person is hoping to accomplish. As we help our friends, we'll fill in the details of that outline together.

Let's drop in on a conversation between Peter and his friend Mike. Imagine that they are having lunch together and Peter has once again complained about not getting promoted to manager. Let's see how Mike listens, gathers information, and encourages Peter to translate his wishes into goals and a plan of action.

Mike: "I've heard you say a number of times that you wish you could be promoted to a manager's position. What do you plan to do to make that happen?" [Reflecting content; open-ended question.]

Peter: "I really don't know that there's much I can do. I'd like to be moving up in the company, but as long as the boss doesn't notice me, I guess I'm stuck where I am."

Mike: "You sound frustrated and think there's not much you can do to get ahead." [Active listening to content, feelings, and implication.]

Peter: "I just want to be happy at work. Right now I'm miserable. I feel that what I do is never noticed."

Mike: "What would you need to do to be less miserable? [More specific question to zero in on Peter's goals and to help him define the problem in terms of himself.]

Peter: "I'd like to know I was getting somewhere in the company."

Mike: "What is 'getting somewhere'? What are you shooting for?" [Specific, open-ended questions to help Peter clarify his goals.]

Peter: "I'd really like to be in management."

Mike: "What is keeping you from getting there?" [Probing, open-ended question.]

Peter: "Well, I'm not sure I have the right skills. And my boss mentioned a poor attitude. . . ."

Mike: "So you're saying that you may need more training and a change in your attitude." [Summarizing content through active listening.]

Peter: "Well, I guess so. But I'm sure the boss would never agree to spending money for my courses, and I can't afford them myself. And I really don't know what's wrong with my attitude."

Mike: "Which is most important, the courses or your attitude?" [Prioritizing problems.]

Peter: "Maybe my attitude, since I keep hearing how that's so important around here."

Mike: "Have you ever asked your boss what he means by a 'poor attitude'?" [Data gathering.]

Peter: "Not really. He's such a hard person to talk to. I just figured he had it in for me and that it wouldn't do any good to talk to him."

Mike: "I get the impression that you think your boss has the problem, not you. It also seems as if you feel defeated before you start, don't get the information you need, and then are frustrated when you don't move up in the company." [Active listening that summarizes implications of Peter's statements.]

Peter: "I hadn't thought about it like that. What do you think is the big deal about my attitude, anyway?"

Mike: "I wonder how you could find that out?" [Question that places the responsibility back on Peter.]

Peter: "Well, I guess I could talk to my boss."

Mike: "That's one thing you could do. Is there anything else besides that?" [Affirming Peter's answer; open-ended question to gather more possibilities.]

Peter: "I could try to find out why other people got promoted in the department. But I don't want to become just another 'yes man' like some of the other guys I know!"

Mike: "I can appreciate that you don't want to just say 'How high?' every time your boss says, 'Jump.' [Active listening.] Yet it seems as if you're unhappy with your status in the company and may be willing to make some changes in yourself in order to get promoted. You may have some choices ahead of you." [Summarizing conversation; pointing toward possible action.]

Peter: "Maybe you're right."

Mike: "What would you like to do next?" [Open-ended question that moves toward action.]

Peter: "I guess I'll talk with my boss about my attitude. It probably can't hurt."

Mike: "When do you think you'll be able to do that?" [Holding Peter accountable for his plan.]

Peter: "Probably by the end of the week."

Mike: "Great, I'll check back with you and see how it goes."

Let's observe several things about this conversation. First, notice that Mike didn't accept Peter's initial goal of being "happy." It was subjective and would be very difficult to measure. We need to help our friends state specifically what they are trying to achieve. Questions like, "What do you hope to change?" "What are you going to do about this situation?" or "What do you hope to be doing, feeling, or thinking differently?" will help our friends pinpoint their goals.

Next, Mike made sure that Peter phrased the problem in terms of himself and not in terms of his boss. If our friends' goals are dependent on somebody else changing first, their plans probably are doomed to failure.

The next time these two friends get together, Mike should check on whether or not Peter followed through on what he said he would do. If he hasn't, Peter may not really want to change jobs as much as he indicates. Mike should find out what he expects to *gain* by reaching his goals, as well as what he could *lose*. This helps to spot any unrealistic expectations ("My salary will double") as well as any fears ("I'm afraid I'd be a poor manager"). It's important that every person count the cost of changing. Refer to chart #4, "Check Your Friend's Goals," for ways to help your friend be specific about change.

Finally, observe how Mike interspersed questions with active-listening responses. You'll be using both these tools in the Personal and Practical section and in role-playing with your study group. Don't forget to practice these skills with your family and friends! They'll appreciate being heard, and you'll have found a new way of communicating with the people around you.

CHART #4: CHECK YOUR FRIEND'S GOALS

1. Does your friend phrase the desired change in terms of what he or she will do or in terms of what someone else must do?

2. When does your friend expect to have the change completed? Is this a realistic deadline?

3. Does the change itself seem realistic and workable?

4. Is your friend's plan phrased in small, reachable goals?

5. Has your friend agreed to it willingly or is he or she doing it only because you've suggested it?

PERSONAL AND PRACTICAL

For Practice

Exercise #1: Perceive content, feelings, and implication.

Directions: In order to practice the active-listening response, read the statements below and write in your notebook the content, feelings, and possible implications of each statement. The implications will direct the types of questions you would later ask each of these friends.

1. "I really like Michael a lot, but I don't know if I'm ready to get engaged. He seems more sure of his feelings for me than I do of my feelings for him. How will I know when I'm ready for marriage?" *Sample:*

content of statement: _____

feelings: _____

possible implications: _____

2. "I heard that Joanne is talking about me behind my back. I won't mind if I never speak to her again."

3. "I'm not looking forward to this move. I know I have no choice in the matter, but I hate leaving the church and all our friends. We'll never experience the same kind of fellowship that we've had here."

4. "Jim and I never seem to have any fun anymore. It just seems as if something is missing from our marriage."

5. "No matter what I do, my father is always on my back. I can't take much more of this!"

Exercise #2: Form the active-listening response.

Directions: Respond to each statement in your notebook by writing how the person is feeling (after "You feel"), the content of the message (after "because"), and the implication (after "you're thinking that").
Sample: Helper: You feel _____
because _____
and you're thinking that _____

1. Friend: "I don't know what to do with my life. I wish God's will were clearer to me. Maybe if I talk with my pastor, he'll tell me what to do."

2. Friend: "The kids at school are all a bunch of snobs. No one ever talks to me. Not that it matters really. Who needs them anyway?"

3. Friend: "I've been really working hard, and Laura doesn't seem to appreciate that when I come home, I just want to relax and not be hit with a million things to do. It makes me feel like not coming home!"

4. Friend: "Sometimes I'm so down that I just don't know if I want to go on. I don't even feel that God cares."

5. Friend: "Since George went into the hospital, my whole life has been upside down. I spend every day there, and nothing is getting done at home. My mother is taking care of the kids, but I worry about them too. The whole thing is more than I can handle."

Exercise #3: Put the active-listening response into your own words.

Directions: Look at the Sentence Builders and Feeling Words charts below. Use the phrases suggested under Sentence Builders to begin your active-listening response. Then from the Feeling Words chart, pick out the word that best describes the emotions the person is feeling. Next take the ten statements from Exercises #1 and #2, and write in your notebook your own active-listening response.

SENTENCE BUILDERS[5]

Here are some sentence starters that you can use when building the active-listening response. After you've been able to identify both the content and feelings of your friend's message using the basic formula, you can move on to putting the active-listening response into your own words. As you get used to this method, it will come naturally to you and you'll find many of your own ways to begin your response.

When you are fairly sure you are perceiving with accuracy, you can say:

> "The way it seems to you is that. . . ."
> "As you see it. . . ."
> "From your point of view it looks as if. . . ."
> "You're feeling . . . because of. . . ."
> "It sounds as if you feel. . . ."
> "You're telling me that. . . ."
> "So what's happening to you is. . . ."
> "When . . . happened, you felt. . . ."

When you aren't sure that you're perceiving your friend's meaning accurately, express yourself tentatively:

"This is just a hunch, but. . . ."
"I guess when that happened, you felt. . . ."
"This may be off base, but. . . ."

When you want to find out if you are perceiving accurately, try:

"I'm not sure if this is right, but you feel. . . ?"
"I am wondering if you're saying. . . ?"
"Do you mean that. . . ?"
"Am I hearing you right that. . . ?"
"Is it that. . . ?"

FEELING WORDS

Abandoned, abused, agitated, aggravated, affectionate, ambivalent, annoyed, anxious, apathetic, astounded, ashamed, attracted, awed.

Bad, beautiful, betrayed, blissful, bold, bored, brave.

Calm, capable, challenged, charmed, cheerful, childish, clever, cold, competitive, condemned, confident, confused, contented, crazy, crushed, curious.

Deceitful, deceived, defeated, delighted, depressed, desperate, devastated, determined, discontented, discounted, disgusted, distraught, disturbed, dominated, doubtful.

Eager, ecstatic, empty, energetic, excited, exasperated.

Fascinated, failed, fearful, foolish, frantic, frustrated, frightened, free, fulfilled, furious.

Glad, good, gratified, greedy, grieved, guilty.

Happy, helpful, helpless, high, homesick, honored, hopeful, horrible, humbled, hurt, hysterical.

Ignored, imposed upon, impressed, indifferent, infatuated, inspired, interested, intimidated, irritated, isolated.

Jealous, joyful, jumpy.

Kind.

Lazy, left out, lonely, lovable, loving, low, lustful.

Mad, mean, melancholic, miserable.

Naughty, nervous, needed, needy, nice, nutty.

Obsessed, odd, optimistic, outraged, overwhelmed.

Panicky, peaceful, petrified, persecuted, perturbed, pitiful, playful, powerful, pressured, pretty, proud, put down.

Quarrelsome, queer.

Rebellious, refreshed, rejected, relaxed, relieved, remorseful, restless, reverent, righteous.

Sad, safe, scared, screwed up, secure, selfish, self-assured, settled, sexy, shocked, silly, skeptical, skillful, solemn, sorrowful, spiteful, stingy, strange, strong, sure, suspicious, sympathetic.

Talkative, tempted, tense, tentative, terrible, terrified, threatened, tired, trapped, troubled.

Ugly, uneasy, unlucky, unsettled, unsuccessful, unsure.

Violent, vehement, vulnerable.

Warm, wary, weak, wicked, wise, wonderful, weepy, worried.

Zany.

For More Practice

1. Go over the Feeling Words list and check off the emotions that you've felt recently. Circle the ones that you've heard expressed by family members or friends. Underline the emotions with which you're uncomfortable. Is there overlap between these different categories? Do you notice any patterns?

2. Observe the way you listen to family members and friends. Do you accurately reflect what they say and how they are feeling? Do you parrot instead of paraphrasing?

3. Try out the active-listening response with someone you know, and ask that person to give you feedback on how accurate you are. With his or her permission, tape your conversation. When you listen to it, observe whether or not your responses "tune in" on your friend's wavelength. Keep track of the questions you ask. Do they invite your friend to keep talking or do they close down communication?

4. Write active-listening responses to these statements in your notebook.

1. "This job is a real drag. Day in and day out I do the same old thing. I wonder if I made the right choice in taking it."

2. "Where were you when I needed help? It's too late now; Sam is filing the divorce papers next week."

3. "I wish I had a job like yours."

4. "Boy, I had a tough day at the office. My boss was really on my case. I wonder if he thinks I'm not doing well enough."

5. "I don't want another wedding invitation! My single friends are all getting married!"

For Further Reading

Read David Augsburger's *Caring Enough To Hear* (Ventura, California: Regal Books, 1982).

Complete the personal exercises in chapters 4 and 5 of Gary Collins' *People Helper Growthbook* (Santa Ana, Calif.: Vision House, 1976).

NOTES

[1] Dr. Thomas H. Holmes and Richard H. Rahe, *Journal of Psychosomatic Research,* Vol. 2 (1967): 21–26.

[2] Gail Sheehy's popular best-seller *Passages* (New York: Bantam Books, 1974) describes the meaning of different events at different times in our lives. Or for a Christian approach to adult development, listen to Dick Keyes's "Human Life Cycle" tape series (Sound Work Associates, P.O. Box 2035, Michigan City, IND., 46360).

[3] For more discussion on the rescuing game, see Muriel James and Dorothy Jongeward's *Born To Win* (Reading, Massachusetts: Addison-Wesley Publishing Company, 1971), pp. 84–89.

[4] Each active-listening response will not necessarily include a reference to each of these areas, but you should touch on them all eventually. In

general, you want to give a response that fits the statement your friend makes.

[5] Adapted from R.P. Walters's *Amity: Friendship in Action,* Reprinted by permission (P.O. Box 7443, Boulder, Colorado 80306: Christian Helpers, Inc., 1980).

‡

CHAPTER 8

SPEAK THE TRUTH: THE SECOND LEVEL OF HELPING

A word aptly spoken is like apples of gold in settings of silver.
—Proverbs 25:11

TRUTH-SPEAKING PRINCIPLES

Our ability to speak the truth in love will be built on our abilities to genuinely accept our friends and listen with understanding. Joined together, these three form the core of every helping response.

Just as Jesus, the incarnate Word, spoke in ways we could understand, we also need to speak to our friends in ways they will understand. This involves using vocabulary familiar to them as well as speaking at a pace, tone, and volume that corresponds to their way of speaking. Speaking clearly helps our friends explore, identify, understand, and take responsibility for their problems. This prepares them for taking action.

The Bible not only teaches us how to listen, but it also shows us how to speak to one another. Paul's instructions to "truth it" to one another imply that we are to speak openly, honestly, and plainly with one another (Eph. 4:15). Truth speaking is precious (Prov. 25:11), enduring (Prov. 12:19a), and should be offered at the proper time (Prov. 15:23).

How can we tell if we are speaking from love for the other person or if we are simply ventilating our own opinions or criticisms? Paul offers us a way to check our attitude and motivation: "Do not let any unwholesome talk come out of your mouths, but only what is helpful for building others up according to their needs, that it may benefit those who listen" (Eph. 4:29). Asking ourselves: "Will what I say be helpful to the other person? Do I have the other person's needs in mind?" will help us determine our true motivation. In addition, Paul specifically notes that we are to get rid of all bitterness, rage, anger, brawling, slander, and malice and to replace it with kindness, compassion, and forgiveness (Eph. 4:31–32).

Truth without love is harsh. Love without truth is impotent. Biblical truth speaking joins love and honesty together: truth speaking is neither derogatory nor belittling, sentimental nor fearful. We shouldn't hesitate to speak the truth, but we must be discerning in *what* we say, *how* we say it, and *when* we say it (Prov. 10:13a, 19). Our tongues are to be instruments of life, not of death (Prov. 15:4; 18:21; see also James 1:26; 3:1–9).

Several tools will help us to speak the truth in love. These include making "I statements," giving feedback, expressing affirmation, giving the big picture, and confronting in love. We'll look at the first four skills in this chapter and focus on confrontation in chapter 9.

SPEAK FOR YOURSELF, NOT FOR YOUR FRIEND

Avoid "You Statements"

If you've ever wanted to respond to the "helpful" advice of, "Don't you think you should. . . ?" with, "Who do you think you are to tell me what to do?" then you know what it feels like to be on the receiving end of a "you statement." With anger or defensiveness you resist being controlled by the other person. That is a common response to a "you statement."

God can command us to specific acts of obedience; however, unless we are in a position of authority (that is, as a pastor or elder), we lack that same prerogative. In general, helpers who make "you statements" define the other person's feelings and thoughts, thereby not allowing the person freedom to examine himself or herself. "You statements" can manipulate a person to act in the way the helper wants.

"You statements" often communicate "I don't trust you to find a solution." This message leaves the friend feeling put down, blamed, or even rejected. He or she can feel a sense of injustice or judgment as the speaker ascribes motives to him or her that are incorrect.

As a result, "you statements" often lead to resistance and resentment. They tend to invite competitive, sarcastic responses like, "Well, who put you in charge, anyway?" In the most extreme situations, the helper's message is totally ignored. The listener rejects the content of the message in an effort not to accept a negative comment about himself or herself.

As friend to friend, we must learn how to replace "you statements" with "I statements." Doing so will enable our friends to nondefensively receive our help.

Take a look at chart #1, "Responses to Avoid," for a list of statements to avoid using. Note that many of these statements lock the other person into a predefined position. "You statements" often give advice that doesn't relate specifically to the friend's particular situation. Good help encourages our friends to develop their own responses rather than limiting them to our advice.

CHART #1: RESPONSES TO AVOID[1]

The following responses may imply negative judgments about our friends' intelligence, freedom, or ability to make wise decisions. The responses marked with an asterisk may be appropriate in *some* helping situations, but they should be used with great care.

1. *Warning, threatening:* You'd better. . . . If you don't, I'll. . . . You'll be sorry if. . . . Beware that*. . . .

2. *Commanding, ordering:* You must. . . . You will. . . . You have to. . . . That's the law*. . . . I'm telling you to. . . . Don't. . . .

3. *Obliging, moralizing:* You should. . . . You ought. . . . It's your duty*. . . . Please do this. . . . There's no other way. . . .

4. *Giving answers, solutions:* Why don't you. . . . I suggest that. . . . Try this. . . . The right way is*. . . . The truth is*. . . .

5. *Arguing, persuading, instructing:* Yes, but.... The facts are.... You're wrong.... Most people.... You'd better....

6. *Judging, evaluating, blaming:* You're mistaken.... Don't you see that.... It will be your fault.... You know that isn't right.... Shame on you....

7. *Excusing, sympathizing:* You couldn't help it.... Everyone does it.... You aren't to blame.... (Use this last one only if the person is blaming himself or herself for someone else's sin or problem.)

8. *Reassuring, minimizing, denying:* You shouldn't worry .... Things can't be as awful as you think....

9. *Interpreting, "psychoanalyzing":* Don't you think that your motive is ...? Unconsciously you are trying to.... You always try to make me mad....

10. *Probing, prying, cross-examining:* Why did you ...? Now be honest.... Are you sure ...? Just what are you trying to hide...?

11. *Impatiently, intolerantly, or irritably:* If I've told you once, I've told you a thousand times.... You never.... You always....

12. *Maliciously, harshly, with ridicule:* You're so self-centered.... How can anyone be so stupid...?

13. *Simplistically, Band-Aiding:* It's not so bad. You'll feel better tomorrow. Don't you know that God helps those who help themselves?

14. *Condemningly or critically:* Everyone knows you shouldn't.... How could you even think of ...? I would never....

15. *Assuming:* I know just what you're feeling.

"I statements" also contain the word "you" and thus can be misused. As the author of this book, I am concerned that when you help your friends, your "I statements" don't become subtle ways of putting them down. You *must* learn how to give feedback without condemning the other person or you'll *never* be a good helper. Notice the last two sentences. Both give directions, but in slightly different ways. The first phrased those directions in terms of my concern as the author of this book. The second was more of a command, threat, or order.

Of course, there will be times when we'll need to confront our friends. But the *way* we speak the truth is crucial. Listen to your tone of voice. *How* you speak often communicates more than *what* you say. Choose your words with care. Using judgmental words like "You're crazy to think that!" or "You're so stupid" are like waving red flags before an angry bull—such words just prepare a person to fight back!

Use "I Statements"

In order to speak for ourselves and not for our friends, we can learn to make "I statements."[2] This counseling technique will enable us to give our friends feedback and to confront them in a nonthreatening manner.

"I statements" are simple, honest statements that define the helper's beliefs, thoughts, values, perceptions, and feelings. Speaking with "I statements" shows our friends respect, allows them room for personal choice, and models a different form of communication.

In order to form good "I statements," follow the formula below. Although it may seem mechanical at first, you'll find that with practice, you can easily integrate it into your everyday conversation. Work toward using your own words so that you don't sound stiff or formal.

Every "I statement" contains three parts:

Part #1: "When you. . . ." The first part of an "I statement" is a description of the behavior you want to talk about. Be as specific as possible when you label the behavior that may be causing a problem, the sin that you want to confront, or the situation with which you are upset.

Part #2: "I feel. . . ." The second part defines how you feel or react to the situation. By stating your response, you take personal responsibility for your reaction.

Part #3: "because. . . ." The third part states the effects of the behavior on others; this helps your friend see the consequences of his or her actions. (Note: As demonstrated in the following examples, the order of the three components can be varied to fit your conversation.)

Let's take a look at some examples. Let's say that you're talking with Laura, a teenage girl in your neighborhood who complains that her parents never let her do anything. Each week she complains that all her friends are allowed to stay out later than she does. You begin to feel like a dumping ground for all her complaints. But, when you ask her why her parents are so strict, she casually mentions that she's being punished for breaking her curfew three times in a row. You're afraid that if you confront her, she'll stop talking to you. How can you talk to her in a way that won't turn her off? Here's a chance to use an "I statement": "Laura, I want to help you, and yet I feel uncomfortable [your feelings] when you talk on and on [Laura's behavior] about how awful your parents are. I'm uneasy [your feelings] because it seems as if you complain a lot [Laura's behavior] and don't see your part in this situation. I don't feel as if I'm really helping you by listening to you talk like this [consequence of Laura's behavior]." In this way you communicate your concern for Laura and help her see her responsibility.

Here is another example. If you've ever tried to help someone who doesn't seem to appreciate your efforts, you may feel like saying, "I always try to help you and you don't appreciate me one bit! Don't you think you should at least say thank you?" If you feel this way, you are blaming your friend for not responding to your help the way you expected. It would be more accurate to say, "I am hurt [your feelings] when I try to help you and you don't acknowledge what I have done [friend's behavior]. I begin to feel that my help doesn't matter [consequences of friend's behavior]." In the first statement you dump the problem on your friend; in the second you take responsibility for your own disappointment.

Notice also that the helper is hiding advice behind a question. "Don't you think you should . . ." is a sneaky way of sliding an opinion into the conversation. "I statements" will keep you from asking questions that answer themselves. Use chart #2, "Use Statements Instead of Questions," to identify the types of situations in which you tend to ask questions instead of making statements.

CHART #2: USE STATEMENTS INSTEAD OF QUESTIONS[3]

The most frequently misused communication pattern is the question. Questions can be concealed ways of offering multilevel messages, of applying hidden pressures, or of manipulating the other person. Notice how the questions listed below are not open-ended. They evoke a specific response from the other person.

Questions lead	*Statements inform*
"Isn't it true that. . . ?"	"I believe that. . . ."
"Wouldn't you rather. . . ?"	"I would rather. . . ."
Questions punish	*Statements report*
"Why did you say that?"	"I don't like what you. . . ."
"What's wrong with you?"	"I'm unhappy with. . . ."
Questions seduce	*Statements invite*
"If you were in charge of this, wouldn't you have. . . ?"	"I would like. . . ."
	"I would prefer. . . ."
Questions command	*Statements request*
"When are you going to. . . ?"	"I would appreciate change."
"Why didn't you get to. . . ?"	"I would like cooperation."
Questions deceive	*Statements disclose*
"Why don't you choose . . . ?"	"I'm happy for you to choose."
"What did you mean by that?"	"I don't understand. . . ."
Questions divide	*Statements unite*
"Are you bragging or complaining?"	"I'd like to hear how you feel about it."
"Do you agree with them or me?"	"I want to know your view."
Questions bind	*Statements free*
"Didn't you once. . . ?"	"I'd like to talk about. . . ."
"Didn't you promise to. . . ?"	"I'm still hoping that we. . . ."

Since "I statements" are an excellent way of facilitating communication, you may want to use them with your family. For instance, let's say that a wife is angry with her husband for criticizing how she decorated the house. Instead of yelling, "You make fun of everything I do," she could use an "I statement" and say, "When you criticize me for how I decorate the house, I feel hurt because it seems that you don't appreciate me."

Her husband, who might typically respond with a sarcastic comment like "Well, you're so busy with the house that I'm surprised you even notice me," could say, "When you're so busy doing things around the house, I feel left out and unimportant because it seems that you never have time for me." "I statements" help each person say what he or she is feeling and thinking, without turning the other person off.

"I statements" are useful not only to deal with problems but also to convey positive comments. The unhappy wife could say, "I feel great when you compliment me on the way the house looks because then I know you appreciate the time and effort I spent." And her husband could reply, "I'm happy that my opinions matter to you."

Remember that the "I statement" formula is a guideline to improve your communication. You can rearrange the three parts to find a style that fits you. For practice, turn to the Personal and Practical section and make "I statements" with the examples given in the For Practice exercise.

FEEDBACK: OPENING THE DOOR TO SELF-AWARENESS

In chapter 1 we saw how we all have the tendency to hide from God, ourselves, and each other. We all have "blind spots"—areas we prefer to ignore, areas we're ashamed of. Our friends' blind spots can be part of their problems. For example, in the last chapter we saw how Peter's poor attitude at work was part of the reason he wasn't being promoted. In his case, Mike was like a mirror, carefully reflecting to Peter things he didn't see about himself. This shed new light on Peter's responsibilities. This aspect of speaking the truth is called feedback.

Feedback gives our friends new information about themselves. It helps them admit their sins and failures, as well as see their strengths and abilities. With this new awareness, our friends will have more choices. As a result, they'll be able to take more responsibility for themselves and their problems.

The ability to give feedback requires many of the helping

skills we've already learned. We draw upon the information we've "heard" with our eyes as well as with our ears. We use the information that we've gained through asking questions and active listening. Then, we take responsibility for our observations by using the "I statement" formula. In all of this, it's important to be patient and to go slow. We don't want to overwhelm our friends with too much information before they are ready to hear it.

When to Use Feedback

Use feedback in the "here and now." One of the main purposes of feedback is to comment on what is happening in the present. This helps the other person immediately become aware of himself or herself. We can use lead-in phrases like "I notice that . . ." or "You look as if . . ." or "Are you aware that . . . ?" to introduce feedback to our friends.

For example, in the course of a conversation with your single friend Cheryl, she begins to complain how the people at church never invite her to do anything. You can give her feedback by simply saying, "You don't think anyone goes out of their way to include you at church. I wonder if you feel left out." Active listening to content, feelings, and implication is the first way of giving feedback.

As the two of you talk, observe what Cheryl is expressing nonverbally. For instance, as she talks, notice how Cheryl's arms are folded across her chest and how her legs are crossed in front of her. She looks mad at the world. Her voice sounds tense and resentful. Your feedback to Cheryl might be, "Are you aware that you sound very angry?"

Imagine that Cheryl answers defensively, "I'm not angry! Why do you say that?" You could respond by saying, "Well, it looks to me as if you've got a spring inside of you that is ready to snap any minute! You say that you aren't angry, but you look and sound as if you are." Feedback also points out inconsistencies between *what* our friends say and *how* they sound and look to us.

If you have a good relationship with Cheryl, and if you're on target with your observations, your feedback will be like a key unlocking the door to her self-awareness. She may begin to think about what you've said and start sharing more of herself: "Well, to be honest, I'm sick and tired of hearing that the church is full of people who love you. I don't have any more friends at church than I do at work. Take Terry for example. Last Sunday he promised to call me during the week and get together next Saturday. I waited and waited, but do you think he called? Of course not! He's a hypocrite like all of the rest who say they care but never follow through. Who needs them anyway? Not me!"

Now imagine that this isn't the first time you've heard Cheryl complain about her lack of friends. In fact, you've thought of calling her and inviting her out, but her sour attitude has kept you from wanting to spend time with her. Another way of using "here and now" feedback is to take information from your own relationship and use it to comment on your friend's problem. You could say, "Cheryl, to be honest, I thought of including you when several of us went out to dinner last week. But when you come across in such an angry and demanding way, I hesitate because I'm afraid that you'll turn everyone off. I wonder if you may be cutting yourself off from other people without even knowing it. Perhaps that's the reason no one invites you out." Thus Cheryl's interactions with you become a part of how she learns about herself.

Feedback is also a way of drawing your friends' attention to their sin. What sins might be underlying Cheryl's problems? She sounds as if she's focusing on herself and on what others should do for her. She's holding a grudge against people in the church, and she seems to be reacting from pride ("I don't need anybody anyway!"). You may want to review the list of problems in chapter 1 to see what Cheryl's problem may be. It appears that Cheryl doesn't accept others or herself. *After* you have accurately listened and reflected her feelings, you could comment, "Cheryl, I wonder if you're aware how preoccupied you seem to be with yourself. When others don't treat you the way you want, you get angry and hold a grudge against them. It seems as if you are unable to forgive them." As we'll see in the next chapter, this type of feedback confronts our friends and encourages them to evaluate what they're saying from a biblical point of view.

In all of these situations, you're giving back to Cheryl information that she has already communicated about herself. Your feedback aims at confronting Cheryl in the most nonthreatening way possible.

Use feedback to share yourself. Feedback is also a way we disclose ourselves. When we talk about our own feelings and experiences, we remove the "I've-got-it-all-together" facade.

Self-disclosure also helps to break down walls of distrust that may separate us from our friends. They see that we also have problems, and as a result they'll feel less alone. Our openness and vulnerability encourages our friends to be more open and honest, paving the way for a more mutual relationship.

Self-disclosure serves as a form of feedback in two specific ways. First, we can share similar struggles. Express this identification by saying: "I also have felt disappointed at church. I was angry when no one came to visit me after my operation. So I called the pastor when I was ready for visitors, and as a result several people came to see me." The fact that you've worked through a similar situation not only gives your friend hope but it also models appropriate problem-solving behavior.

In the same way, we also can share our reactions to our friends. Use an "I statement" and say to Cheryl, "I am worried when you say that you're ready to give up on trying to make friends at church because then it seems as if you'll end up with even fewer friends than before." Sharing your concern tells Cheryl that she is important to you and that her problems and feelings matter to you.

Keep in mind that when you talk about yourself, the conversation shouldn't start revolving around you. Avoid the "let's-see-whose-story-is-worse" syndrome. When you share your own feelings:

- Don't add your burdens to a person already in pain.
- Don't distract your friend from his or her problem.
- Don't talk about yourself too much or too often.
- Don't let it become a "pity party," with the two of you exchanging complaints on how awful life is.
- Don't imply that your friend must experience things just the way you do.

Use feedback to summarize your conversation. Feedback is a helpful way of pulling together different subjects that your friend has talked about. Look for patterns in the problems you have shared. For instance, you could say to Cheryl, "Are you aware that you sound angry with many of the people in your life? You don't seem to have many friends at work or at church." In this way you give Cheryl the opportunity to connect different parts of her life so that she'll see how she is distancing herself from a lot of people.

Use feedback to see if what your friend heard is what you said. Do you remember playing "whisper down the lane" or "telephone" as a child? If so, then you know how communication can get really mixed up. As we saw in chapter 5, this occurs most frequently when the *intent* of the sender's message is not the *impact* on the listener. You can use feedback to minimize this misunderstanding. Check to see if you understand your friend's message by saying, "Cheryl, let me play this back to you and make sure I've heard you right. You seem to feel left out and angry that no one calls you. You're disappointed because Terry said he'd contact you and he didn't. Now you sound as if you are ready to give up on everyone at church." Once again your feedback takes the form of the active-listening response, reflecting the content, feelings, and implications of Cheryl's statement.

In the same way, if you're unsure that your friend understands what you have said, ask, "What do you think I'm saying?" When she puts it into her words, you'll find out if she heard what you intended to communicate. If she hasn't, you may not have been clear and you may need to rephrase your comments. Carefully watch your tone of voice and body language and think, "What am I conveying to my friend?" Both your speaking filter and your friend's listening filters can prevent your message from being accurately received.

AFFIRM YOUR FRIEND: GIVE ENCOURAGEMENT

By now you might be feeling that if speaking the truth always involves helping your friends see their problems, then you'd just as soon not take the job! Happily, truth speaking also has a more enjoyable side. Paul instructs us that the purpose of speaking the truth is to *build each other up* (Eph. 4:16). One way we build each other up is through encouragement and affirmation (Rom. 12:8; Heb. 3:13; 10:24).

The first way we can encourage our friends is to help them discover their talents. Through feedback we can point out abilities and strengths of which they may be unaware. Christians are often guilty of false humility. Pretending that they can't do much, they hide their God-given talents. As Christian helpers, we must encourage our friends to use their gifts rather than bury them (Matt. 25:14–30).

Encouragement is not flattery. Encouragement affirms the development of a friend's unexpressed gifts. For example, you can reach out to the shy young man in your Sunday school class by encouraging him to express his musical talents. You can help a friend who thinks she has nothing to offer the church by turning her concern for others into the gift of hospitality. In the same way that Jesus saw the undeveloped talent of poor fishermen, we can nurture our friends' talents.

A second type of encouragement is to acknowledge a friend's work, effort, or achievement. Take note when Cheryl invites the singles group to her apartment rather then waiting around to be asked out; compliment Peter when his boss remarks on his changed attitude. Noticing our friends' accomplishments encourages them to use their own resources rather than depend on us. But be respectful and not patronizing; give your friends a handshake or a hug, don't pat them on the head.

We don't have to wait until our friends have hurdled all their problems before we applaud their accomplishments. Small steps count too. Our friends can feel discouraged and lose sight of their progress. Note each step that Cheryl takes toward becoming less bitter and more friendly herself. The fact that you notice her efforts may give her just the inspiration she needs to continue.

A third way to encourage a friend is by making clear, positive statements. A family I know begins their day by giving each other "affirmations." Like verbal hugs, these are ways they openly communicate their love and appreciation for one another.

The church should be a place where we naturally affirm and encourage each other. Opportunities exist in the pulpit, the pew, a Sunday school class, or a committee meeting. For instance, write your pastor or elders a note saying that you appreciate the work they do and that you pray for them. Don't be afraid to give compliments. Tell a young, single woman, "You really look nice today," or mention to a junior high student, "I thought your answers in Sunday school were really good."

A fourth way that you encourage a friend is to affirm his or her point of view. Consider how rejected you feel when someone important to you constantly challenges your opinions. Then again, think about how good you feel when this same person takes your viewpoint seriously. In the same way, we join our friends and show them that we're on their side when we agree with some part of what they're saying. The next time you're tempted to disagree with a friend, first find something with which you can agree.

Encouraging and affirming a friend serves one final purpose: it buffers feedback and confrontation. Cheryl will be more likely to hear your comments about her attitude if you've first acknowledged her efforts to make friends. In general, most people have an easier time admitting their failures when they have a safety net of success and confidence underneath them.

GET THE BIG PICTURE

An old story describes a group of blind men who came across an elephant. Each man felt a different part of the elephant's body and concluded it was something different. The man who felt the elephant's legs thought it was a tree trunk; the man who felt the elephant's side thought it was a wall; and the one who felt the elephant's tail thought it was a rope. Although each observation was accurate, the conclusions the men reached were wrong.

The blind men needed someone to take a look at the *whole* picture. Similarly, sometimes our friends will get stuck seeing only one aspect of a situation. They are so close to a particular problem that they can't begin to put it into perspective. As observant helpers, we help our friends see the bigger picture.

For the Christian, God's Word defines the bigger picture of the world around us. In fact, God *is* the bigger picture behind every sorrow, accomplishment, conflict, trial, or joy we experience. Beyond space and time, God's perspective of history is radically different from ours.[4] Although we can't claim to know all God's purposes, we can help our friends prayerfully seek out a biblical perspective on their lives.

We'll learn how to relate a biblical worldview to a friend's problem in the next two chapters. For now, let's apply the skills we've already learned to helping a friend discover the bigger picture.

What Else Is Going On?

Let's take the example of your friend Robin. She is worried because her husband, Dan, has been withdrawn lately. He comes home from work, gives her a peck on the cheek, stretches out on the sofa, and hides himself in the newspaper. She automatically assumes his silence means he's angry with her. She begins to worry over what she has done wrong, decides she hasn't done anything at all, and then gets angry at Dan for being mad at her. Robin does all this without ever finding out what is bothering Dan! She desperately needs to see the bigger picture.

If you were helping Robin, your first job would be to ask her some open-ended questions. Questions like "What else is going on right now for Dan? Could there be any other reasons why he is keeping to himself?" will help her see the larger picture.

Let's say that after thinking a minute, Robin remembers that Dan recently said he wasn't going to be able to meet an important deadline at work. Stepping outside of her own perspective, Robin then discovers that other things may account for Dan's behavior. Her selfish preoccupation with herself prevented her from focusing on Dan.

Part of your job as Robin's friend will be to encourage her to look at the situation from every possible angle. And if Robin is a Christian, she'll need to see her response to Dan from God's perspective. When she pulls inward, is she serving God or is she only thinking of herself? How would Jesus have responded to Dan? What sin was involved on her part? Working with your friend to think through her responses also will help her find new ways of integrating her faith into her daily life.

How Many Ways Can You Peel a Potato?

People sometimes get stuck because they don't see the choices available to them. Another part of speaking the truth is helping our friends discover new possibilities and alternatives.

Maureen, a former client of mine, taught me this aspect of helping. A married woman in her thirties, Maureen dreaded her mother's visits because inevitably she would criticize the way Maureen managed her home. Maureen couldn't do anything right in her mother's eyes.

One day Maureen said to me, "According to my mother, I can't even peel potatoes right!" I looked at her and asked her very simply, "Maureen, is there only *one* way to peel potatoes?" A smile spread across her face as she considered my question. From then on Maureen learned that not only were there several ways of peeling potatoes, but that she had more options in many other situations too. As a result of discovering her choices, Maureen experienced more control over her life. Her life wasn't boxed in between narrow lines anymore.

Sometimes people get stuck when they meet a situation they think they can't change. Maureen could have given up and said, "Well, since I can't change my mother, I guess I'll just have to do things her way!" If she had, she would have been confusing what she *can* do with what she *can't* do. Thinking correctly that she *can't* change her mother, she would have falsely concluded that she had no other choices. "I can't" limits a person's alternatives as well as his or her responsibility. Maureen *could* peel potatoes her own way as well as manage her home as she chose.

If you have a friend who is limiting his or her choices, give your friend that feedback ("Are you aware that there are many things you say you can't change?") and ask your friend to consider what other options and alternatives he or she has ("Are there other ways of doing that?").

So far we've learned how listening attentively and responding with an accurate paraphrase shows your friend that you've heard and understood him or her. These skills convey *comfort*. Using your speaking skills, you can give your friend feedback, affirmation, and a broader perspective. As we'll see in the next chapter, these are all different aspects of *confrontation*.

When we put the active-listening response together with one of the speaking responses, we have the outline for every helping response. In other words:

ACTIVE LISTENING + TRUTH SPEAKING = HELPING RESPONSE

Now that we've learned these skills, we've come a long way toward being effective friends and helpers.

PERSONAL AND PRACTICAL

Study the Scriptures

1. Read Ephesians 4:29–32. Compare verse 31 with 32. What does Paul instruct you to put off? What does he say to put on instead? Think about the last time you spoke to someone in bitterness or anger. What could you have said instead?

2. Read Isaiah 50:4 and Proverbs 21:23. What are some characteristics of a truth speaker?

3. Read Proverbs 29:20. In what situations do you tend to speak hastily? What can you do about this problem?

4. Read Proverbs 15:1. What is the author's main point in this verse? Think of a time when your harshness triggered someone's anger. Think about the different speaking skills you studied in this chapter. What could you have said instead?

5. Read Luke 6:45. According to Jesus, what determines the words that come out of our mouths? Think of a time you recently "spoke the truth" to a friend. What was your heart attitude? How did that affect what you said and how you said it?

6. Read 2 Corinthians 7:4, 6–7. Paul made himself vulnerable to the Corinthian church and shared some of his own feelings. What were these feelings? What effect might his vulnerability and self-disclosure have had on the Corinthians?

For Practice

Directions: Use the "When you. . . , I feel. . . , because . . ." formula and rewrite the following statements in your notebook:

1. "It was really stupid of you to tell the boss that we could get the project done by this weekend. Now we're both in hot water!"
2. "You should know better than to go out with a guy who has a reputation like his. Now look at the mess you're in!"
3. "Don't interrupt me when I'm talking!"
4. "I've never met anyone as lazy as you!"
5. "You know I'm only trying to help you. Why don't you ever take my advice?"
6. "I can't believe you lied to me!"
7. "You always seem to have the perfect answer to everything."

8. "Your birthday card really was a surprise."
9. "You always put my friends down."
10. "Look who took out the trash for once. It's nice to see someone else doing something around here besides me."

For Thought

Directions: Read the cases listed below and think about what you could say to each person. In your notebook, write a brief paragraph that discusses the following points:

- The content, feelings, and implication of the person's message.
- Main problems (refer to categories from chapter 1).
- Themes and patterns to the person's problem.
- Types of helpful feedback you could give.
- Ways that you might use self-disclosure.
- Ways that you could affirm the person.
- Other ways to see the person's problem.

FRANK

Your friend Frank is unemployed and lonely. He feels that everything he tries backfires. He shrugs off people's input or suggestions with "Yes, but . . ." and seems to want to give up on finding a new job. He has a tendency to monopolize conversations and doesn't seem to understand what other people are saying to him. He is argumentative and defensive and doesn't take feedback very well.

SHARON

Sharon is a person who can't say no and as a result gets herself overcommitted. She serves on several different church committees, works in the PTA, and is a den mother for her son's Boy Scout troop. She begins to resent her responsibilities but continues to overextend herself. She doesn't know why she feels angry, and she sees no way out of her situation.

MARSHALL

Twenty-five and single, Marshall is angry that his girlfriend just broke up with him. He figures there's nothing better to do than make the round of the local bars and get drunk.

For Further Reading

1. See chapters 2, 3, and 5 of David Augsburger's *Caring Enough To Confront* (Ventura, California: Regal Books, 1981) for a further discussion of how to use "I statements" in daily situations.
2. Read Lawrence Crabb and Dan Allender's *Encouragement* (Grand Rapids: Zondervan Publishing House, 1984) for further discussion of encouragement as a way of speaking the truth to others.

NOTES

[1] Adapted from Paul Miller, *Peer Counseling in the Church* (Scottdale, Pennsylvania: Herald Press, 1978), p. 104 and Dr. Thomas Gordon, *P.E.T., Parent Effectiveness Training* (New York: Peter Wyden, Inc., 1970), pp. 41–44, 110, 113.

[2] Adapted from Dr. Thomas Gordon, *P.E.T., Parent Effectiveness Training,* pp. 115–38.

[3] Based on David Augsburger's, *Caring Enough To Hear and Be Heard* (Ventura, California: Regal Books, 1982), p. 113.

[4] For further discussion on how God sees things as they truly are, see Jerram Barrs, "Christianity True to the Way Things Are," in *What in the World Is Real?* (Champaign, Illinois: Communications Institute, 1982), p. 3.

‡

CHAPTER 9

CONFRONT BIBLICALLY

Therefore each of you must put off falsehood and speak truthfully to his neighbor, for we are all members of one body.

—Ephesians 4:25

By now we've gained many different skills to use in talking to our friends, family members, neighbors, or anyone with whom we come in contact. Now we'll learn to use these same skills to confront our friends. Look again at the diagram of the helping process (introduction to Part III) and see how the skill of confrontation is built on a foundation of love, acceptance, listening, and speaking the truth. Patiently building a solid helping relationship with our friends will earn us the right to confront them.

CONFRONTATION PRINCIPLES

Confrontation is speaking the truth while showing concern for the other person. Although most people don't think of it like this, confrontation is really a way of loving someone. Truly caring enough to be honest is a clear demonstration of committed Christian love, although this is often risky and difficult to accomplish.

Confrontation is an invitation to growth, *not* a demand that our friends conform to our wishes or standards. It requires sensitivity and empathy, setting it apart from condemnation or rejection. It's offered firmly but not insistingly. Biblical confrontation seeks to build up rather than tear down; it attempts to restore rather than to alienate.[1]

Confrontation accomplishes several purposes. First of all, confrontation helps our friends become aware of their sin and encourages them to turn from it (James 5:20). We want to help our friends develop a sorrow that leads to repentance (2 Cor. 7:9–10). (This is different from *forcing* a confession out of someone. That "repentance" is often shallow and artificial, with a person only confessing because he or she "should.")

Second, confrontation provides our friends with more information about themselves and it illuminates their choices. In this way, confrontation helps our friends take responsibility for their decisions and actions.

Third, good confrontation skills demonstrate to our friends appropriate ways of communicating disagreement and of resolving conflict. Being responsible in the way we confront our friends models good interpersonal skills of how to give and receive confrontation.

Although we shouldn't be afraid of pointing out sin, one author recommends that in restoration, "The emphasis on gentleness is crucial . . . . Restoring another person is not like fixing a broken appliance that will run after being kicked a few times."[2] As we combine speaking the truth with compassion, we follow the biblical pattern of joining holiness with love.

Two of the Greek words we studied in chapter 3, *noutheteo* and *parakaleo,* enrich our understanding of this delicate balance between love and truth speaking. Let's review them and see how they are related to confrontation.

Confrontation Is Nouthetic

If you remember, the word *noutheteo* means "to teach," "to admonish," "to warn," "to rebuke," "to reprove," or "to confront." Literally it means "to place something before someone's mind."

Paul writes that the goal of nouthetic confrontation is to "present everyone perfect in Christ" (Col. 1:28b). The purpose of confrontation is to help another person grow in maturity (Eph. 4:13). As we confront nouthetically, our goal is not to shame

(1 Cor. 4:14), but to warn (2 Thess. 3:15). We'll need knowledge of the Word of God in order to accomplish this (Col. 3:16). All true biblical confrontation is ultimately a confrontation with God, not with us.

We must be ready to confront several behavior patterns and attitudes: our friends' relationship to God, their sin and its consequences, ways in which our friends are not taking responsibility for themselves, and weaknesses they may not be aware of. This latter category may or may not include sin. In the last chapter, for example, Cheryl may not have been aware of how she was alienating the people with whom she wanted to be friends. As we saw in chapter 2, confrontation involves identifying problems and then speaking the truth about these problems.

Confrontation Is Parakletic

In chapter 3 we saw that the word *parakaleo* means "to advocate for," "to help," "to exhort," "to cheer on," "to encourage," or "to comfort." Confronting parakletically involves speaking the truth while simultaneously being on the person's side. Being empathic while confronting shows our friends that we are working for their benefit, not to win an argument or to get our point across.

The author of Hebrews tells us that the purpose of parakletic confrontation is to "encourage one another daily, as long as it is called Today, so that none of you may be hardened by sin's deceitfulness" (Heb. 3:13; see also Heb. 10:25). Paul uses the same word when he urges us to live lives that are worthy of God (1 Thess. 2:11–12). We confront our friends because we want them freed from the destructive nature of sin and because we covet godly lives for them.

But how can our friends be released from sin? An essential aspect of parakletic confrontation is helping our friends receive the *comfort* of the gospel. Confrontation must include forgiveness. If it doesn't, we encourage our friends to face their sin and then we abandon them with no way out. Paul himself knew that without forgiveness confrontation leads to crippling despair (2 Cor. 2:7). Confrontation paired with a comfort that forgives offers hope for change and makes new life possible.

This is particularly important for our friends who fear facing their sin. We must remind them of God's marvelous comfort: "If we confess our sins, he is faithful and just and will forgive us our sins" (1 John 1:9a). Receiving God's love and comfort through human helpers breaks down a person's defenses and prepares the way for genuine confession of sin.

Biblical confrontation requires that we lovingly speak the truth to our friends. Although the truth is often painful to speak as well as difficult to receive, when we "truth it" to one another, we call each other to deeper levels of godliness and holiness.

HOW DO WE CONFRONT OUR FRIENDS?

Getting Ourselves Ready

In order to understand the many steps involved in confrontation, let's look at a situation in which you might be asked to help. We'll imagine that Ann, the wife of your friend Gary, calls you one evening. She tells you that in the last month Gary has been working overtime three or four nights a week. She feels that really isn't necessary and wonders if he is using work as a way to avoid her, neglect the children, and ignore his household responsibilities. On top of this, Ann worries that Gary's overtime is really a cover-up for an affair. She asks you if you would be willing to talk to him, and you agree.

Before approaching Gary, you need to evaluate the information that you've received as well as your personal response to Ann's story.

First of all, you must separate facts from suspicions. One of your first tasks will be to find out more information from Gary. Is he working that much overtime? If so, why? What is he trying to accomplish during those hours? In order to avoid confrontation that is based on gossip, rumors, or suspicions, get *all* the facts before you confront. (Many helpers fall into the rescuer temptation at this point. They hear a disturbing story, fail to get all their facts together, and end up rushing in to save someone who may not be "drowning.") Don't assume Gary's guilt until you've also heard his side of the story.

Next, you'll want to evaluate whether or not it's wrong for Gary to be staying at work rather than be at home. Are there any biblical principles that can help you answer that question?

At the same time, consider your own personal reaction. Do you think Ann is just another nagging wife who doesn't understand the importance of a man's work responsibilities? Or do you strongly sympathize with her and feel that Gary is neglecting her and the children? In the first case you might dismiss Ann's worries as unimportant. In the second you might find it difficult to talk to Gary without voicing strong disapproval or rejection. The third option would be to reflect God's attitude: hating sin and its destructive effects and having confidence in the power of Jesus' forgiveness. This last attitude will enable you to approach Gary as a committed Christian friend.

The next step is to examine your emotional response toward Gary. What feelings are aroused in you as you think that Gary may be neglecting his family? Do you feel shocked, disgusted, or angry? Do you feel protective of Ann and their children? Or perhaps you might feel a twinge of jealousy, wishing you had that same time away from your family. Like your opinions and attitudes, your feelings also can influence your response to Gary. If you have a strong emotional reaction to Ann's story, it would be wise first to calm down before confronting Gary. (Your emotions can be good *if* they are channeled and if they motivate you to do what is right.)

Next, examine your motives for confronting Gary. Perhaps it's simply because Ann has asked you to talk to him. But other motives could also lurk beneath the surface. Test yourself by asking, "Am I for or against Gary?" Look for any traces of pride: "Do I want to make Gary look bad so that I look better?" It is important that you confront Gary in a way that communicates you have his best interests at heart.

Confrontation should not be punishment. Don't say, "Look at what you've done. How can Ann ever trust you if you act so irresponsibly toward your family?" That probably won't move Gary toward genuine confession and repentance. As we've seen many times, confrontation is an expression of God's love.

Don't use confrontation as an opportunity to ventilate your anger, frustration, or your revenge. On the other hand, don't refrain from confronting because you're afraid of hurting him. Gary's needs, not your own, should be uppermost in your mind.

Remember, we are to speak the truth *in love*. You can say, "Ann is upset because you've been working late a lot of evenings." But don't say, "You treat Ann horribly by working late. You should be ashamed of yourself," which attacks Gary personally. Your confrontation should indicate clearly what is fact, feeling, or hypothesis. Saying to Gary, "Ann was wondering if your overtime was necessary" is very different from, "You must be covering up for an affair." Don't make assumptions, analyze motivations, or jump to conclusions. Confront observable, concrete data whenever possible.

All of your attitudes, feelings, and motives will be communicated in your nonverbal behavior. Picture yourself talking to Gary. What is your body language saying to him? Are you scowling and standing with your arms crossed? Listen to yourself. What is your voice communicating? Do you sound critical? Try to imagine the messages you are sending Gary and how he'll feel receiving them. You want to confront in a way that will maintain a positive influence in his life.

Finally, consider the relationship you have with Gary before confronting him. Confront at a level proportionate to the depth of your relationship. If you have known Gary for several years and the two of you are close friends, there is probably a bond of trust and acceptance between you that will permit confrontation. But if Gary and Ann just moved into your neighborhood and Ann had no one else to turn to but you, you'll first need to establish those bonds of trust. If Gary is a Christian, you'll have even greater freedom and responsibility.

Getting a Friend Ready

Not only do we prepare ourselves, but we also must prepare our friends. For example, if you try to show Gary his areas of sin or weakness while he is on the defensive, you and he will both be frustrated.

You can prepare the groundwork for confrontation by first carefully choosing *when* to confront your friend. Confrontation comes later in the helping process because it takes time to win a person's trust. Don't back your friend into a corner by beginning the conversation with direct confrontation. For example, if you begin by saying to Gary, "Ann called me up and said you were cheating on her" before you have listened to his side of the story, you'll put him on the defensive and he may not open up to you at all.

Second, be sensitive to what else is going on in Gary's life. If he is experiencing stress in other areas, it will be difficult for him to listen to confrontation at that particular moment. For instance, if his car broke down on the way to work that day, Gary will have a hard time thinking about anything else. Ask yourself, "What does Gary need right now? Will he be able to hear me?"

Third, be empathic. Empathy will decrease Gary's defensiveness and increase his receptivity to what you are saying. Being aware of Gary's conflicts and problems will help you be more understanding and compassionate. Your sensitivity to his feelings may make the difference between his receiving or rejecting your words.

Finally, don't forget to confront in private (Matt. 18:15). Gary will turn off immediately if you make dinner out with him and Ann the opportunity to discuss their family problems.

Let's imagine that you think through these issues and decide that you and Gary are both ready to have a talk. You phone him and arrange to get together for lunch. Immediately you're faced with your first challenge: How do you begin the conversation?

It's a good idea to be honest and begin by letting Gary know that Ann called you and enlisted your help. Relay what she told you so that he is aware of what you know. Follow this up with a genuine statement of concern: "I hope that you don't feel put on the spot by my coming to you like this. I don't know your side of the story, but since Ann was so upset, I agreed to talk with you. I want you to know that I care about you, your relationship to the Lord, and your family."

Let's pick up the conversation at this point:

Gary #1: "I can't believe Ann talked to you behind my back. I hate it when she talks about our family problems with other people. And on top of it all, she has the nerve to accuse me of messing around with another woman! After all I do for her! That really makes me mad!"

Helper #1: "You feel betrayed that Ann talked to me without telling you, and you're angry that she thinks you might be seeing another woman. [Showing understanding and empathy through active listening. This tells Gary that you hear his side, which will help him be less defensive.] Perhaps if you tell me what is going on at work, I can help clear up some of the misunderstanding between you two. How many nights are you working late?" [The helper's invitation for Gary to explain his side of the story and open-ended question will encourage Gary to talk and provide more information.]

Gary #2: "Well, we're working on a new project and there's a lot of pressure to get it done. I guess I do end up staying late three or four nights a week. But I can't really say no to my boss when he piles the work on me, can I?''

Helper #2: "You're under a great deal of pressure to work on this new project and to do what your boss asks you to do. [Acceptance through active listening.] You're also saying that you're staying late three or four nights because of your extra work. That means there really isn't another woman in your life. Is that correct?'' [Checking the facts.]

Gary #3: "That's right. I enjoy my work. This project is fun, and it makes me feel better about myself than I have for ages. Hey, I've never been given this much responsibility before. And besides, who needs another woman? I've got enough trouble with the one I've got at home!''

Helper #3: "So you're saying that all your time at work is dedicated to this new project, which you really enjoy. But what do you mean when you say that you've got trouble with 'the woman at home'?'' [Active listening, open-ended question to follow up on Gary's comment.]

Gary #4: "Well, it's not as if we're having major problems or anything like that. It's just that I always feel as if nothing I do ever matters. All I'm good for is bringing home the weekly pay check. Ann doesn't appreciate how hard I work. All she does is nag, nag, nag about the house. And the kids could care less about anything—they're always off doing their own thing. Now at work it's a different story. There someone notices that I'm worth more than just paying the bills or mowing the lawn!''

Now we're getting more to the heart of the matter. Gary is telling you that although there isn't another woman in his life, his job, rather than his family, has become the major source of his personal satisfaction. Let's see how you could confront this:

Helper #4: "You've really been feeling unappreciated at home and your job is now giving you the recognition you miss. [Active listening.] Although I can understand that you want your family to appreciate you, I wonder if consistently staying late at work is the best way to gain recognition. I'm concerned about how that affects your family too.'' ["I statement."]

Gary #5: "Oh, I don't know. If Ann really wanted me to be home more, she'd show it by nagging me less when I'm there.''

Helper #5: "Now you're indicating that you really could be home more evenings if only Ann would nag you less. Does that mean you really don't need to be staying late three or four nights?'' [Data gathering, using feedback to confront Gary's inconsistencies.]

Gary #6: ''Well, I'm not sure. It's hard to get the work done during the day with so many people in the office. I find it easier to concentrate when everyone's gone.''

Helper #6: ''It seems that another part of the problem is that you might not be working efficiently during regular office hours.'' [Feedback.]

Gary #7: ''Hmmm. I never thought of that. But still, who wants to be home each night with a nagging wife? If Ann were more appreciative and supportive, I wouldn't mind coming home at night!''

Although Gary has partially admitted that he has poor work habits, he's not assuming responsibility for his decision to work at night. First, it's his boss' fault for asking him to do the extra work; now it's Ann's fault for not appreciating him. Gary keeps blaming others for his own choices.

Take a minute to review the types of problems that people face (outlined in chapter 1). Which ones apply to Gary? Although he began by being honest, his last answer sounds defensive. This indicates that he may be hiding from his sin to avoid feeling guilty. He may also feel ashamed that he's not fulfilling his responsibilities as husband and father.

Gary's pride is also involved; he feels hurt that he's not getting the recognition that he thinks he deserves at home. As a result of putting his own needs first, his priorities are now out of order and his family is suffering. In addition, he doesn't seem genuinely accepting of himself or Ann. He also seems to have a distorted view of marriage. Most importantly, his family problems are probably symptomatic of Gary's poor relationship to the Lord and subsequent neglect of his responsibilities.

Lead Your Friend Into Self-Confrontation

Our second challenge is to help our friends confront themselves. In some ways it would be a lot easier just to point a finger at Gary and say, ''Look at what you're doing, you sinner!'' It's a lot harder to be like Nathan, who cleverly led King David into confronting himself (2 Sam. 12:1–15). Helping our friends to see themselves honestly will prevent them from arguing with us. Their reflection, not our fingers shaking in their faces, will be their confrontation.

Use your friend's words. Listen carefully to Gary's description and then use his own words when you give him feedback. For instance, you could continue your conversation with Gary like this:

Helper #7: "Gary, first you told me that you were working overtime because your boss asked you. Now you're implying that you could get the work done if you could concentrate better during the day. And then you keep coming back to the fact that if only Ann nagged you less, you would be home in the evenings with her. [Summarizing the conversation using Gary's words.] It sounds to me that you're blaming your boss and Ann for what really is your decision to work late." [Feedback.]

Gary #8: "Well, I'm not sure it's really as simple as that. I really am trying to do my best."

Notice that the helper uses simple language that gets right to the point. The helper doesn't editorialize on Gary's behavior, but rather replays it for him so that Gary can see the implications of what he's saying. The helper matches Gary's vocabulary so that Gary will understand and not feel "psychologized."

Observe your friend's nonverbal behavior. People communicate how they're feeling through their body language, facial expressions, and tone of voice. For example, as Gary talks, you may notice that his voice sounds slightly embarrassed and defensive. Now he's squirming around in his chair and has a hard time looking you in the eye. You could comment on this by saying:

Helper #8: "I notice that you look uncomfortable as we talk about the real reasons why you're working late. Even though you say you're doing your best, you look and sound as if you don't feel so great about what's happening at home." [Feedback, pointing out inconsistencies between Gary's verbal and nonverbal behavior.]

Gary #9: "Well, I feel really caught in the middle and don't see any way out. My boss is expecting me to get this project done, and Ann is too demanding. I guess Ann will just have to accept the fact that I have to put in overtime."

Gary still isn't admitting that he can do anything to change the situation. You can help Gary confront himself more by employing step 3:

Ask leading, open-ended questions. An important aspect of self-confrontation is asking questions that enable our friends to look at the implications of their behavior. Good leading questions help our friends to think through the consequences of their decisions and actions. We want to avoid closed questions that limit a person's response. A question such as "Why are you hurting Ann like this?" communicates your opinion rather than probing Gary for his. (Review chart #2, "Use Statements Instead of Questions," in chapter 8.) Instead, try saying:

Helper #9: "The fact that you look ashamed makes me wonder if you are being totally honest with me and with yourself. [Feedback] You say that you don't know a way out of this dilemma, but I wonder if you have considered every way of getting your work done during regular office hours." [Self-confrontative question. This is very different from saying, "Don't you know that spending that much time away from your family is wrong? Why can't you just stop goofing around and get your work done during the day?" That question not only does the counseling work *for* Gary instead of leading him into self-confrontation, but it also belittles.]

Gary #10: "Well, I guess I could try working harder during the day. But that's pretty tough with all the phone interruptions and people coming by to talk. It really is so much easier to work at night. But you're right. I do feel bad about it."

Helper #10: "It seems as if you think of ideas but then give up on them pretty easily. [Feedback.] Can you tell me more about what you feel bad about?" [Open-ended question to help Gary confront himself.]

Gary #11: "Well, to be honest, I feel lousy that I've lost touch with the kids. We used to do a lot more together as a family. It was like we were all friends. And Ann and I used to get along better too. But not now. Yeah, and the house gets me down too. There's always something that needs fixing. You have to admit, it sure is a lot to tackle."

Helper #11: "You feel bad that your family isn't as close as you once were, and you feel discouraged about all that needs to be done around the house. The job looks pretty big to you."

Gary #12: "Yeah, it would take so much work to get Ann and me close again, to get the family back together, and to fix up the house. Sometimes I wonder if it's really worth the effort. Besides, who will really appreciate what I'm doing?"

Now that Gary is being a little more honest with you, you can go further with him. His honesty is necessary in order for him to take responsibility for his behavior. Your next step then is to:

Confront your friend's value system with the Word of God.
In order to help Gary evaluate his behavior, you want him to
consider whether he is violating any of his own values as well as
any of God's standards. Follow up his comments by saying:

Helper #12: "You feel as if you're not sure your family is
worth your effort. [Active listening.] When you say that no one
will appreciate what you do, I wonder what your real motivation
is for caring for your family. ["I statement."] Let me ask you
this, Gary. What do you think of a father who doesn't spend
enough time with his wife and children?" [Confronting Gary on
his values.]

Gary #13: "I always thought it wasn't right, but to be
honest, I really don't know if I've got what it takes to be a good
husband and father."

Helper #13: "You're doubting whether or not you can
fulfill your responsibilities to your family. [Active listening.] It
seems that you haven't done that so far. [Feedback.] What does
the Bible say about all this?" [Open-ended question.]

Gary #14: "I think it says somewhere that God will help us
do what we are supposed to do. But it's tough balancing
everything at home and at work!"

At this point Gary has begun to admit that he has gone
against his own values and biblical standards. But he has not
committed himself to changing the situation. Your final step is to
help Gary think through the choices he is making.

Help your friend make a decision. It's very tempting at this
point to tell Gary what you think he should do. But that's not
your job. Instead, you want to help him make a responsible
decision. Try to avoid red flag words like "should" and
"ought," which imply the direction you think he should take.

Helper #14: "Although you've said you aren't handling
your responsibilities at home well, so far you haven't committed
yourself to doing anything different. [Feedback.] What do you
think will happen as a result?" [Open-ended question to help
Gary consider the consequences of his behavior.]

Gary #15: "Well, I guess Ann will still be pretty upset with
me."

Helper #15: "Not only that, but did you ever think that her
nagging may increase as you spend less and less time at home
with her and the children?" [Helping Gary get a bigger perspective on the situation.]

Gary #16: "Well I certainly don't want that!"

Helper #16: "I didn't think so. But isn't there more you need to consider? Specifically, I'm wondering what God's response is to how you are not properly caring for your family responsibilities right now."

Gary #17: "I suppose He isn't too happy with me either."

Helper #17: "What does that mean to you? What do you plan to do given the fact that God isn't pleased and Ann is pretty upset?" [Open-ended question to encourage Gary toward a biblical plan of action.]

Gary #18: "Well, I suppose I really need to stop working overtime and be home in the evenings. But I really don't know how I'll do all that and still get everything at the office done."

At this point Gary has expressed his first commitment to change. When this happens, a careful helper will find out *why* Gary plans on changing. He might be saying that he'll change just to get you off his back! Genuine repentance is a change of mind that leads to a change in *life*. If a person agrees to change without genuine internal commitment, he or she will not follow through on that promise. To have permanent results, obedience must be truly embraced within.

Honest confession should motivate your friend to take action. In the next chapter we'll see how you can help Gary translate his decision into specific changes. But first, let's look at some times when more direct confrontation is necessary.

In general, it's best to ask open-ended questions that lead your friend into confronting himself or herself. But, there are a few exceptions to this rule. If Gary repeatedly refused to admit that he was neglecting his family, then the Bible commands us to get more involved. If you've carefully confronted a friend using the steps listed above and he or she still refuses to admit or turn away from that sin, then you need to follow the instructions in Matthew 18:15–17.

Here Jesus teaches that if a person fails to listen to private confrontation, then we must bring others to assist in speaking the truth to him or her. If the person still refuses to listen, then he or she must be brought before the elders. Ultimately, church discipline may be necessary. This is a serious matter that must be handled very carefully.[3]

Second, we take a more active role when a friend is going through a crisis. As we'll see in chapter 11, a friend in crisis is often unable to think clearly. At that time, we'll need to give more direct suggestions and advice. But this is a short-term role.

As soon as possible we'll help that friend draw from his or her own resources to avoid dependency on us.

Third, we'll need to be more actively involved if a person is threatening to hurt himself, herself, or another person. We obviously are not going to stand by and watch one friend put a gun to his head or watch another beat her child. These are obviously extreme situations that require more direct intervention.

Temptations to Avoid

Because of the risks involved, some of us are tempted to avoid confrontation for several reasons. First, we are tempted to "underspeak" and not confront a friend when we should.

Second, we are tempted to err in the opposite direction and "overspeak" by forcing our opinions on our friends. It's hard for us to realize that we can't *make* another person change. We must be patient and pray that the Holy Spirit will show our friends how they need to change. Remember, we are not alone as we counsel. We must rely on the Spirit to convince our friends of the truth.

Third, we may confront our friends adequately but fail to minister comfort. Remember, forgiveness is an integral part of the entire helping process.

Fourth, we are tempted to confront the sins of others but to ignore our own. Our help will be more genuine and our counsel more believable if we are humble enough to admit our own weaknesses and sin. In fact, the times that I have shared my own struggles against sin have often been the most significant interventions for the friends whom I have helped. Remember that our own Christian lives can be the most powerful confrontation. To the extent that we honestly confront and confess our sins and receive forgiveness, we show our friends how they too can be free from the "sin that so easily entangles." Our personal knowledge of God's holiness and love is the most solid foundation for helping others. It equips us to incarnate God's example of loving confrontation.

PERSONAL AND PRACTICAL

Study the Scripture

1. Compare Galatians 5:15, 20 with Galatians 5:22. Pick out the behaviors that are related to how we speak to

one another. Which behaviors does Paul instruct us to put off? What are we to replace them with? How does this relate to biblical confrontation? What is the role of the Holy Spirit in this (see vv. 25–26)?

2. Read Galatians 6:1 and 1 Corinthians 10:12. What is Paul's warning to us as helpers? What principles of confrontation are implied in these passages?

3. Read Luke 17:3–4. How do Jesus' words relate to our theme of confrontation and comfort? Think of a situation where friends or family members repeatedly sinned against you. What was your response to them? What would it have taken for you to forgive them?

4. Read Proverbs 18:21 and James 3:5–6, 9–10. Why is the tongue considered to be so dangerous? What sins of the tongue must you avoid when you confront a friend?

5. Read Matthew 12:34–37; 15:17–20. What was your heart attitude the last time you confronted someone? How did this influence what you said or how you said it?

6. Read Ephesians 4:15–16. What is the reason Paul gives for speaking the truth? What difficulties do you experience in being honest with another person? What areas do you find difficult to confront in another 1person's life? Over the next few days, notice if you hold back from saying certain things to people. Is there a pattern to the things you won't speak the truth about?

7. Read Ephesians 4:29. What should be the goal of what we say to one another? Consider verses 31 and 32. What is Paul's antidote to sinning with our mouth? Consider someone against whom you've sinned with your mouth. How could you have responded to that person instead?

8. Read Proverbs 9:8b; 12:15; 13:18b; 15:31–32. What do these verses teach about the person to whom your confrontation is addressed? What should you do if your friend refuses to listen to you?

For Thought

Review the cases presented at the end of chapter 8. Write a brief paragraph on how you would confront each person. As you think of what you would say, consider the following points:

- What is your purpose in confronting this person? What do you hope to accomplish?

- What feelings are aroused in you as you talk to this person? What is your response to his or her problem?
- Is there sin involved? How can you be sure? If so, what do you think it is? How would you point out the sin?
- How can you show love if the person persists in sin?
- Is the person experiencing guilt or shame? If so, how could you respond to each? If not (as in the case of ignored guilt) what would you say?
- What are the facts of the situation? What are the types of problems the person is facing (refer to chapter 1)? What else may be going on for that person?
- What questions would lead this person into confronting himself or herself?
- How could you speak the truth and show forgiveness at the same time?
- What would you do if the person resisted hearing what you had to say?
- How might you be tempted to "underspeak"? How about "overspeak"?

For Further Reading

1. Read Jay Adams' *Competent To Counsel* (Phillipsburg, New Jersey: Presbyterian and Reformed Publishing Co., 1970) for further discussion of nouthetic counseling.
2. Read David Augsburger's *Caring Enough To Confront* (Ventura, California: Regal Books, 1981) for practical suggestions on how to confront.
3. Review pages 106–09 of Lawrence Crabb and Dan Allender's *Encouragement* (Grand Rapids: Zondervan Publishing House, 1984) for their concern about giving premature advice when helping a friend.
4. Read pages 153–57 of William Kirwan's *Biblical Concepts for Christian Counseling* (Grand Rapids: Baker Book House, 1984) for his discussion on biblical confrontation.

NOTES

[1] Much of the following material on confrontation has been adapted from Gerard Egan's *Face to Face* (Monterey, California: Brooks-Cole Publishing Co., 1973), pp. 133–34.

[2] Dick Keyes, *Beyond Identity* (Ann Arbor: Servant Books, 1984), p. 155.

[3] For further exposition of this passage, see Jay Adams' *Competent To Counsel* (Phillipsburg, New Jersey: Presbyterian and Reformed Publishing Co., 1970), pp. 225–28 as well as his *The Christian Counselor's Manual* (Phillipsburg, New Jersey: Presbyterian and Reformed Publishing Co., 1973), pp. 52–60.

‡

CHAPTER 10

DIRECT TOWARD ACTION: THE THIRD LEVEL OF HELPING

Obedience is the road to all things. It is the only way to grow able to trust him. Love and faith and obedience are sides of the same prism.

—*George MacDonald*

Therefore let us learn to shake off the things that stop us from coming to Jesus Christ . . . . So that we may yield ourselves with a free heart to God and be earnestly minded to obey him and to give ourselves wholly to him, for so it is his will to have us joined to him.

—*John Calvin*

We have learned how to help our friends confront themselves and acknowledge their problems. Now it's time to learn how to help them put muscle behind their words and translate their insights into action. This includes helping our friends develop appropriate responses to what they are facing, establish a plan of action, and then follow through on that plan. In doing this, we'll teach problem-solving skills they will use in future situations.

As you approach this last step of the helping process, don't forget your job description: you're a coach, not a lifeguard.

ACTION PRINCIPLES

We've seen that when we offer comfort and join our friends, we are *parakletic* helpers; when we confront and speak the truth, we are *nouthetic* helpers. Similarly, when we encourage our friends to take action, we are fulfilling a third helping function. You could say that we are *dynamic* helpers, derived from the Greek word *dunamoo,* which means "to enable" or "to strengthen." Our job at this point is to enable and strengthen our friends to take action so that they will solve the problems entangling their lives.

Scripture emphasizes the renewal of the mind as a precursor to change (Rom. 12:1–2; Eph. 4:17–24; 1 Peter 1:13–14). This renewal eventually should be reflected in observable changes in behavior. In particular, a Christian's changes should be marked by Christ's lordship of his or her life.

Just as it's difficult for us to break old habits and sinful patterns, it also will be difficult for our friends. Why is it so hard to stop being impatient, jealous, sarcastic, lazy, bitter, or proud? Why is there a gap between what we *know* we should do and what we actually *do*? One theologican explains that this happens because sin is really knowledge that refuses to take responsibility for itself.[1] Therefore, true repentance occurs only when knowledge and responsibility come together. In other words, genuine repentance is one that fully admits to sin and guilt, believes Christ's forgiveness, sees God's mercy, and consequently decides to change.

As the Word of God exhorts us and our friends, this change must involve putting off sin and putting on new, godly behaviors (Eph. 4:22–24; Col. 3:10; 1 Peter 4:3–6). The work of "putting off" includes repentance and turning away from sin. "Putting on" involves replacing that sin with godly living. See chart #1, "Put On—Put Off," for a list of Scripture references that match sins to be put off with godly habits to be put on.

CHART #1: "PUT ON—PUT OFF"[2]

"Throw off everything that hinders and the sin that so easily entangles" (Heb. 12:1b).

PUT OFF	SCRIPTURAL INSIGHT		PUT ON
Lack of love	1 John 4:7–8, 20	John 15:12	Love
Judging	Matt. 7:1–2	John 8:1–11 Gal. 6:1	Self-examination

Bitterness	Heb. 12:15 1 Thess. 5:15	Col. 3:12	Compassion and kindness
Unforgiving spirit	Matt. 18:23–35	Mark 11:26 Col. 3:13	Forgiveness
Selfishness	Phil. 2:21	John 12:24 Matt. 10:38–39	Death to self
Boasting	1 Cor. 4:7 James 4:13–16	Prov. 27:2 Rom. 12:3	Humility
Pride	Prov. 16:18	1 Peter 5:5 Gal. 6:3	Humility
Arrogance	1 Sam. 15:23	1 Peter 2:13, 14, 17	Submission
Rebellion and disobedience	2 Tim. 3:1–9 Rom. 1:26–32	Exodus 19:5 1 Sam. 15:22 Matt. 7:21	Repentance and obedience
Impatience	Luke 10:40 Num. 20:10–13	James 1:2–4; 5:7–8 Rom. 12:12	Patience and trusting God
Ungratefulness	Rom. 1:21	Eph. 5:20	Thankfulness
Discontent and complaining	Num. 11:4–6	Phil. 4:11–13 1 Thess. 5:16–18	Contentment
Covetousness	Exod. 20:17	Col. 3:5	Not having evil desires
Irritation to others	Eccl. 7:9	1 Cor. 13:4	Forbearance
Jealousy	Prov. 27:4	Phil. 2:3–4	Trust, Preferring others
Conflict	James 3:16	Luke 6:31	Esteem others
Violence	Prov. 16:29	1 Thess. 2:7	Gentleness

Anger	James 1:19–20 Matt. 5:21–22	Gal. 5:22–25 Eph. 4:26 1 Cor. 13:4–6	Self-control, Love and kindness
Murder	Exod. 20:13	Rom. 13:10	Love
Gossip	1 Tim. 5:13	Prov. 26:20	Confidentiality
Lying and bad language	Eph. 4:25, 29 Col. 3:8, 9	Eph. 4:31 Zech. 8:16 1 Tim. 4:12	Speaking the truth in love
Evil thoughts	Matt. 5:28	Phil. 4:8	Pure thoughts
Stealing	Exod. 20:15	Eph. 4:28	Working for others
Complacency	James 4:17	Col. 3:23	Diligence
Hypocrisy	Matt. 6:2, 5, 16; 23:27	1. Thess. 2:4–6	Integrity
Other gods	Exod. 20:3–4	Col. 1:18	Christ is Lord
Lost first love	Rev. 2:4	1 John 4:10, 19	Meditate on Christ's love
Worry (fear)	Matt. 6:25–32	1 Peter 5:7	Trust God
Doubt (unbelief)	Mark 9:24	1 John 6:29 Heb. 11:1	Faith in God

In order to become "dead to sin but alive to God" (Rom. 6:11), all Christians must realize that they are constantly engaged in a spiritual battle (Eph. 6:12–18). We'll all be able to fight this "good fight" only if we are outfitted with God's equipment: His Word, the Holy Spirit, prayer, encouragement from others, and the capacity He has given us to make right choices. It's by exercising our wills and by relying on God's power and grace that we can make godly choices and resist sin (Gal. 5:14–6:10).[3]

LET'S MOVE!

Get Ready . . .

Are our friends ready to take action and to make definite changes in their lives? In order to answer this, we need to ask ourselves the following questions:

- Are my friend's problems clearly identified?
- Does my friend have a clear idea of the goal(s) that he or she is trying to reach? Are they biblical goals?
- Is my friend looking to the grace of God for power?
- Is my friend assuming responsibility for the situation?

If our friends can answer these with a definite yes, then they are prepared for action. If our friends answer any of these questions with a no, then we need to retrace our steps. To help them answer the first three affirmatively, we must return to active listening, open-ended questions, and confrontation.

If a friend is not assuming personal responsibility, then we must encourage him or her to "rewrite" the problem. Our friends need to be the subject, not the object of their statements. For example, Gary needed to see that *he,* not his boss or Ann, made the decision to work late. Let's begin a second conversation with him and see how to move him dynamically through ten different action steps. (For the sake of this example, the following is happening during only two conversations. Frequently it will take your friend longer to go through all ten action steps.)

1. Assume responsibility. When we left the previous conversation, Gary had just begun to consider the consequences of his sin and its effects on his relationships to God and Ann. He had made a tentative decision to stop working overtime and to be home in the evenings. But he wasn't sure how he would do that and still get his work done. An observant helper would help Gary be more specific by asking:

Helper #1: "I'm glad you're thinking of coming home on time and trying to get your work done during regular office hours. [Active listening.] What could you do to concentrate better during those hours so you could complete your work then?" [Open-ended question that directs Gary to consider his choices.]

Gary #1: "Well, I've been thinking about that. I figured I'd try to work real hard for about a week and see if anyone at home notices what I'm doing."

We have our first problem! "I'll work real hard" is a pretty vague plan. Gary's time frame (one week) is also unrealistic. But most important, his goal—to get his family's attention and recognition—is not biblical. He is still focusing on change in order to *get* rather than to *give*.

Helper #2: "Gary, although you've admitted that you need to change your work habits and come home on time, it seems as if you're willing to try it only if it pays off. [Feedback.] When you do that, I'm concerned because it seems as if you're still not assuming your family responsibilities. ["I statement."] God's Word says that your responsibility to Ann and the children is separate from anything you might receive in return." [Giving a biblical perspective on Gary's role.]

Gary #2: "Well, maybe that's true. But what should I do first?"

Helper #3: "Let's figure out some specific goals. What are you trying to accomplish?" [Open-ended question to help Gary establish his goals.]

Gary #3: "I guess to become a better husband and father."

Helper #4: "If you were a 'better husband and father,' what would you be doing differently now?" [Open-ended question to help Gary be more specific.]

Gary #4: "I suppose I'd really have to change my work habits."

Helper #5: "What work habits do you think need changing?" [Forcing Gary to be more concrete.]

Gary #5: "I guess I could tell the secretary to weed out the important phone calls. I could answer those and let her handle the rest. I hate to say it, but I suppose I'll have to cut off all those chats during the day too!"

Helper #6: "That sounds like a good start on the office problem to me. [Affirmation.] How about your family? What do you think are the first steps to take with them?"

Gary #6: "Well, I guess it would be to spend that evening time with them instead of at the office."

By acknowledging his failures, Gary has come out from hiding and has begun to be more honest with you and himself. You then can help him take the next step:

2. Confess sin. Scripture teaches that we are to confess our sins to God and to one another (Prov. 28:13; James 5:16).

Although it is painful, confessing our sin is a necessary component of change. More than commitment to "putting off" sinful behavior, it's also the only way out of guilt. In addition, confession prepares the way for forgiveness, reestablishes broken relationships, and begins the process of "putting on" new behavior (see Ps. 32:1–7).

How could you help Gary confess his sin?

Helper #7: "It seems you're really admitting how you've neglected your family and how you need to be a better husband and father. [Active listening.] Have you said these things to God, to Ann, and to the children?" [Probing question that encourages Gary to make a complete confession.]

Gary #7: "Not really. I've always had a hard time admitting I've been wrong. And since I really haven't been praying much lately, it's hard to say that to God too."

Helper #8: "You seem embarrassed. [Active listening to feelings.] I often have a hard time admitting when I'm wrong too. What has helped me is realizing how merciful and forgiving God is." [Self-disclosure that points toward biblical truth.]

Gary #8: "Now that I think about it. I've been neglecting Ann and the kids for quite awhile. Do you really think God can forgive me for the way I've acted toward them in the past? I don't even know how to begin to talk to Ann about this."

Like many of us who have become used to hiding our sins, Gary is afraid of being totally open. By the time he finally recognizes his sin, he is close to being engulfed with despair. But with a proper understanding of God's holiness as well as His forgiveness, Gary is free to confess his sins. At this point you can do several things. First, look at Scripture passages that describe God's forgiveness (Isa. 53; Psalms 32, 51 and 130; 1 John 1:1–2:2). Second, as his helper you have the important job of demonstrating to Gary the power and freedom of forgiveness through Christ. You could reach over and touch his arm and say,

Helper #9: "I know that it's really hard to come face-to-face with our sins. [Showing understanding.] But what I have found to be so amazing, is that God's Word promises that in Christ, we are now new creatures and cleansed from our past sins. [Self-disclosure and reminder of God's Word.] Those are pretty big things that God promises us!"

Third, you want to encourage Gary to rehearse with you what he will say to Ann and the children. This gives him a chance to put his thoughts into words in a less-threatening environment. (This type of rehearsal is helpful whenever a friend is preparing to *say* or *do* something new.)

Imagine that Gary carries through on this assignment and confesses his sin to God, Ann, and his children. He still has a long way to go to becoming a more godly Christian and a more responsible husband and father. Accordingly, your next step is to help him to:

3. Apply the Word.   Although the Bible gives us many guidelines on how to live our lives, application of Scripture to specific problems isn't always easy. As helpers, we want to avoid two extremes: either giving pat answers that simplify problems and say more than God's Word truly says or not including the Bible in the counsel we give. To avoid misrepresenting God's Word in any way, we must pray that the Holy Spirit will guide us in choosing *which* Scriptures to use, *when* to use them, and *how* to use them.

We can use the Scripture many different ways to help a friend. One Christian psychologist writes that these include using the Bible as a source of confrontation and instruction, as a standard by which a person should judge his or her thoughts and actions, as a way to restructure a person's ethical system and reshape a person's habits, and as a source of comfort.[4] (See Appendix B for a list of Scriptures to use when you are counseling.)

Let's see how you could use the Bible while helping Gary. He has confessed his sins of irresponsibility to God and his family, and he has promised to stop working overtime so that he could be home in the evenings. But two weeks later he tells you he's still unhappy because nothing much has changed at home. He's not sure if he really made the right decision after all. How could you respond to him? Remember that breaking old habits is never easy. The way Gary is dragging his feet is not unusual.

Helper #9: "Gary, I'm pleased to see how you followed up on our last conversation. [Affirmation.] But you seem ready to give up on your responsibilities to your family all over again! [Feedback.] Have you thought about what God's Word directs you to do? It may be a good idea for us to look at Scripture together and figure out just what your responsibilities as a husband and father are."[5]

Notice that the helper doesn't club Gary over the head with the Bible, but instead tries to lead Gary into applying scriptural principles to his life. Similarly, the helper doesn't confront him with his or her own opinions or judgments. We want to help our friends judge their thoughts, desires, and actions by the standards set down in the Bible, not by our standards.

If you were helping Gary, what passages could you study together? Consider looking at Ephesians 5:25–31 and 6:4; 1 Corinthians 13:4–8; Mark 9:35 and 10:31; and Deuteronomy 6:4–7.

As Gary responds to God's Word, his thoughts will be restructured and his habits will be reshaped. At this point, "putting off the old" and "putting on the new" becomes concrete. A good helper will help Gary through this process by asking questions such as, "What do you think loving Ann includes?" or "How have you frustrated your children? What can you do instead?" Each of these questions emphasizes a different aspect of how Gary needs to change. (The questions we ask will influence the direction of our conversations. Keep your friend's goals in mind when deciding what to ask.)

Just as Gary needs to be *confronted* by God's Word, he also needs to experience its *comfort*. Gary needs to understand that God forgives guilty sinners who repent and that He accepts even the most shameful parts of us. Prayerfully consider which Scripture verses would minister to Gary. Often parables, like the Prodigal Son in Luke 15, convey the fullness of God's love, forgiveness, and mercy in ways that our own words can't communicate.

Get Set

We've seen that a preliminary step to taking action is assuming personal responsibility. But how does a person determine the extent of his or her responsibility? People are often confused between what they *can* and *can't* do. Part of our job is to help them clarify this question.[6] To do that, let's take a look at the next action step:

4. Determine the limits of responsibility. Throughout our lives we encounter situations that we can't change. A factory closes down and jobs are discontinued; a granddaughter is raped; a close friend moves away. Some situations are beyond our control.

But we each have control and responsibility over our *response* to those events. In other words, when we face a situation that we *can't* change and that isn't under our control, we must learn a godly response to that situation. Although it isn't easy, this is something we *can* do.

Gary, for instance, needs to decide what he can and can't do. He *can* make Ann more important than his job by ordering his work day so that he is home in the evenings; he *can't* force Ann to appreciate him more. Although she might never change, Gary still has a responsibility to be a godly, loving husband. In addition, Gary *can* trust that God stands alongside him, using these circumstances to refine and mature his faith.

Next, we help our friends:

5. Prioritize problems. When our friends first begin to recognize their responsibilities, they often will feel overwhelmed by the mountain of problems that need to be addressed. As we've seen, part of Gary's problem is that things have piled up at home. Not only does Ann need attention, but when he took a good look around him, he discovered that his daughter is hanging out with a bad crowd at school, and his son is failing math and science. Looking around the house, he saw that he hadn't cleaned the gutters, put up the storm windows, cleaned up the yard, balanced his checkbook, or tuned up the car. No wonder he felt as if he had a lot to tackle! How can you help him?

First of all, remember that you provide an outside perspective on his situation. You can help him distinguish small hills from large mountains. Begin by asking him to list and prioritize his responsibilities. Perhaps Gary's list would look like this:

1. Strengthen my relationship to God.
2. Do more things that Ann enjoys.
3. Help my son with his homework.
4. Spend time with my daughter and find out about her friends.
5. Balance my checkbook.
6. Winterize the house.
7. Clean up the yard.
8. Get the car tuned up.

When you encourage Gary to focus on the most important tasks, he commits himself to working on his relationships to God and to Ann first. (Action steps 8 and 9 will explain how you can help Gary break down even these responsibilities into smaller tasks.)

After he has worked on these two relationships for awhile, he promises to spend more time with the children too.

6. Evaluate past successes and failures. In the process of getting ready to take action, consider how Gary has tried to solve his problems in the past. What has and hasn't worked for him? If he says that he has tried "everything," make sure you ask for details. He may have repeated the same solution over and over again without exploring other alternatives. This attitude can be a cover-up for his reluctance to try new options or for his attitude of self-pity.

Finding out what Gary has already tried also will help him draw from past successes and avoid past failures. Perhaps he'll remember a time when he felt closer to God. Asking a question like, "What did you do differently then?" may remind him of the personal Bible study he has since abandoned. Similarly, asking, "What do you think is interfering with your relationship to God now?" may help him avoid similar sins now and in the future.

7. Evaluate available resources. Sometimes our friends get stuck because they think they are alone—without outside assistance or without a way of escape from their troubles. But God's Word promises that He has not left us alone or without an exit (Deut. 31:6; 1 Cor. 10:13). He has given us a host of resources that will enable us to tackle our problems.

First, our friends can draw on the resources of God's Word to direct their thinking, to shape their decisions, and to provide much needed comfort. In the same way, we need to encourage them to draw upon the power and presence of the Holy Spirit. Within this context, prayer is an important resource for each Christian. Prayer is the means by which we communicate and maintain our relationship with the living God.

Second, the church, as Christ's visible body on earth, is another important resource. At the moment of conversion, each Christian becomes a member of the family of God. The body of Christ must support, encourage, build up, exhort, and love each believer. The Christians whom we counsel need the support of this team, including the support of their pastors and elders.

Third, our friends also should be able to draw on the support and encouragement of family and friends. Although not everyone has a wide network of friends, most people have a few people to whom they can turn for support. Asking "Who else could help you in this situation?" will help your friend remember this resource. (You may be called on to help people who are truly isolated and without friends. If that is the case, then part of your job is to help them develop relationships that will ease their isolation and provide support.)

Fourth, God has placed several resources within each of us: our abilities to reason, feel, understand, figure out, learn, and decide. Our friends can draw upon these resources when they consider the consequences of their behavior and when they figure out new ways of acting. Encouraging our friends to exercise their God-given talents also will help them see what they can offer others, taking their minds off themselves and their problems.

Fifth, our friends have material resources. We can ask our friends to draw on their financial and physical resources as well as their resources of time.

Go!

8. Brainstorm about alternatives. Our next task is to help our friends figure out how they will reach their goals. We need to be creative. We can pull ideas from a friend's reservoir of past experiences and bank of future possibilities. For example, ask Gary, "What can you do to improve your relationship to God?" and "What are some things you and Ann could do together?" Encourage him to write down every possibility—even those that seem silly or crazy. Don't be afraid to draw from your own experiences also. This brainstorming process will show him that he has many choices.

In order to improve his relationship to God, Gary replies that he could:

1. Have a half-hour Bible study every morning.

2. Go to church twice on Sunday and attend the weekly prayer meeting.

3. Read more Christian books.

4. Hold family devotions every evening after supper.

He and Ann could:

1. Go out for dinner once a week.

2. Attend a couple's Bible study.

3. Jog together three times a week.

4. Take a course together at a local adult evening school.

5. Join a bridge group together.

Although these are good suggestions, they're probably not feasible all at once. For a plan to work, it must be realistic, practical, and obtainable.

In order to determine the viability of each solution, Gary needs to consider such factors as time requirements, available resources (including finances), and his family and work obligations. Then he must determine the pros and cons of each decision. Asking Gary "How will having a half-hour Bible study affect you and the other people in your life?" and "What will you lose or gain if you take Ann out to dinner every week?" will help him anticipate the possible benefits or losses resulting from his decisions.

After sorting through these alternatives, Gary should:

9. Develop a plan of action. Gary's next step is to form a plan that is self-directed and self-monitored. He'll be more likely to follow through on changing if he has input into designing, carrying through, and monitoring his own progress.[7] Help Gary select a few ideas from the brainstorming process. These ideas will become his first steps toward reaching his goals. They should be small, measurable, and concrete so that Gary can see some immediate success.

Let's assume that Gary decides that he's going to spend twenty minutes before work each morning in Bible study and prayer. He also plans to attend the church's weekly prayer meeting with Ann. Since their budget is tight, he'll take her out to dinner every other Friday night and find something less expensive for them to do together on the alternative weeks. In a sense, he's assigning himself "homework" that will help him carry out his plan.

As a part of this homework, encourage Gary to study and/or memorize related Scriptures. These could include Colossians 3:19; Ephesians 5:25, 28, 33; 6:4; 1 Timothy 3:4, 5; and 1 Peter 3:7.

A journal also can be helpful at this time. Encourage Gary to record his goals and the steps he's taking to meet them. He could keep track of the Bible passages he's studying and situations in which he applies them. Similarly, he could record the activities he and Ann do together. This record will confront and encourage him as he remembers where he started and where he's headed.

Finally, our friends can take the last action step:

10. Evaluate skills. In order for our friends to complete their plans successfully, they must have certain skills. In Gary's case, does he know how to study the Bible? Has he ever been taught how to apply the Word to his daily life? If not, he may need specific instruction in order to accomplish his first goal. In the same way, Gary also may need help in showing Ann that she's special to him.[8]

It's not our job to teach our friends every skill they need. Eventually Gary may need to learn how to budget his money, how to relate better to his daughter, and how to manage his time. Don't feel as if you have to teach your friend each skill he or she lacks. Part of your job is to refer your friends to the appropriate sources of help.

We must make sure we follow up on our friends. Check back with Gary and see how he's doing on his goals. You could say, "I have been praying for you and am wondering how your Bible study time is going" or "What did you and Ann do this week?" These questions promote accountability and show him that he and Ann are important to you.

OBSTACLES TO TAKING ACTION

We all face a battle when trying to break old habits and sinful patterns. One part of us wants to stop, another part doesn't. Old habits, like old shoes, are comfortable and familiar. New habits, like new shoes, are often painful to break in but worth establishing after the pain is over. Even the apostle Paul knew what it was like to fight this battle (Rom. 7:15–20).

Whenever we move toward a goal, we meet various obstacles. Let's take a look at how these obstacles, many of which involve sin, might prevent Gary from taking action.

Faith That Lacks Action

A friend's lack of commitment to Christ will be his or her first obstacle to action. For example, Gary's work, rather than the Lord, had become the top priority in his life. But even after Gary decided to stop working overtime, he still had difficulty coming under Christ's lordship. We might hear Gary's unwillingness to do this in a variety of ways:

Statement #1: "If I stop staying late at work, will it pay off? Will Ann give me the appreciation I need?" Gary is trying to find a reason to put his own desires first. His hesitation shows that he's not trusting that God will bless his obedience to Him.

Statement #2: "If God asks me to love Ann, then I guess that's the cross I'll have to bear." Gary's attitude of martyrdom is not the same as genuine commitment to Ann. True love for others springs not from self-pity but from appreciation for God's love and from dedication to His Word.

Statement #3: "I must wait on God. He's really the only one who can change my heart toward Ann." This statement reflects a superficial understanding of Christian responsibility and is a rationalization for not changing. The passive Christian often confuses his or her own responsibility with God's.

Motivation Matters

Change requires self-discipline, effort, and hard work. Often people think they want to change, but they may not want it enough to actually *do* something different. Gary's inadequate motivation might be heard in statements such as:

Statement #1: "If Ann wants me to spend more time with her, I guess I'll just have to." This statement shows that Gary's motivation lies outside himself, not inside. He's changing only because he "should," and he's removing himself from the process.

Statement #2: "It sure would be nice to spend more time with Ann, but I can't because this project needs to be completed." "I can'ts" and "yes, buts" often hide "I won'ts." If Gary meets your suggestions with a form of "yes, but," you may suspect that what he really wants is a sympathetic listener rather than someone who will encourage him to change.

Statement #3: "I've told Ann that I'm sorry a million times, but she says that's not good enough. What more can I do?" A ritualistic request for forgiveness is not the same as genuine repentance. If Gary really wants to change, he'll add effort to his apology.

Statement #4: "I don't feel like loving Ann when she is so cold and distant." One of the easiest ways to avoid the responsibility of changing is to rely on emotions. We must acknowledge our friends' feelings and then help them to separate their emotions from their responsibilities.

Statement #5: "I've sinned so much, God can't possibly forgive me." A person who thinks he or she is unforgivable is also saying he or she is unchangeable. As we saw in chapter 1, this is actually a form of pride. Gary is resisting God's sanctifying power and is giving himself an excuse not to change.

Statement #6: "My mother always said I was just like my father and would never make a good husband. I guess she was right." Although we do learn a lot about ourselves as we grow up, it's our responsibility to filter out the messages that are false. Gary is responsible to decide which voice he'll believe—his mother's voice telling him he's hopeless or God's promises telling him that Jesus gives him power to change.

We need to listen for the possible *implication* of our friends' messages in order to detect these motivational problems. Think about what Gary is deciding when he makes these excuses and use this information to give him feedback: "I know you said that you wanted to learn to love Ann, but when I hear you say that you can never be a good husband, I wonder if you really plan to work at your marriage."

Fear Inhibits Action

People often are afraid of the risks involved in changing. The fear of the unknown combined with the safety of the familiar are very real obstacles to change.

Gary might communicate his fears by saying:

Statement #1: "I'm afraid I'll fail at being Ann's husband. I always mess things up. Why should I even bother trying?" People who lack self-confidence believe that not trying is better than trying and failing. Unable to face their failures, they give up too easily. Friends like this need to be reminded that Jesus is always present with them and that self-confidence comes from what we learn from our failures as well as our successes.

Statement #2: "But what if I try loving Ann the way the Bible says I should, and she just laughs at me? Or worse yet, what if she ignores me?" The fear of rejection also can inhibit action and can keep a person trapped in old behavior patterns.

Statement #3: "The guys at work are going to think I'm such a jerk for being yanked around by Ann. They all work late, and none of their wives can nag them into coming home early.

How can I face them?'' Embarrassment and shame also can be obstacles to change. As we saw in chapter 1, shame is concerned with how we appear to others. In this situation, Gary is afraid of how his peers will perceive him. Thus his pride prevents true obedience.

Our job is to help our friends stare down their fears. The simple question "What is the worst thing that could happen to you?'' will often help our friends see that their fears are unrealistic. We also must look together at God's reassuring promises that we don't need to be afraid (Matt. 6:25–34; 10:29–30). In this way we help our friends fight off the ghosts of "what ifs'' that limit their lives.

Problems with the Action Plan

Sometimes our friends fail to reach their goals because their plans are too difficult, unrealistic, or inappropriate. You'll know this has happened if you hear Gary say something like:

Statement #1: "I told Ann that I'd show she was important to me by buying her some new clothes and by taking her out to dinner every week. I wish I hadn't promised her that because I really can't afford it. Now I'm stuck doing it.'' If Gary tries to do more than is realistically possible, he'll end up frustrated with himself and angry with Ann. He needs to find more appropriate ways to reach his goal.

Statement #2: "For the last week I've tried hard to really love Ann, but she has warmed up to me only a bit.'' Gary has an unrealistic expectation of how soon change should happen. He will be frustrated and disappointed if he's expecting Ann to change her attitude toward him immediately.

Statement #3: "I just want to be a better husband. I can't figure out why nothing has happened.'' If Gary's goals aren't clearly defined, he'll have difficulty taking action. Breaking down large, vague goals into small, measurable steps will help him achieve success.

Sometimes a friend may stay stuck. At that point the two of you may agree that since your counsel hasn't helped, it would be wise for him or her to speak with a professional Christian helper to help determine what is preventing biblical change.

WE CAN HAVE PROBLEMS TOO

Our friends aren't the only ones who face obstacles at this point. Let's look at two common pitfalls helpers experience at this stage of the helping process.

"Why don't you hurry up and change?"

As you are helping a friend, you may find yourself wanting him or her to change faster. "Why can't Gary just treat Ann like a Christian husband should?" you might ask yourself.

Be patient and don't push your friend too hard, too soon. Although Gary's lack of progress may look as if he's failing to practice what you have discussed with him, he'll move at his own pace. Furthermore, God's timing in changing Gary may not be the same as yours. Sanctification doesn't happen overnight.

"Why can't you do things my way?"

Impatiently, we often want to make decisions for our friends. This often gets communicated as plain, ordinary advice.

Keep in mind that our goal is to encourage our friends to stand alone with Jesus as soon as possible. Therefore, advice giving should be given humbly, carefully, and sparingly. Advice should be given not to load them down with guilt but to help them enter the fullness of life that following Christ involves. We want our friends to grow in Jesus' way, not ours.

Congratulations! You're now equipped with the basic helping tools. You have learned how to comfort through acceptance and listening, how to confront through speaking the truth in love, how to follow up with comforting forgiveness, and how to exhort a friend to action dynamically. In the last three chapters, we'll study how to use these skills in some special helping situations.

PERSONAL AND PRACTICAL

Study the Scriptures

1. Read Acts 3:1–10. How was Peter a link between Christ and a person in need? What help did Peter give? Who is

a "lame beggar" in your life? What do Peter's actions model for you?

2. Read 2 Timothy 3:16 and consider three ways to use Scripture. How do these fit into the action stage of helping?

3. Read 2 Corinthians 10:5 and 1 Peter 1:13–14. According to these verses, what are the prerequisites for taking action?

4. Read Ephesians 4:22–32. List at least five sets of behaviors to be "put off" and others to be "put on" (see also Col. 3:8–14).

5. Read Matthew 26:36–39. What does Jesus model about facing suffering? What were the feelings He expressed? What did He decide to *do* in spite of His feelings? How is this related to action step 4 (determine the limits of responsibility)? How could you use this passage when helping a friend?

6. Consider the following verses: Ecclesiastes 3:1–11; 7:14; Romans 8:18, 28; 1 Peter 1:3–9; 4:12–19. Why do we face hurt, trials, and suffering? How are we to respond to suffering? How could you apply this to a person who is angry about the death of a family member, a divorce, or an illness? What do you need to be careful of as you use these verses?

7. What problems do you think you might encounter as you direct someone toward change and action?

For Thought

Directions: Read over the two situations described below and write out how you would help each of these people. Include answers to the following:

- How do you think this person is feeling? Why?
- What are his or her problems (refer to categories from chapter 1)?
- What thoughts, behavior, or sin would you need to confront?
- What Scripture verses would you use when talking to him or her?
- What plan of action is necessary?
- What steps would you encourage this friend to take?
- What obstacles might you or they encounter?

● How would you minister forgiveness to him or her?

JIM

Jim joined your office staff a month ago. You want to get to know him better, so you invite him to lunch. You find out that he just recently moved his wife and two children from Florida, hoping he would be able to advance professionally and earn more money in your city. He just became a Christian last year. His wife, Maureen, is Catholic and isn't sure what Jim's becoming "born again" is all about.

The second time you get together for lunch, Jim mentions that Maureen seems to have changed since they moved. She cries readily and isn't getting any housework done. Boxes are still stacked up all over the place. The kids' toys are everywhere, and he's lucky if he can find a clean shirt to wear to work! Jim admits that he's so tired and frustrated that when he comes in the door, he and Maureen immediately start fighting.

PATRICIA

Patricia, who is thirty-three, has been a close friend for five years. Over time, you've come to see that she is a perfectionist—she always has to do things right. As a result, she usually excels in what she does. She's been promoted to a high-level position on her job; she's headed several committees at church; she dresses beautifully; and when she entertains at her apartment, everyone is impressed at how everything is "just right."

Recently you've noticed that she doesn't seem to be her normal, happy self. When you ask her about this, she confides that the man she had been dating just broke off their relationship, claiming that she was too critical of him. This isn't the first time this has happened to Patricia, and it seems to her that she'll never find someone to love her. She has even begun to doubt God's love for her.

For Further Reading

1. Read chapters 18 and 19 of Jay Adams' *The Christian Counselor's Manual* (Phillipsburg, New Jersey: Presbyterian and Reformed Publishing Co., 1973) for his ideas about helping a friend to take action and change.
2. Read Jay Adams' *The Use of Scriptures in Counseling*

(Phillipsburg, New Jersey: Presbyterian and Reformed Publishing Co., 1975) for suggestions about how to use Scripture when counseling.

3. Read chapter 11 in Eric Berne's *Games People Play* (New York: Grove Press, 1964) for more information on the types of games helpers sometime play.

4. Read chapter 9 of Lawrence Crabb's *Effective Biblical Counseling* (Grand Rapids: Zondervan Publishing House, 1977) for a more in-depth discussion of the relationship of feelings, thoughts, and behavior. He writes about how to challenge a person's assumptions in order to produce biblical thinking.

5. Read chapters 13 and 15 of Sinclair Ferguson's *Know Your Christian Life* (Downers Grove, Illinois: InterVarsity Press, 1981) for a clear discussion of putting off the "old man."

6. Read pages 158–61 of William Kirwan's *Biblical Concepts for Christian Counseling* (Grand Rapids: Baker Book House, 1984) for his discussion of how counseling ends when a person begins to serve others.

7. Read chapters 20–26 of Paul Welter's *How To Help a Friend* (Wheaton, Illinois: Tyndale House Publishers, 1984) for his discussion of how to help a friend choose a plan of action.

8. Read chapters 10 and 11 of Everett Worthington's *When Someone Asks for Help* (Downers Grove, Illinois: InterVarsity Press, 1982) for his discussion of how to help a person rethink his or her situation in order to formulate a suitable plan of action.

NOTES

[1] Os Guiness, "Knowing Means Doing," tape available through Sound Word Associates, P.O. Box 2035, Michigan City, IN., 46360.

[2] Adapted from H. Norman Wright's *Training Christians To Counsel* (Santa Ana, California: Christian Marriage Enrichment, 1977), pp. 37–40.

[3] Marty Voltz, "The Battlefield of the Mind," *Insight* Vol. 2, No. 1 (October 1983): 34–38.

[4] Waylon Ward, *The Bible in Counseling* (Chicago: Moody Press, 1977), pp. 17–18.

[5] For the sake of this example, confession of sin and application of the Word is taking place at two different times. This doesn't always happen. Consulting the Word should be incorporated throughout the helping process.

[6] The "serenity prayer" reflects this dilemma: "Lord, give me the serenity to accept the things I cannot change, the courage to change the things I can, and the wisdom to know the difference."

[7] Everett Worthington, *When Someone Asks for Help* (Downers Grove, Illinois: InterVarsity Press, 1982), p. 182.

[8] An excellent book for couples who want to improve their marriages is Wayne Mack's *Strengthening Your Marriage* (Phillipsburg, New Jersey: Presbyterian and Reformed Publishing Co., 1977).

☦

CHAPTER 11

CRISIS INTERVENTION AND INITIATING HELP

Then I heard the voice of the Lord saying, "Whom shall I send? And who will go for us?"
And I said, "Here am I. Send me!"

—*Isaiah 6:8*

EQUIPPED FOR A CRISIS

How Did Jesus Help in a Crisis?

Jesus, your close friend Lazarus is sick and dying. Please come quickly before it's too late!" We can imagine Mary and Martha's panic as they watched their brother get sicker and sicker. Let's look at John 11 to see how our Lord responded to the crisis.

First of all, Jesus did not panic. With a calm control that came from trusting his Father's power and will, Jesus deliberately delayed going to Bethany. As Jesus explained, He waited for Lazarus to die so that more people would come to faith (vv. 15, 42). (We would rarely have the divine reasons to wait two days as Jesus did, although sometimes we may need to wait before intervening in a crisis.)

After this initial delay, Jesus did intervene. He announced His intention to go to the family, and He followed through, even though it was dangerous for Him to go into Judea.

In Bethany, Jesus was greeted by the same rebuke from both Mary and Martha: "Lord, if you had been here, my brother would not have died" (vv. 21, 32). Did Jesus get angry with the two sisters for their rebuke? No, He understood that Lazarus' death caused the sisters to feel sad, anxious, and afraid. As Lazarus' friend, Jesus shared some of these same emotions. Scripture tells us simply but eloquently that "Jesus wept" (v. 35).

Jesus then went a step beyond visiting the bereaved family. He went to the tomb where Lazarus was buried, even though the tomb would have a strong odor. And there Jesus fulfilled His promises and raised Lazarus from the dead. Our Lord often went to difficult, uncomfortable, or unpleasant places in order to do His Father's work.

Throughout this crisis, Jesus maintained an outsider's perspective. Although He was obviously touched by the situation, He didn't lose control. Our Lord responded with compassion and clear thinking, both of which are vital in a crisis.

Jesus also *used* this crisis. He taught believers more about Himself and brought unbelievers to faith (vv. 25, 45).

Types of Crises

Your phone rings at three in the morning. Sleepily you wonder who could be calling at this hour. Suddenly, you are wide awake as you hear the panic in your brother-in-law's voice. Your sister, who has been experiencing some problems with her first pregnancy, has started to bleed uncontrollably. You have been thrown into a *situational* crisis.

One of your good friends at work is approaching retirement. You notice that the closer the time comes for him to leave the company, the more depressed he becomes. Instead of being his cheerful, joking self, he is moody and curt. You are observing a *maturational* crisis.

A crisis is a sudden and unexpected event or series of events that is life changing and emotionally significant. It often involves a loss, the threat of a loss, or a radical change in a person's relationship with some important person or situation.[1] Past coping mechanisms are often insufficient during crises.

Situational crises, as the word implies, are events related to specific situations that not everyone encounters. A car accident, an unwanted pregnancy, sudden financial loss, a child who runs away from home or is kidnapped, infertility, losing a job, physical assault, an operation, a homicide, a life-threatening illness, a divorce, a nervous breakdown, a drug overdose, a burglary, or a fire all have the same thing in common: they are unexpected events often outside a person's control.

On the other hand, maturational crises are more common and do not occur as suddenly. They are related to stages we each experience. Typical maturational crises include pregnancy, birth, a child leaving for first grade, the birth of siblings, adolescence, a child leaving home, beginning a career, marriage, retirement, and death. Although these events don't always result in acute crisis, they represent changes in a person's environment or life-style. As a result, these events can produce stress both for the person going through the transition and for the other people in his or her life.

The Chinese characters that represent the word *crisis* mean both "danger" and "opportunity."[2] Crises are dangerous because they threaten to overwhelm our friends and can begin a downward spiral that results in despair, bitterness, or apathy. On the other hand, crises can be opportunities for our friends to mature and grow in their love *for* God and usefulness *to* God (Rom. 5:3–5; James 1:2–4; 1 Peter 1:6–7).

How people react to crises. Since it's difficult to face something frightening, painful, or stressful, the first response is often denial: "I can't believe this is happening to me" is a common reaction to losing a loved one, hearing a doctor diagnose cancer, or having a spouse announce that he or she is filing for a divorce.

Crises also leave people feeling shocked and numb, with a sense of unreality that feels like a nightmare. People experience "sensory overload" as they try to integrate what has happened into their life. They are overwhelmed by what has happened as well as by all the possible consequences of the event.

Because of this, people in crisis often find that their rational thoughts are blurred by strong emotions: fear, anxiety, hopelessness, helplessness, confusion, and anger. They may bounce from one emotion to the next. For instance, when Ann first wondered if Gary was having an affair, she might have gone from fear to anger to despair as the full implications of that possibility sank in.

During crises, people who normally can solve their problems find themselves relying on those around them. As a result, they may wonder if there is something wrong with them. They may feel guilty and ashamed for not being able to handle the situation better. We need to reassure our friends that their dependency is temporary and that they soon will be able to manage things on their own again.

Crises affect people differently. What looks like a crisis to you may not be one for someone else. For instance, you may not be threatened by speaking in front of people, whereas the thought of speaking in front of a group may cause another person to panic. A flat tire on a dark, lonely road would make me anxious, but my husband would simply get out his spare tire!

The intensity of a crisis will depend on a number of different factors: the person's personal strength, his or her successful handling of past crises, how personally threatening the crisis is, the strength of the person's walk with the Lord, and who the crisis affects. In general, the more severe a crisis is, the greater our friend's needs will be and the more involved we will become.

In order to determine the intensity of a crisis, keep in mind that the closer the crisis comes to a person, the more threatening it will be. Review chart #2, "Is Your Friend Under Stress?," in chapter 7 to see what types of events produce the most stress. Furthermore, the intensity of a person's crisis will be affected by who is involved. For example, although it would be frightening for you to witness a car accident, it would be devastating to stand by helplessly and watch your parents, spouse, or child be hit by a car. Then again, it would be even more overwhelming if you were in the car yourself.

Like a stone that causes ripples in a pond, a crisis also will radiate out, influencing the lives it touches. For instance, consider a couple who gets divorced. Not only does their decision directly affect their children but it also affects their parents, friends, pastor, acquaintances at work, fellow church members, and neighbors. Although the ripple effect will vary according to the person's relationship to the divorcing couple, the divorce will change life for those who know the couple. For instance, some people may have new responsibilities (grandparents may be asked to assist with child care), new fears (friends may think "That could have been us!"), or new questions (neighbors may think, "How do I act when I meet her in the supermarket?").

The relationship you have with your friend is very important during a crisis. It may be tested and tried to its limits as your friend expects more from you than usual. Your presence and help can make the difference between your friend's *collapse* ("I'll never be able to go on") or *conquest* ("I'm amazed at how I learned to trust God during the hardest time of my life."). Let's see how we can be effective helpers during a crisis.

HOW CAN YOU HELP IN A CRISIS?

Helpers will be more active during crises because our friends require our immediate attention. The helping process is accelerated since problem solving must be done rapidly and efficiently. Just as we wouldn't respond to a drowning person by giving swimming lessons, a person in crisis needs *immediate* help.

Overall, one of our main roles will be to remain *outside* the situation. We must be the one to have an objective, unemotional perspective on what is happening. We can help our friends consider the implications of what they are facing as well as reassure them that their feelings and reactions are normal and temporary. If the situation allows it, we must encourage our friends to wait until these feelings have passed before making any important decisions. Our goal is to help our friends resolve the immediate crisis, reduce their intense feelings, and return to their precrisis coping level as soon as possible.

How can you tell if you are the one to help in a crisis? To answer this, you will need to assess if you are the most suitable person to intervene in the situation. Ask yourself, "Do I know how to help or should my friend find someone who knows more than I?" Your answer will be determined by how immediate the danger is and what other resources are available.

The Moment of Crisis—What Will You Do?

Donna is one of those teens who floats in and out of your youth group. When she does show up, she stays on the fringes. Occasionally a vulnerable, scared young girl pokes through her tough exterior, only to disappear. Her parents recently divorced after years of arguing and fighting. Donna is living with her mother, but at seventeen, Donna can't wait to be out on her own.

When Donna comes to today's youth group meeting, she looks different. She has gained some weight. Her face is made up even more heavily than usual, and her wild, stylish clothes create an aura that she is on top of the world. But her scared, anxious eyes betray this false confidence.

After the meeting, Donna uncharacteristically hangs around until all the other kids have left. "Do you have a few minutes?" she asks. A few minutes of silence pass and then she blurts out, "You have to help me, I'm pregnant!" She turns away and starts to cry.

You're stunned. What should you say? A crisis has been tossed right into your lap. What will you do?

Let's imagine walking through this crisis with Donna. As we go through the following steps, note that they often overlap. Use them as a general guideline, not as a rule book.

Ten Steps of Crisis Resolution

1. Be with the person. The first step is to establish contact with the person. Since you and Donna are already together, this is simple. Sit down with her, touch her arm, show her your concern in a calm voice that communicates your availability. If Donna had told you about the pregnancy over the phone, you would want to talk briefly with her but arrange to get together as soon as possible. A person going through crisis often needs someone to actually physically *be* with them.

At the same time, remember all that you learned about showing love and acceptance. Donna needs support, not judgment. She has gone out on a limb and trusted you with an immense burden. Be sure you are worthy of that trust.

2. Use active listening to define the problem and to hear the person's feelings. Try to identify quickly the major elements of this crisis. Gather your information by asking pertinent questions and listening attentively. In Donna's case her problems include: figuring out who she needs to tell about the pregnancy, what their response might be, what to do about the baby, and eventually how this pregnancy will affect her life. Listening to the way Donna is perceiving the crisis also will tell you how she plans to resolve it.

Donna's face, voice, and body posture will communicate how she is feeling about her pregnancy. Obviously, the fact that her tears broke through her tough exterior shows she is upset. Put yourself in her shoes and consider how scared, confused, embarrassed, and angry with yourself you would be. Use your active-listening skills to acknowledge Donna's emotions, but don't allow her feelings to interfere with resolving the crisis.

3. Assess immediate needs. Like a dam that finally bursts, Donna suddenly floods you with her fears. "What am I going to do? I want to keep the baby, and my boyfriend, Alan, says he'll marry me, but I'm scared what my parents will say. My friends tell me I'm crazy to have the kid. They all think I should have an abortion. I think I should drop out of school and get a job to save some money. What do you think God wants me to do?"

You need to help Donna sort through all these concerns by helping her to distinguish her immediate needs from those she can attend to later. Find out whether there are medical, financial, physical, or legal needs that must be taken care of *immediately*. In Donna's case, it's important *first* to verify that she is indeed pregnant by making sure she has had a pregnancy test.

Donna also is facing the immediate pressure of telling her parents. This is more pressing than deciding if she should marry Alan, leave school, or get a job. Although these are also important issues, they can be handled after the immediate concerns are dealt with.

4. Summarize the problems and their main components. Using your active-listening skills, summarize Donna's problems and their implications. "It seems to me that you are worried about several things: how your parents will react to your news, what to do about the baby, whether to marry Alan, if you should stay in school or get a job, and your relationship to God."

It's often helpful to have your friend make a list of her problems and then subdivide each one. Donna's list might look like this:

1. Talk with my parents. With or without Alan?
   a. Will Mom want me to leave home?
   b. If so, where will I go? Maybe I can live with Dad.

2. Talk with Alan's parents. Should he and I get married? Now or later?

3. What should I do about the baby?
   a. Should I keep the baby?
   b. Should I place the baby in foster care?
   c. Should I give up the baby for adoption? (Some unwed mothers might consider abortion as an alternative. If

so, then your counseling will need to include whether
or not this is a viable option. For more information on
this topic, consult the For Further Reading section at
the end of this chapter.)

4. What does God want me to do? I don't feel I can even
   pray.

5. Should I finish school?

6. Should I get a job? If so, where?

Making a list will serve two functions. It will keep Donna
from feeling overwhelmed. And it will help you remain *outside* of
her situation. This prevents you from "catching" her feelings of
panic and confusion.

5. Focus on one problem at a time. Beginning at the top of
Donna's list, the two of you can tackle each problem. The way in
which her parents respond to her pregnancy will directly affect
her other decisions. For instance, if Donna's parents totally
oppose her keeping the baby, her options would be quite
different than if they agreed to help her keep the child. Looking
at one problem at a time, noting its ramifications, consequences,
and possible solutions, will help Donna make careful decisions.

6. Evaluate what has been done so far. Find out what steps
Donna has already taken. Perhaps she has seen her doctor, the
pregnancy was confirmed, and she is in her second month. She
talked with the doctor about her options, and the physician
volunteered to help her with a private adoption. But Donna isn't
sure that she wants to take that route. If you feel unequipped to
answer all of her questions, go on to the next step.

**7. Explore community, family, church, and personal re-
sources.** You may want to help Donna get in touch with a local
crisis pregnancy center. (For help in referring people in crisis,
see chart #4: "Where to Refer" in chapter 13.) Then find out
who else could help her now. A relative or a family in the church
might be willing to assist. Establishing other resources also will
take the pressure off you.

Next, encourage Donna to think about how she has
successfully responded to previous problems. Perhaps she will
remember how confused and angry she felt when her parents
divorced. She felt like running away from home but instead she

met with her school counselor who taught her how to talk things out with her parents. Encouraging her to use these past coping skills will reinforce her own problem-solving abilities and prevent her from totally relying on you.

8. Make a plan of action. Donna is now ready to develop a plan that will move her toward resolving this crisis. Following her list, she decides to talk to her parents with Alan. She hopes they will support her decision to get married and keep the baby. She also plans to talk with her pastor about her questions about God and her future with Alan.

Now you need to help Donna consider some of the obstacles she might meet. For instance, is her plan realistic? Is she ready to get married? Is this really the best thing for her, Alan, and the baby? Questions like these may prevent Donna from prematurely jumping into marriage.

People in crisis often underestimate what they are experiencing and overestimate what they can handle. Is Donna saying things like, "We're old enough to take care of ourselves. Alan and I don't need anyone's help!"? What will happen if her parents don't let her marry Alan and order her to give the baby up for adoption? When initial plans fail, frustration, guilt, and anger often result. Therefore, it's also important to establish an alternative plan.

Be resourceful and creative as the two of you consider other alternatives. One possibility is to allow her parents some time to get used to her pregnancy. Donna also might consider visiting a Christian crisis pregnancy center to discuss other options. Brainstorming about all her choices and weighing the advantages and disadvantages of each one is an important part of crisis resolution.

9. Give realistic hope. Make sure you are encouraging and hopeful. You can say something simple like, "I know you're overwhelmed by this situation and have a hard time seeing how it will turn out. Although you're in the middle of making some very difficult decisions, God promises that there *is* a way out and that He won't leave you alone now."

10. Follow up. Even after the moment of crisis is over, stay in touch with Donna. People often hold themselves together during a crisis but fall apart later. Make sure Donna carries out her plan. Find out how her parents are doing. They may be wrestling with their own reactions of guilt or anger and need some help too. Donna also needs to straighten out her relationship with God. Finally, talk to Donna about how this pregnancy affects her future. Conversations about her sexuality, her relationships with men, and her thoughts about motherhood would be appropriate.

Finally, be aware that a major temptation of helping a friend in crisis is to encourage too much dependency. Although a crisis is a time of "rescuing" a "drowning" person, your rescuing efforts should be limited. You will avoid prolonged dependency (and the frustration of having a friend who seems to go from one crisis to another!) by remembering that our goal is to help our friends return to functioning on their own. Remember the motto: be a coach, not a lifeguard.

SUICIDE: A SPECIAL CRISIS

How to Detect a Potential Suicide

We can't study all the different types of crises we might encounter, but we need to consider one that is truly life threatening—suicide.

Most people have thought about hurting or killing themselves at one time or another. Reasons for contemplating suicide can vary: a loved one dies; a business fails; life seems to lack meaning and purpose. When a person's world appears to be caving in, suicide can appear to be an attractive way out.

In order to determine if someone is truly suicidal, we need to do the following six things:[3]

1. Listen to the person very carefully. A person who talks about suicide should never be ignored, even though a cry for help may be difficult to discern. Comments like, "I feel like throwing in the towel" or "I wish I could just check out of life" may indicate suicidal wishes. A question like, "Do you think people who kill themselves go to hell?" also can indicate similar thoughts. Studies show that most people talk about suicide before attempting it.

Is your friend saying good-bye to people? Do you hear complaints that there is nothing to look forward to in life? Does your friend *sound* or *look* hopeless, depressed, helpless, dissatisfied, or apathetic? Any of these may indicate a despair that often precedes a suicide attempt.

Sometimes people talk about suicide as a way to gain attention. Don't *assume* this is the case by minimizing a person's feelings or intentions. If your friend is talking about suicide, consider *all* the following information. If you decide that your friend isn't seriously considering hurting himself or herself, professional counseling may be recommended to determine why your friend is going to such extremes to get attention.

2. Note individual characteristics. A decade ago men over forty were targeted as the ones most likely to commit suicide. Since women have achieved equal opportunity in the work force with corresponding equal stress, their suicide rate has also increased.[4] Unfortunately, suicide has become an attractive option for members of both sexes in the younger age group also. Suicide now ranks second as the cause of death among adolescents and college students.[5]

In addition, a person who is impulsive, unstable, or abuses drugs or alcohol is also more likely to commit suicide. If the suicidal thoughts of the person you are talking to are confused, distorted, or bizarre (symptoms of psychosis), seek professional help immediately.

3. Find out if the person has a plan. One of the most important ways to determine how serious your friend is about suicide is to find out if a *specific* plan has been arranged. The danger to a person's life is dramatically increased if the person has the means to accomplish that plan and if the plan is a sure way of dying. The man who talks about cutting his wrists is not in as much danger as one who recently purchased a gun and is thinking of shooting himself in the head. A person who has previously tried to kill himself or herself is also a greater risk than one who has never attempted it before.

4. Check the person's life for stress. The death of a loved one, a divorce, a separation, or an end to any intimate relationship may precipitate a person's thoughts to "chuck it all." In situations like these, the person may be motivated by an irrational thirst for revenge or an escape from the stressful situation. In some instances, guilt over misperceived mistakes or accurately perceived sins also can prompt suicidal thoughts.

Losing prestige, status, a job, money, possessions, health (either through a serious operation or life-threatening illness), freedom (through incarceration or a physical handicap) all can precipitate thoughts of suicide. In an effort to maintain personal control, some people prefer taking their own life rather than experiencing the helplessness of events beyond their control.

On the other hand, a person who gains new responsibilities

also may experience stress, thus also becoming a potential suicide candidate. For example, a person who receives a promotion may feel anxious about not fulfilling his or her new job requirements and may look for a way out.

5. Look for sudden changes. As you talk to your friend, take note of anything that seems unusual to you. If he or she has been depressed and then suddenly improves, the change in behavior may signal that the person feels relieved because death is approaching soon. Find out if your friend's life is in order. If he or she is giving away possessions, buying or updating insurance, or paying long-standing bills, then he or she may be serious about ending it all. Similarly, a once-talkative friend who begins to withdraw may be beginning to detach himself from his or her relationships. A teenager who begins to lose interest in what he or she once enjoyed and begins to take more physical risks may be showing suicidal tendencies.[6] Loss of appetite, changes in sleep patterns, and complaints of physical or emotional exhaustion are symptoms of depression that often precedes suicide.

6. Find out about the person's support system. People who live alone, who cut themselves off from others, or whose family is distant and uninvolved are higher suicide risks than those with close relationships. Rationalizing that their behavior affects no one or that their family and friends would be better off without them, these people deny the effects of their actions.

Similarly, a person without faith in Jesus Christ is spiritually alone and cut off from God. Therefore, he or she is more likely to consider suicide than a Christian who is in fellowship with God and other believers. This doesn't prevent some "religious" people from committing suicide, however.

What You Can Do to Help

1. Be a person who can talk about suicide. If you suspect that your friend is considering suicide, don't be afraid to bring up the subject. People often hesitate to talk about suicide, fearing they'll give their friend the idea. On the contrary, a person considering suicide will feel relieved that someone is willing to talk about it. But don't think that if your friend talks about suicide, it won't be attempted. That isn't true. *All* talk about suicide should be taken seriously and necessary steps toward prevention should be taken.

2. Be aware of the dynamics of suicide. People who want to kill themselves often are dissatisfied with some part of their life. For instance, a teenage boy who feels different from all his peers because he's never had a girlfriend may think the answer is to kill himself. You need to help him find ways of developing more social skills so that he will not feel the need to kill himself.

Other people use suicide attempts as a means of communication. Unhappy with how they are being treated, suicide can be a disguised message to an important person in their life. People like this need to learn to *say* what they are feeling, rather than to act out their emotions in a self-destructive way.

3. Be a bridge to referral. Probably one of the most important things you can do for someone contemplating suicide is to help him or her find professional help. If the danger is imminent (if your teenage friend is on the phone, and he has a gun to his head), your response will be immediate. You will first convince him to put the gun down, get someone to be with him immediately, and then consider possible hospitalization so that he will be temporarily protected from himself. If, however, he casually mentions that he has been out looking at guns lately, you may want to ask him why he's looking at guns and then, if it appears appropriate, to recommend that he see a professional counselor.

Finally, we must remember that since we are image bearers of God, suicide is a serious spiritual problem. It not only reflects a person's dissatisfaction with himself or herself but it also violates the sixth commandment.

INITIATING HELP

Just as crisis intervention requires special sensitivities, so we will use special skills in helping friends who don't know they need help. Many times we will see problems in our friends' lives before they come to us for help. How do we initiate the helping process? We're not professional counselors with clients who make appointments with us; we are friends who want to help others. How do we begin to approach our friends? To answer that, let's first look at how Jesus accomplished this.

How Did Jesus Initiate Help?

From the moment Adam fell, God took the initiative. It wasn't as if a group of people got together and went to God and said, "We need help. Please send us a Savior." Rather, God knew our hunger, spiritual poverty, and needs. He sent Jesus into the world to answer these needs. In spite of our lack of initiative, we have received divine help.

Jesus continued this pattern of taking the initiative by going to the people who needed Him. Although at times people went to Him with their requests, many times He approached people and began conversations. He called the twelve apostles to follow Him; He offered spiritual truth to the Samaritan woman; He healed the blind man; He dined with tax gatherers; and He went to be with sinners. Jesus was not afraid to go to sick and needy people and to offer comfort, help, and healing.

HOW DO WE INITIATE HELPING A FRIEND?

Be Prepared

Marge is a middle-aged woman in your Bible study who has a tendency to monopolize every discussion. She always manages to spin off from the main topic to one of her many personal problems. Since these remarks distract the other members of the Bible study, you, as the group leader, decide to talk to her.

Before you say anything, remember that established relationships are the best avenues to providing help. If Marge is new to your Bible study, it may take some time to establish enough of a relationship that you feel comfortable talking to her about her behavior. On the other hand, if you have known Marge for several years, it will be easier to begin a conversation with her.

Next, you need a loving attitude that communicates, "You matter to me. I'm not saying these things to criticize you or put you down. I want to help you." Be a helper who can confront and listen without being condescending and without getting overwhelmed by the other person.

Get Involved

Now what do you do next? How do you break down the barrier that seems to separate you from Marge? First, remember to use all of your empathetic listening and speaking tools. Put yourself in her shoes for a minute. Why does she have such a need to talk about herself all the time? What do you know about her personal life that may indicate some unhappiness or dissatisfaction from which she is unintentionally seeking relief? At the same time, be careful not to overanalyze her. Check out your perceptions through active listening and open-ended questions.

Begin your conversation by using open-ended "I statements." In private you could say to her, "Marge, I want to talk about something that may seem very personal to you. I'm not sure that you're aware of how much you talk about your personal matters in the Bible study. Sometimes you bring things up that are really unrelated to what we are talking about. As the group leader, I have a hard time when you go off on tangents because I an afraid we won't cover our material for that day and that other members won't get a chance to talk. I'm also not sure that it's the best time for you to share your personal problems."

Now give Marge a chance to respond to you. She may or may not be aware of her tendency to monopolize conversations. She may be defensive and totally resist what you are saying, or she may be open to further suggestions on other ways to get help with her personal problems. Either way, it's very important that your goal is to help Marge, not to run her life.

Be Careful

When you reach out and get involved with the people around you, you are responding to Christ's command to love and serve others. As you do this, keep in mind the following guidelines:

1. Don't solicit business for yourself. Remember that you're a lay helper and a concerned friend. Be prepared to help people you know, but don't offer help to someone you don't know just because someone has asked you to help that person. (The exception would be if you are a recognized lay counselor, whose responsibility is to help those in trouble.) Know your limits. Don't try to help in situations where you lack adequate information or training.

2. Don't meddle. There is a difference between helpers and busybodies. Talking to Marge because you heard a rumor that she and her husband were splitting up and you want to hear the *real* story is motivated out of curiosity rather than concern. The people to whom we offer help may feel vulnerable. Respect them by giving help that will benefit them, not that will satisfy your own need to be involved.

3. Don't help for the wrong reasons. Similarly, don't offer help to satisfy your own feelings. Don't talk with Marge just because you pity her or would feel guilty if you didn't; she'll sense your attitude and resent your "help."

4. Don't barge in. Reach out carefully, respectfully, and with sensitivity. Make statements of availability that allow your friend the option of taking or refusing your help. Take your cues from the other person. If Marge avoids eye contact and keeps changing the subject, she's probably not ready or willing to talk right now. Pounding on a locked door won't open it, but patience and love may eventually unlock it.

5. Don't take it personally if someone refuses your help. Respect the other person's right to say no. You can follow all the rules of helping, be the most kind and compassionate person that you know how to be, and still have your help refused. Don't reject your friend by subtly communicating, "Well, if you don't want my advice, then I guess that's just *your* problem." Instead, you could give feedback: "I feel frustrated right now because I would like to help you, and yet it seems as if you really don't want that now." Leave the door open for another helping opportunity by concluding, "If there ever is a time when I can be of help, please let me know."

A WORD ABOUT THE TELEPHONE

The phone has become an important vehicle for giving help. A person's first request for help may come to you through a phone conversation. Or you may first sense something is wrong in a telephone conversation, and you may begin to give help right then.

Helping by phone is different from helping face-to-face because we can't observe our friends. This is a potential handicap for both us and our friends. They won't be able to tell if we're really listening to them unless we give empathic, sensitive responses. We'll lack visual cues to help us determine what they are experiencing. We must therefore listen well to gather this information. Be sensitive to tone of voice, silence, and word choice. What does your friend's shaky voice or hesitant comments or short, clipped speech communicate?

Be aware that some people may prefer the subtle anonymity that accompanies talking on the phone. Talking on the phone is less risky and requires less personal commitment to change.

As a result, the phone can also be abused by friends who call every time something goes wrong. Don't allow telephone counseling to go on indefinitely. If you do, you'll be supporting your friend's dependency on you, and you'll feel angry and imposed upon.

PERSONAL AND PRACTICAL

Study the Scriptures

1. Review John 11:1–45. Under what circumstances would you delay before intervening in a crisis? What six things did Jesus do in this crisis?
2. Read Acts 16:16–40. What different crises did Paul and Silas encounter? How did God use them? What were the outcomes? How could you use this Scripture passage when helping a friend?
3. Read James 1:2–8. What is the writer's message about trials and temptations? In what crisis situation could you refer to this passage? What temptation must you avoid in using this?
4. Read Luke 19:1–9. How did Jesus respond to Zacchaeus' interest in Him? In what way did Jesus initiate help with the tax collector? In what circumstances might you invite yourself to someone else's home? What should you be careful of in doing this?

For Thought

Directions: Read over the following situations and write a brief description of how you would help these people. Include answers to the following:

- What are the main aspects of this crisis?
- What is the person feeling? Why?
- What are the first things you would do to help?
- What further steps would you take?
- How would you use active listening, "I statements," and feedback?
- What plan of action is necessary?
- How would you communicate hope?
- How and when would you follow up on this person?

LISA

Lisa calls you on the phone, and you sense she's been crying. She tells you that her father just called long distance to say that her mother, who hadn't been feeling well lately, was hospitalized today. The doctors suspect she may have cancer of the liver. As a nurse, Lisa knows that this disease is often fatal. She starts asking you questions: "Do you think I should fly home? If I do, who will watch the kids? How can God take her now? We were just starting to get along!"

MARK

You see your friend Mark in church, and he looks really down. When you ask him what's going on, he tells you that he lost his job on Friday. He's worked in the same office since college and is really worried about going out into the job market again. He's not sure if he'll be able to get unemployment, and financially things look really tight. He wonders about how he'll pay the mortgage, car payments, and other bills. Life looks pretty bleak for Mark, and he thinks God isn't providing very well for his needs.

PAULA

You've noticed some changes in Paula. She alternates between being withdrawn and apathetic or cynical and bitter. You hear through the office grapevine that her boyfriend broke off their engagement and that she didn't get the promotion she was expecting. When you try talking to her, she almost laughs in your face, "Don't even bother trying to be nice to me. What's the use of going on when nothing ever works out for me? How can you believe in a loving God when life is so screwed up?"

For Further Reading

1. Read Selwyn Hughes' *Helping People Through Their Problems* (Minneapolis: Bethany House, 1981) for more suggestions about how to help a person face a crisis.
2. Read Lisa Halls Johnson's *Just Like Ice Cream* (New York: Bantam, 1982) for an easy-to-read novel about a young girl who becomes pregnant and receives spiritual

help from a Christian friend. This book is helpful for teenagers struggling with their sexuality.

3. Read Linda Roggow and Carolyn Owens's *Handbook for Pregnant Teenagers* (Grand Rapids: Zondervan Publishing House, 1984) for a realistic approach to dealing with teenage pregnancies. This book addresses the spiritual dimension of helping pregnant teenagers.

4. Read Robert B. Somerville's *Help for Hotliners: A Manual for Christian Telephone Crisis Counselors* (Phillipsburg, New Jersey: Presbyterian and Reformed Publishing Co., 1978) for a practical guide to telephone and crisis counseling. This book incorporates Scripture and gives the reader many practice cases.

5. Read Dr. and Mrs. J. C. Willke's *Handbook on Abortion* (Cincinnati: Hayes, 1971), a question-and-answer handbook that discusses everything from what is human life to some of the ethical issues related to abortion.

NOTES

[1] Glenn Whitlock, *Understanding and Coping with Real Life Crises* (Monterey, California: Brooks-Cole Publishing Co., 1978), p. 3.

[2] Donna C. Aguilera and Janice M. Messick, *Crisis Intervention: Theory and Methodology* 5th Edition Revised (St. Louis: The C.V. Mosby Co., 1986), p. 1.

[3] The following is adapted from Gary Collins' *How To Be a People Helper* (Santa Ana, California: Vision House, 1976), p. 106; and Aguilera and Messick's *Crisis Intervention,* pp. 166–71.

[4] Aguilera and Messick, *Crisis Intervention,* p. 168.

[5] Ibid., p. 166.

[6] Darrell Sifford, "Teen Suicide: Why It's Rising," The Philadelphia *Sunday Inquirer,* May 6, 1984.

‡

CHAPTER 12

HELPING NON-CHRISTIANS AND PEOPLE FROM OTHER CULTURES

We loved you so much that we were delighted to share with you not only the gospel of God but our lives as well.
—1 Thessalonians 2:8

When I teach lay counseling, I'm often asked two questions: How do I help a non-Christian and how do I help someone from another culture? To my students' dismay, I don't give out any magic formulas.

Helping non-Christians or people from another culture is in many ways similar to helping our Christian friends. Our non-Christian friends often have the same needs and problems as believers do, and we use the same tools and skills to help both. However, helping non-Christians and people from another culture poses several new opportunities as well as new problems. It's these new elements that we will explore in this chapter.

JESUS AND THE UNSAVED

How did Jesus relate to the "unsaved" Jews, Greeks, and Samaritans? How did He help them and simultaneously share the Good News of salvation?

What Did Jesus Do for Nonbelievers?

Jesus got involved with sinners; He didn't just love from a distance. Jesus touched those who were outcasts of society: the prostitutes, the demon possessed, the lepers, the tax collectors. Jesus' involvement included crossing cultural barriers. Going against the social customs of the times, He talked with a woman from Samaria (John 4:1–26) and a woman from Syrian Phoenicia (Mark 7:24–30). Not only was Jesus' behavior unusual because these two people were women, but they were also Gentiles. What an unheard of breach of etiquette!

But Jesus' identification with sinners didn't mean that He agreed with their life-style. Jesus accepted the adulterous woman without accepting her sin. He confronted the sin without condemning the sinner (John 8:1–11). He loved her without giving license to her sin. "The paradox of agape love is that we accept our neighbors unconditionally and with open arms and at the same time desire moral purity for their lives. If Jesus is our Lord, our compassion will be shaped by his moral absolutes. Christ both was merciful and made judgments. . . . Indeed, it was his love that prompted his judgment."[1]

An intrinsic part of Jesus' embodiment of holiness was that He consistently spoke the truth. As the perfect teacher, He tailored His message so that His listeners would understand Him. When Jesus spoke to the Samaritan woman at the well about her problems and needs, He used imagery about water and wells; He used elements common to her life to point to her need for salvation (John 4).

Remember, Jesus spoke the truth even when it was risky and difficult. He taught in inhospitable synagogues; He preached to hostile crowds; He confronted the Pharisees; and He boldly answered government officials. Although we may find it difficult to speak the truth, Jesus promises that His presence and power will be with us (Luke 21:12–19).

Jesus' message of truth included the need to obey God. He challenged His listeners to put their faith into action. Fishermen had to drop their nets to follow Him. The rich young ruler had to give of his wealth to the poor. The Pharisees had to learn how to do more than just tithe their spices.[2] Jesus' call to repentance is a call to obedience.

HELPING A NON-CHRISTIAN

Even though we'll find helping non-Christians is similar to helping Christians, we also should be aware of significant differences. First, non-Christians usually are unaware of their spiritual needs. As a result, their views of the world, their values, and their ideas probably will revolve around themselves rather than God. Their approaches to life, the choices they make, and the conclusions they reach will be different from those of committed Christians. And whereas your goal when talking to Christians is to help them become *more like Christ,* your goal in talking to non-Christians is to help them see their spiritual condition and *need for Christ.*

Jesus instructed us to give a thirsty person a cup of cold water. In the same way, we must begin helping our non-Christian friends by first responding to the needs they are expressing. By doing so, we establish our care and trustworthiness. This then becomes the springboard for sharing spiritual truths. Let's look at an example.

Tricia: The Woman Whose Debt Was Greater Than She Thought

You're raking leaves in your front yard when your neighbor Tricia, a nominal church attender, pulls into her driveway with a screech, slams the car door shut, and goes stamping up the porch into her house.

"Hey Tricia!" you call to her, "What's up? You look like you're ready to kill somebody!"

She looks up at you, startled. In her anger, she hadn't noticed you. She walks over to your yard and starts talking. "Oh, I'm really burned up. I was just at the camera store getting a new wide-angle lens for David's birthday. When I went to put it on my Visa card, the clerk said I had gone over my line of credit! He took my card, called the store manager, and made a really big scene. I've never been so humiliated in all my life!"

"I'd be pretty embarrassed and upset too," you answer sympathetically.

"Yeah, I had no idea I had charged so much. The clerk told me we owe $3,000! I knew it was bad—but not that bad! What they don't know is that all my other charges are pretty high too. Wait until David hears about this—he's really going to blow up."

"You're worried what David is going to say when he hears the news."

"That's putting it mildly! I wished I'd never let them raise our line of credit. Suddenly I feel as if we're over our heads in debt! I can't get over it. I started working part time so that David and I could enjoy things a little more—and look what happens. I mean, what is life about if you can't enjoy some of the better things the world has to offer? There's got to be more to life than just paying the mortgage and gas bill every month! I begin to wonder if it's all worthwhile. We seem to be going deeper and deeper into debt instead of getting ahead. You never seem to get yourself into a mess like this! How do you avoid it?" Tricia turns to you for an answer.

Suddenly, a simple neighborly chat has changed. Tricia has reached out for your help. What are you going to say? Can you help her in a way that will encourage her to look at her spiritual needs? Here's an opportunity to use your helping tools, not as mechanical techniques, but as part of a normal, everyday conversation. When you answer Tricia, you'll want to remember the following:

1. Look upward. Before responding to Tricia, silently ask for God's guidance and wisdom.

2. Look inward. Take a quick look at your own reaction to Tricia. Do you feel shocked, angry, superior, or disapproving? Before you say anything, make sure that your attitude is humble and that you are ready and willing to help.

3. Love and welcome. Now you are ready to focus on Tricia. It may help to remember what your values and life were like before you became a Christian. You may even face similar temptations now! Think how much harder it is then for an unbeliever to understand what is really important in life. Like the woman at the well in John 4, Tricia doesn't even know what she needs.

4. Gather your data. Find out if overspending is a problem that she and David have faced before. What helped them get out of debt then? What prompted her to get a job? What were she and David hoping to do with a second income? What do material things mean to her? All of these questions will help you to better understand Tricia's situation.

5. Listen to content, feelings, and implications. If you listen well, you can hear that Tricia has two different levels of problems. On one level she is talking about her high Visa bill, her debt, and David's reaction. But underneath these worries there is a deeper level of frustration. She isn't meeting her goals in life; she was hoping that money would bring her security, comfort, and pleasure; and she is envious of others who seem more content than she is. Responding to these deeper concerns will form a bridge to a discussion of spiritual matters.

Usually our non-Christian friends and relatives don't come right out and ask us about the gospel. Instead, they'll make statements about their lives or ask questions that indicate they are searching for love, truth, or meaning to this life. Listen hard for these questions, for they will offer opportunities to show how the gospel meets these universal needs. Chart #1 provides a list of these types of questions and statements. Consider also any that you have heard (or made) yourself.

CHART #1: LEAD-INS TO THE GOSPEL

1. "Why should I bother changing anyway?"

2. "What does my life mean in the whole scope of things?"

3. "I don't think I'll ever find someone who can love me."

4. "No one seems to care about me except you."

5. "What in the world am I doing with my life?"

6. "Why do I care so much about what others think of me?"

7. "I've made a mess of my life. I've failed totally. Nothing I do can make a difference now."

8. "I just can't seem to accept myself the way I am."

9. "Why do I feel guilty all the time?"

10. "I wish I'd goof up less. I keep trying to stop doing the wrong thing, but I just can't seem to do it myself."

11. "You seem so much happier than I am. Why is that?"

6. Disclose yourself. In Tricia's case, she asked you a personal question. You now have an open door to discuss how you have been able to handle your financial temptations. This is an appropriate time for self-disclosure. Let's pick the conversation up at this point.

Helper: "To be honest Tricia, I struggle with overspending

too. The thing that helps me is figuring out why I want to buy some new clothes or things for the house. Often I realize that when I'm feeling down, shopping becomes my 'temporary fix' to make me feel better. In the long run it doesn't really fix anything at all.''

Tricia: "Yes, I know what you mean. The old saying 'money can't buy happiness' is really true.''

Helper: "It looks as if you're caught in the same thing that I was—buying things to feel happy or secure. This may sound surprising, Tricia, but I've begun to see that the only lasting form of happiness and security comes in a relationship to God.''

Tricia: "What do you mean, like going to church and things like that? I go every once in awhile, but it doesn't do much for me.''

Helper: "I wonder if you've ever thought about why you go to church or about who God is. I know I didn't for the longest time.''

Tricia: "Well, to be honest, I have a hard time believing all that stuff the minister says about God. With the world being such a mess, it's hard to believe that there really is a God who is in control of everything. Don't you think that's pretty old-fashioned?''

Don't get defensive because of Tricia's questions! A positive response to the gospel often begins with curiosity. We must listen patiently and encourage our friends' inquiries. Then we'll be ready to respond with the truth and not with arguments.

7. Make "I statements." Remember that the *way* in which you speak the truth will often determine whether or not you are heard. This is especially important when talking to non-Christians because you don't want them to feel attacked or badgered. As Peter writes, we must "always be prepared to give an answer to everyone who asks us to give the reason for the hope that [we] have. But [we must] do this with gentleness and respect" (1 Peter 3:15).

You could respond to Tricia in a variety of ways:

Helper: "When you express doubt over God's existence, I know what you mean. I felt the same way before I began to read the Bible. I'd love to share with you what I've learned about Him.''

Helper: "I'm concerned when you say you don't know what life is about if it's not having a lot of nice things because I've found that life is more than that.''

Helper: "I understand when you say that God seems out-of-date today. But I'm concerned when you say that because I know you're missing something very important."

Note that all these statements first receive Tricia's questions undefensively and then return with a personal statement. Like invitations, they open the door for Tricia's response.

8. Use your friend's language. When Tricia asks for help, don't slip into "Christianese" and say, "Well, when the Lord saved me, bringing me out of slavery to sin and into a life of glory, I began to see the light. I decided that I had to turn from all my evil ways and take up my cross and follow Him." Don't devalue the gospel by speaking in archaic language ("Verily, verily, I say unto thee. . . .") or by using doctrinal words ("Jesus justifies you, imputes you with His righteousness, and then sanctifies you by the power of His Holy Spirit."). Instead, use your own words to talk about how God has worked in your life.[3]

9. Confront carefully and cautiously. In order not to make your non-Christian friends feel attacked and defensive, respect their abilities to reason and to make decisions. Ask indirect questions that involve them and help them to examine themselves. These will encourage your friends to think through their assumptions and presuppositions. Communicate respect through your tone of voice. A warm, caring voice will show you are genuinely interested.

10. Use the Word. Don't forget to refer to specific Scripture passages as it is appropriate. This shows your friends how the Bible is authoritative and relevant to every struggle and problem they experience. (For someone who is totally unfamiliar with the Bible, you may want to read from a modern-language version, like the Good News Bible or the New International Version.)

If Tricia has seemed interested in what you've been saying so far, suggest that the two of you could look at the Bible together. You could look at Matthew 6, where Jesus clearly says that life is more than money, fancy clothes, or fine food (Matt. 6:19–34; see also Luke 12:16–21). Or you might want to look at how our Lord responded to a first-century "yuppie" in Mark 10:17–23.

As you read these passages with Tricia and as the Spirit is working in her life, she will see that Jesus is not old-fashioned at all! In fact, His words speak to her very personally. In Matthew 6, God promises that if Tricia searches for His kingdom and His righteousness, He'll provide for all her needs. Reading verses 25–33 could lead to a conversation about God's kingdom, His righteousness, and then to a broader discussion about who God is and our sin and separation from Him.

Be careful not to use the Bible in a superficial way. We don't want to "paste a verse" over our friends' problems. Similarly, we don't want to use the Bible as a hammer, beating our friends over the head with it. We must encourage them to think about what we have said and to consider it for themselves.

Once again, we must be patient. Although the main part of the conversation with Tricia took place on one occasion, this is the exception rather than the rule. Most discussions about spiritual concerns will happen over a period of time. Some people will hungrily devour the gospel in one sitting, but most want to take time to digest what they've heard. Make sure that you follow up on your conversations at a later time. As you have sparked your friends' interest and encouraged their questions, they'll want to learn more.

11. Encourage action. If Tricia comes to understand her sin and indicates a desire to trust in the Lord and obey His Word, don't be afraid to encourage her to repent of her sin and believe in the Lord Jesus Christ. Sometimes Christians are so afraid of being pushy that they leave their friend hanging, without helping him or her take this most important step.

After Tricia has made a commitment to follow Christ, your job will be to help her grow as a new Christian and to show her how to apply her faith to her life. At the same time remember that Tricia's new faith may be a "crisis" for the people around her. Depending on the religious beliefs of her family and friends, she may meet with hostility, confusion, cynicism, or indifference. Tricia will need your support as she takes her first wobbly steps as a new believer.

But what if Tricia doesn't become a Christian? What if she shuts you out and you never even get to talk about the gospel? What then? Your responsibility to love and welcome remains the same; you never know what seeds you will plant as you do. This also will keep the door open to further conversations.

HELPING SOMEONE FROM ANOTHER CULTURE

The landscape of America has changed. Many of us no longer live in exclusively white, middle-class, Protestant neighborhoods, or black neighborhoods, or Roman Catholic neighborhoods. Depending on what part of the country you live in, the family who lives next door may be Mexican or Laotian; your co-worker may be Jewish, Muslim, or atheist. Similarly, the person sitting next to you in church might be from Puerto Rico, Belgium, or India. You don't have to be a missionary to a foreign country to meet someone from another culture.

How do you reach out to someone from a different culture, race, or religion? Even more fundamentally, *who* is someone from a different culture? Although our discussion will focus on people from other countries, the principles also apply to the American subcultures that aren't distinguishable by skin color, language, or holidays. These subcultures include people like the elderly, the handicapped, and prison inmates.

What is culture? One missionary wrote that culture is the sum total of all our lived experiences, providing us a system of values to direct our activities.[4] To some extent, our culture will dictate what we believe, how we act, how we solve our problems, and how we live our lives.[5]

What follows is an overview, not a thorough description, of how to apply our helping skills to someone from another culture. Keep in mind that we need to be flexible and treat these principles as broad guidelines rather than absolute rules.

Principles of Cross-cultural Helping

Know yourself. None of us approaches the job of helping others without prejudice. Even this book is biased! It's written from the perspective of a woman who is the daughter of German Jewish immigrants, who became a Christian in the early seventies, who married at twenty and was widowed at twenty-seven, who worked as a Christian counselor in suburban Philadelphia, Pennsylvania, and then who remarried and moved to Matthews, North Carolina. Your helping will include biases from your background also. In order to be ready to talk to someone from another culture, we need to understand how our personal background influence the help we give.

Think for a minute. What are your stereotypes about Puerto Ricans or Cambodians? How did your parents talk about blacks (or whites)? What are the stories that you hear (or tell) about Jews, Poles, or Italians? What past events prevent you from relating to a person from another culture as a unique person rather than as a member of a group that, for example, burglarized your relative's home or took your neighbor's job? We need a posture of humility and learning rather than of power, superiority, or bitterness when we help someone from another culture.

Know the other person. Each of us is simultaneously like all the rest of humanity, like some of humanity, and yet like no other person at all. Let's take a brief look at each of these categories.

1. Like all humanity. How are you and I similar to one another, and to a Berber nomad, a British model, or a Bangkok businessman? Obviously, the biggest common denominator is that we are all members of the human race and have all been created by the same God. As a result, we all share physiological, psychological, sociocultural, and spiritual characteristics.[6]

2. Like some of humanity. But an American still will be quite different from the nomad in Morocco, the model in Great Britain, or the businessman in Thailand. On the other hand, as different as they may be, a New Englander and a Texan will resemble one another more than each would resemble a Berber nomad. Even though they represent two subcultures within the United States, they share the same American culture.

3. Like no other person. We all have the same basic human nature, some of us even share the same cultural background and yet, like the unique pattern of a snowflake, we are each one of a kind. Every person in this world has a set of distinguishing characteristics that is as particular as a set of fingerprints: a person's physique, family background, geographical environment, social status, personality, mental ability, and emotional makeup all contribute to making a person a unique human being.[7]

Use Your Helping Skills

Build trust and develop a relationship. Four ways of showing acceptance are particularly applicable to cross-cultural helping.

First, we must join the person with whom we're talking. We communicate love when we accept the other people as they are right now, even though they are culturally different from us. As one author writes: "To begin the communication or counseling process with people where *they* are instead of where *we* are is psychologically and biblically defensible."[8]

Second, we can anticipate people's needs and do practical things for them. My former pastor's wife reached out to an unmarried, pregnant woman from Romania by taking her to childbirth classes and serving as her labor coach. I had one friend who shared Thanksgiving with a family from Scotland, while another opened her home to an African college student.

Third, we can be understanding and refrain from judging the other person. We must be especially careful to separate the universal requirements of Scripture from those that are culturally specific.[9] A Christian can worship in a different type of building or use music different from yours—without being *wrong*.

Fourth, we show acceptance by being empathic. Although it may be difficult, we must try to understand why people from another culture think, talk, or behave the way they do. For instance, did you know that a man from an Asian culture may have difficulty simply receiving your help because of the shame that it would bring to his entire family? Or did you know that many Africans have difficulty talking about their personal lives to strangers? Multitudes of misunderstandings can develop if we try to help without adequate understanding about the other person's culture.

Listen carefully and be sensitive to differences. "Listening" to someone from another culture can involve reading up-to-date books about our friends' cultures and keeping informed of their country's role in world activities. Both of these will show interest in who our friends are and where they have come from. (Be sure to confirm what you learn with your friend. Sometimes the media distorts or slants information.)

The reward of good listening can be great. A missionary to a Muslim country befriended a neighbor by simply listening to the woman's personal and family problems. Even though the missionary had been her neighbor for less than a year and barely knew Arabic, one day she was rewarded with the highest compliment: "You are my closest friend," her neighbor said. Through listening, this missionary had formed a bridge to this woman's heart.

What are some of the specific differences we need to listen for when we're helping someone from another culture? Here are five that commonly surface in cross-cultural helping.

1. Differences in basic communication. The way you speak, how much you disclose about yourself, your tone of voice, and the pace you set while speaking probably will be different from the communication style of someone from another culture. For example, silence is considered dignified in many Asian cultures; Americans panic if a conversation pauses for only a few seconds. Furthermore, the Japanese tend not to speak directly about a subject and have difficulty coming right out and disagreeing. Their "maybe" or their "yes" can sometimes mean "no." We must be sensitive to cultural practices without forcing our style of communication on others.

2. *Differences in language and vocabulary.* Words can have different meanings in different cultures. This is true even among English-speaking countries! An American missionary visiting England tells of traveling with a British friend. When her friend pointed to the side of the road and said, "I had a flat there," the missionary replied, "That's too bad." She didn't realize that her friend was showing her where she had had an apartment, not where her car had broken down!

3. *Differences in nonverbal communication.* Our body posture, facial expressions, eye contact, and touch all communicate a great deal. Since much nonverbal expression is culturally specific, it's easy for misunderstanding to occur between people from two different cultures. What is acceptable to one can be highly offensive to another.

For example, whereas in America it's polite to look directly at someone with whom you are talking, in some areas of Africa direct eye contact can communicate anger or sexual advance. Similarly, the Japanese are taught from childhood to look down rather than straight at a person.

Communicating through physical contact also varies cross-culturally. Hungarians, for example, greet each other with a big bear hug. Although some Americans might not find that too offensive, consider how put off a reserved Britisher might feel when greeted with such affection!

Latin Americans also are comfortable with physical contact and consider it a normal part of how they communicate. To them, a touch on the forearms, hands, or the back is a way of saying "I hear you. I agree with you." Again, this can be quite disconcerting for someone who isn't comfortable with touch.

Body space also may vary from culture to culture. A friend came back from a trip to North Africa having jokingly nicknamed the natives "space invaders." Although they were perfectly comfortable making sure she was listening by talking within inches of her face, she found it difficult to listen in such tight quarters!

4. *Differences in customs, values, and beliefs.* Several years ago at a retreat, I noticed that a young Korean woman was

upset during our discussion of the role of the Christian wife. When I asked if I could help her, the newlywed told me about some misunderstandings she was having with her American husband. After listening to her, I suggested that she speak to her husband and make her feelings known. What I failed to take into consideration was that my advice went counter to her culture— that was not the Korean way for a wife to relate to her husband! My well-intentioned help, therefore, was ineffective.

5. *Differences in concepts of time and priorities.* As Americans we live in a time-oriented society. We structure our days for maximum efficiency: we think punctuality is a virtue, and we manage every minute of our time. What a surprise it is for Americans to find out that some Africans, for example, are event oriented, and time has little importance. A party, for example, begins when the guests arrive, not at 7:30. Australians also have a different approach toward time. If they promise that your watch will be repaired "tomorrow," they might not understand your frustration if the job is not done the next day. For them "tomorrow" is not an exact description of a specific time but rather a reference to some time in the future.

We must be sensitive to all these cultural differences, for if we aren't, we can easily jump to the wrong conclusions. We could end up feeling hurt if a Korean doesn't take our advice, frightened when a man from Columbia takes our hand, or angry if a Ugandan is late for lunch. Furthermore, if we aren't culturally sensitive, we risk being offensive and losing our credibility as caring, compassionate Christians.

Speak with understanding. After we have effectively shown that we understand the other person, we still must be careful. We must continue to ask questions and not assume that we know everything. As we said before, we can be prejudiced by our stereotypes, past experiences, or the media. Even the generalizations found in this section should be used as guidelines, not as absolutes. Make sure that the other person understands what you are saying. Since misunderstandings due to language and cultural differences can easily occur, ask your friend to rephrase your message. Remember, good communication requires that the message *sent* is the message *meant*.

Although we differ from people of other cultures, we also must remember that we are all *people*. Tears have no accents and smiles no skin colors. Particularly, as fellow members of the body of Christ, we are joined together by a faith that has no cultural limitations.

I realized this one night during a vacation in Switzerland several years ago. I was feeling homesick and a bit sad. Suddenly I thought I heard some singing outside. I leaned out my window and caught the faint sound of young German and French voices from a Boy Scout camp down the road. Listening more intently I recognized only one word—"Hallelujah"—as it echoed off the mountains and across the valley. Tears came to my eyes as I realized that the same God whom I worshiped in Willow Grove, Pennsylvania, was being praised in Kandersteg, Switzerland. Suddenly, I was home.

PERSONAL AND PRACTICAL

Study the Scriptures

1. Read Mark 7:31–35 and 8:22–25. How are these two situations similar? What role did the friends play in each person's healing? How does this apply to you as a helper?
2. Consider Paul's conversion in Acts 9:1–19 (see also 1 Timothy 1:12–13). What does Paul's example teach us about the attitudes we should have towards non-Christians?
3. Read James 1:22, 27; 2:14–17. What do these verses say about sharing our faith? Why is James 1:27 considered to be the "acid test of religion"?
4. Read 1 Corinthians 9:22. Find examples in Paul's letters of how he became "all things" to all people. How could you copy his example when talking to someone who is Muslim? Black? Puerto Rican? Jewish? What are some of the things of which you need to be careful?
5. Read Exodus 23:9. Who are some modern-day strangers (aliens) in our midst? (Examples: Vietnamese refugees, a widow in a church full of couples.) How do you think these strangers feel? How can you demonstrate acceptance, empathy, and welcoming love to a stranger in your church or neighborhood?

For Thought

Directions: Choose one of the situations and answer the following questions:

- What events are going on in this person's life?
- What is this person feeling? (If it's a family situation, how are other family members feeling? How would their feelings affect the person you're helping?)
- How are you different from the person you are helping? How would this affect how you help him or her?
- What steps would you take to help him or her? Specifically, what would you say or do to help in this situation?

1. Your (non-Christian) co-worker (make the race different from your own) tells you that his (her) father has just been diagnosed with lung cancer and has been given three months to live.
2. Your Jewish friend knows you are a Christian because you talk about your church and the Bible study you go to. Your friend is sarcastic whenever the conversation turns to religion and thinks you are a fool to believe that the Incarnation really occurred.

For Further Reading on Evangelism

1. Read Harvey Conn's *Evangelism: Doing Justice and Preaching Grace* (Grand Rapids: Zondervan Publishing House, 1982) for a challenging call to practical, compassionate Christianity, or what he calls "holistic evangelism."
2. Read Jim Peterson's *Evangelism As a Lifestyle* (Colorado Springs: Navpress, 1980) for practical advice about putting your faith into your life.
3. Read Rebecca Pippert's *Out of the Saltshaker: Evangelism As a Way of Life* (Downers Grove, Illinois: InterVarsity Press, 1979) for a fresh approach to evangelism; chapters 9 and 10 discuss integrating evangelism into your conversations.
4. Read Ernest C. Reisinger's *Today's Evangelism* (Phillipsburg, New Jersey: Craig Press, 1982). For a description of what the evangelistic message must be and some abuses of modern evangelism.

For Further Reading on Cross-cultural Counseling

1. Read David Hesselgrave's *A Theory of Christian Cross-cultural Counseling* (Grand Rapids: Baker Book House,

1984) for a comprehensive, scholarly treatment of Christian cross-cultural counseling.

2. Read Thom Hopler's *A World of Difference* (Downers Grove, Illinois: InterVarsity Press, 1981), which challenges the white, middle-class Protestant church to reach people from other cultures; this book includes many interesting cross-cultural insights into familiar Bible passages.

3. Read Marvin Mayers's *Christianity Confronts Culture* (Grand Rapids: Zondervan Publishing House, 1974) for case studies, exercises, and questions that encourage the reader to examine his or her own biases and to think cross-culturally.

NOTES

[1] Pippert, *Out of the Saltshaker: Evangelism As a Way of Life* (Downers Grove, Illinois: InterVarsity Press, 1979), pp. 89–90.

[2] See also the parable of the sower in Matt. 13:18–23.

[3] Similarly we don't all describe our faith in the same way. New Christians may not know all the "proper" terms to describe their conversion. A person from a different church background or culture may not use typical evangelical terms.

[4] Thom Hopler, *A World Of Difference* (Downers Grove, Illinois: InterVarsity Press, 1981), p. 13.

[5] David Hesselgrave, *A Theory of Christian Cross-cultural Counseling* (Grand Rapids: Baker Book House, 1984), p. 198.

[6] Ibid., pp. 153–54.

[7] Ibid., pp. 253–58.

[8] Ibid., p. 243.

[9] For more information on separating the two see Hesselgrave, *A Theory of Christian Cross-cultural Counseling,* p. 231.

‡

CHAPTER 13

LOOKING UPWARD, INWARD, AND OUTWARD: A REPRISE

> Speaking the truth in love, we will in all things grow up into him who is the Head, that is, Christ. From him the whole body, joined and held together by every supporting ligament, grows and builds itself up in love, as each part does its work.
>
> —*Ephesians 4:15–16*

Two more helping jobs remain to be examined. First, how do we involve others when helping our friends? Second, how can we prevent problems from occurring?

LOOKING UPWARD: SOME BIBLICAL PRINCIPLES OF REFERRAL

As we've already seen, the first person to whom we should be referring our friends is God. "Surely God is my help" (Ps. 54:4a) reminds us that our help is impotent without God's *power, wisdom,* and *direction* (see also 2 Cor. 3:5).

Seeking wisdom is a good thing (Prov. 3:13; 4:7). Sometimes God will reveal His wisdom directly to us through the Bible, but sometimes He'll show us His wisdom in the counsel of other helpers. We are wise when we realize our limitations, admit our lack of knowledge, and seek additional help.

This principle is clearly demonstrated in Matthew 18:15–17. Here Jesus teaches about how to deal with a person who has sinned and then refuses to listen. Although this passage deals specifically with confronting someone who has sinned, there is another broader application: we need to bring in other helpers when our help is ineffective.

LOOKING INWARD: REEVALUATE YOURSELF

Take a few minutes to write a paragraph summarizing the highlights of your training as a lay counselor. Compare what you have just written with the goals you set for yourself in chapter 1. What goals have you met? Which ones have you been unable to reach? Were some of them unrealistic? If you still consider them to be obtainable, record them on the bottom of the "Evaluate Your Skills" form below. What do you plan to do differently to reach those goals?

Next, let's see if your helping skills have improved. Make two copies of the "Evaluate Your Skills" form and fill out one copy yourself and ask the same person who gave you feedback for the self-evaluation forms in Part II to fill out the other copy. Now compare the two ratings. How are they similar or different? Talk about any significant differences with your evaluator. He or she may be able to see areas of growth that you don't.

You probably will notice areas of improvement. On the other hand, you may be like one of my students who rated himself lower *after* this training than *before*. "I really wasn't honest when I first filled this out," he explained. "Now I realize how poorly I *really* help people!"

EVALUATE YOUR SKILLS

Directions: Listed below are many of the skills we have studied. Beneath each statement is a series of numbers. Circle the number that best describes you now, at the end of your training. Mark with an asterisk three skills that you want to practice consciously in the weeks ahead.

1. I show that I attend to my friends through my open body posture, eye contact, and keeping track of what they are saying.

Rarely   1   2   3   4   5   6   7   8   9   10   Usually

2. I show genuine acceptance and caring for my friends.

Rarely   1 2 3 4 5 6 7 8 9 10   Usually

3. I'm aware of my temptations as a helper, and I know how to guard against them.

Rarely   1 2 3 4 5 6 7 8 9 10   Usually

4. I maintain an attitude of hopefulness and encouragement while helping another.

Rarely   1 2 3 4 5 6 7 8 9 10   Usually

5. I can reflect to my friends the content and implication of their message.

Rarely   1 2 3 4 5 6 7 8 9 10   Usually

6. I can empathize with and reflect the feelings my friends are experiencing.

Rarely   1 2 3 4 5 6 7 8 9 10   Usually

7. I can make "I statements" and share my personal reaction to my friends and their situations.

Rarely   1 2 3 4 5 6 7 8 9 10   Usually

8. I can relate Scripture verses to my friends' situations.

Rarely   1 2 3 4 5 6 7 8 9 10   Usually

9. I can confront my friends without condemning them.

Rarely   1 2 3 4 5 6 7 8 9 10   Usually

10. I can help my friends take action to change their situation.

Rarely   1 2 3 4 5 6 7 8 9 10   Usually

11. I am comfortable initiating the helping process.

Rarely   1 2 3 4 5 6 7 8 9 10   Usually

12. I know how to help in a crisis situation.

Rarely   1 2 3 4 5 6 7 8 9 10   Usually

13. I can integrate my faith into the help I give to a non-Christian friend.

Rarely   1   2   3   4   5   6   7   8   9   10   Usually

14. I know *when* and *where* to refer my friends when they need help that I can't give.

Rarely   1   2   3   4   5   6   7   8   9   10   Usually

What goals will I want to work toward (pick one or two)?

How will I work toward them?

Who will hold me accountable to these goals?
When will I report to this person?

Although you might not have read this book in order to grow personally, you may now be aware of some areas that need work. For instance, now you may realize your own inability to apply God's Word to your life. You may decide to talk with a good friend, your pastor, or other qualified helper in order to overcome these problems. You will be a better helper once you have received the help you need.

If you are feeling ashamed for not improving your helping skills as much as you had anticipated, remember that you can honestly *confront* yourself with your failure because you can also *comfort* yourself. God's acceptance, love, and forgiveness extend even to imperfect helpers.

Self-evaluation keeps us returning to God. From Him we receive the ability to accept ourselves and our friends. But our confidence isn't in ourselves or our techniques but rather in what *God* will accomplish in us and in our friends.

Now that you have better listening and attending skills, you are more likely to observe other people's problems. But you probably will realize quickly that you are unable to help in every situation. You'll be more likely to give help when you *can,* and to get outside help when you *can't.* Being a bridge to other sources of help is one of the most important jobs a lay counselor can perform.

LOOKING OUTWARD: GETTING OTHERS INVOLVED

When we involve others in the helping process, we guard against the "lone-helper" syndrome, which gives too much power and not enough accountability to any one helper. If you can be a part of a team of helpers, you'll be less likely to fall into this temptation and you'll gain the support of other helpers.

Before we involve others in helping our friends, we must tell our friends that we plan to talk about their situation to someone else. (When we first begin to help our friends, we should promise not to gossip [Prov. 11:13; 17:9; 1 Peter 3:10], but we don't promise never to talk with others. That promise will get us in trouble if our friends need more help than we personally can provide.) Then we must carefully choose to whom we talk. Our friends have opened the treasure chest of themselves to us; we don't want to destroy their trust.

When to Get Additional Help

How do you know when your help is insufficient? How do you know when it's time to bring in a more skilled helper?

Two basic questions will help you make that decision: First, am *I* effective? Second, does my *friend* have a problem I'm equipped to handle?

Look at yourself. Use chart #1, "When to Refer: Look at Yourself," to evaluate yourself. The first four questions describe reactions that could interfere with providing good help. Other emotions such as dislike, boredom, irritation, jealousy, discouragement, frustration, and competitiveness could also prevent us from being caring helpers.

The remaining questions evaluate your involvement with your friend. If you answer more than half of these with a yes, then you've become overly involved and probably have slipped into a rescuing pattern. In addition, if your friend repeatedly tells you, "You're the only one who really cares and understands," then you have another clue that you've climbed onto the lifeguard stand! (Note: The last three questions reveal symptoms of helper burn-out, which usually comes from rescuing and taking on too much responsibility instead of trusting God.)

What should we do if we have been rescuing our friends? We must examine our motives for helping, use feedback to discuss whether or not our friends are subtly asking us to solve their problems, talk about their expectations, and then decide how we can help differently in the future. Most importantly, stop rescuing! Cut back on the amount of time that you spend together, refrain from giving direct answers, and remember whose problem this is!

CHART #1: WHEN TO REFER: LOOK AT YOURSELF

1. Am I frightened by my friend's problem (drug or alcohol abuse, violence)?

2. Am I angered by my friend's problem (child abuse, marital fighting)?

3. Am I physically attracted to my friend?

4. Am I reacting negatively to him or her because of his or her age, ethnic group, or subculture (e.g., adolescents, Hispanics, drug abusers)?

5. Am I regularly spending more than two hours per week with this person?

6. Do I find that I'm not able to stop thinking and worrying about this person?

7. Am I always talking about this person to my family and friends?

8. Am I taking time from other important activities (family, work, recreation) for this person?

9. Am I afraid of drastic consequences (suicide, marriage collapse) if I stopped helping this friend?

10. Am I trying to fix all the problems my friend is bringing to me?

11. Do I feel responsible when this friend makes mistakes?

12. Do I want my friend to change more than he or she wants to change? (Am I working harder at change than he or she is?)

13. Is my friend dependent on me?

14. Am I beginning to feel as if this is my problem, not his or hers?

15. Am I beginning to resent my friend when he or she calls or stops by to talk?

16. Am I beginning to dislike my friend? Do I feel manipulated for extra time or other favors?

Look at your friend. In order to recognize which problems require the help of a more skilled helper, look at chart #2, "Serious Problems and Their Symptoms." These problems, which you'll encounter only occasionally, either have been present in your friend for a long time or have been severe for a short time. As you look at this list, don't be too quick to diagnose a friend (or yourself)! If you're not sure if someone you know fits one of these descriptions, talk it over with a psychologist, your pastor, or another mental health worker. For further help in deciding if you should be helping your friend, answer the questions in chart #3, "When to Refer: Look at Your Friend." If you answer any one of them in the affirmative, a referral to a professional counselor is appropriate.

CHART #2: SERIOUS PROBLEMS AND THEIR SYMPTOMS[1]

Problem	Symptoms
Neurosis	Severe fear, which limits a person's ability to function normally. Source of worry is internal conflicts and serious self-doubts.
Deep depression	Loss of pleasure, appetite, and energy; sleep disturbance, feelings of worthlessness, long periods of crying.

Psychosomatic illness	Variety of possibilities: Ulcers, abdominal pain, headaches, backaches.
Extreme family or marital difficulties	Arguing, fighting, spouse or child threatens to or does leave home. Child having school problems. Signs of physical abuse. Sexual problems.
Alcohol abuse	Unable to stop or cut down drinking. Drinking every day. Binges or blackouts.
Drug abuse	Varies according to particular drug. Generally, inability to function normally at school or work. Change of friends. Change in personality or behavior.
Suicide threat	A plan and means to the plan. Saying good-bye. Feelings of hopelessness, despair, loneliness, guilt.
Eating problems: Anorexia	Significant weight loss. Preoccupation with fear of becoming fat even when person is thin. Extreme dieting and exercise. Extreme concern with body image.
Bulimia	Binge eating followed by self-induced vomiting. Heavy use of laxatives. Extreme concern with body image.
Organic Problems: Delirium	Consciousness is clouded; person can't sustain attention. Disorientation, poor memory. Misinterpretation of things. Illusions, incoherent speech. Altered sleep cycle. Happens quickly.
Dementia	Loss of intellectual abilities. Inability to think concretely and learn new things. Impaired judg-

	ment. Recent memory impaired. Personality changes. Happens slowly.
Psychosis:	Out of touch with reality.
Schizophrenia	Altered form and content of thoughts. Altered mood, affect, and judgment. Auditory hallucinations. Not split personality.
Manic depression	Expansive mood, a lot of physical activity without tiring. Fast speech, racing thoughts. Delusions of grandeur. Impulsive behavior. Flamboyant. Can alternate with severe depression.
Psychotic depression	Delusions of worthlessness and extreme sinfulness.
Personality Problems:	
Borderline	Impulsive and unpredictable self-damaging behavior. Pattern of unstable relationships. Inability to control anger. Unstable moods. Questions about identity. Often feels empty or bored. Sees life as all good or all bad.
Antisocial	Inability to be consistent at work. Irresponsibility as a parent. Frequently breaks social norms: steals, sells drugs, fights, lies, is sexually promiscuous. Fails to honor debts or to plan ahead. No sense of right or wrong. Sees no consequence for behavior or need for punishment.
Dependent	Allows others to assume responsibility for his or her life. Can't function independently. Lacks self-confidence.

CHART #3: WHEN TO REFER:
LOOK AT YOUR FRIEND

1. Is my friend experiencing a deeply ingrained, lifelong pattern of behavior (e.g., homosexuality, chronic depression)?

2. Is my friend feeling as if he or she is losing control over himself or herself?

3. Does my friend need a skill that I can't teach (e.g., assertiveness training, financial management)?

4. Does my friend need medical attention/drugs?

5. Does my friend need vocational guidance/testing?

6. Does my friend need the attention of a government agency (child abuse, financial need)?

7. Can someone else better help my friend (family, church members, friends)?

8. Is my friend responding to my help and meeting his or her goals?

9. Does my friend's problem persist in spite of the fact that I've tried various ways of helping him or her?

10. Does my friend's problem seem to be getting worse?

The last criteria you can use in deciding whether or not to refer a friend, is to determine if he or she is benefiting from your help. If you keep on trying to help but the other person never seems to change, then either the person is not ready or willing to change or you may not have the necessary helping skills. Bring in another helper 1) if your relationship never returns to a mutual friendship; 2) if every time you get together the conversation is always about your friend's problems; 3) if your friend seems too confused, manipulative, angry, mixed up, or stuck.

Where to Find Additional Help

Your friend's needs and the services available in your community will determine where you find help for your friend. Familiarize yourself with the social services in your community by looking in your phone book. Have available the phone numbers of your pastor, the police, your local mental health and mental retardation clinic, and a twenty-four-hour suicide hotline. Chart #4 is a list of other services that your friends may need occasionally.

CHART #4: WHERE TO REFER[2]

Your community has many referral sources. Most will be listed in the blue pages of your telephone directory. In addition to the following suggestions, state and county agencies often can provide local referral information.

Problem	Consider Referral to:
alcoholism	Alcoholics Anonymous, general hospital, physician
child abuse, neglect	State Department of Children and Family Services, Child Welfare Agency, National Child Abuse Hotline 1-800-422-4453
depression, bizarre behavior, anxiety, confusion	Christian psychologist or psychiatrist, mental health and mental retardation services, hospital (for emergencies)
drug problem	general hospital, counseling clinic, Christian psychiatrist
financial	state or local welfare agency, United Fund, church, bank, loan company
gambling	Gamblers Annonymous, United Way, pastor, Christian psychologist or counselor
handicap	Society for the Blind, Retarded Children's Society, United Fund office, local service club

legal problems	lawyer, legal aid society
marriage, family, sexual problems	pastor, Christian marriage counselor, psychologist, social worker, counselor
missing person	police department
poisoning	general hospital, emergency ward
pregnancy	physician, pastor, 1-800-BETHANY
runaway	youth service bureau, National runaway switchboard 1-800-621-4000
senior citizens	area office on aging, meals on wheels, family services for older adults
spiritual problem	pastor, Christian counselor
suicide threat	suicide prevention center, Christian psychologist, psychiatrist, mental health clinic, pastor, emergency ward of hospital
vocational	private employment agency, state department of vocational rehabilitation, school guidance counselor, Christian psychologist

Who Are the Best Helpers for Your Friend?

How do you find the most suitable helper for your friend? Let's look at three different types of helpers to whom we might refer our friends: Christian nonprofessionals and professionals, and non-Christian professionals.

Nonprofessional Christian helpers. Sometimes our friends' problems will not be serious enough to warrant professional help, but we still may feel unqualified to help. In this case, we can consider referring our friends to a more qualified layperson. Look around your church. Who is a sensitive and caring listener?

Whom do other people trust? Whom do others go to for help? Who possesses the wisdom gained through a variety of life experiences?

As you look for a suitable helper, consider someone who has worked through emotions and difficulties similar to your friends' problems. A woman who has struggled with the problem of infertility, for example, may be the best helper for your friend who has given up on having any children of her own.

The church is a resource network. Although fellow church members may not be professional counselors, they may have areas of expertise that our friends need. A nurse can provide advice to your elderly neighbor whose wife just had gallbladder surgery; a lawyer can give appropriate counsel to a woman whose husband is filing for divorce and wants custody of the children; a carpenter can help a single woman maintain her home. Be ready to use the gifts and talents of others.

Professional Christian helpers. First, consider the pastor a full-time professional Christian helper. Many pastors counsel church members as an integral part of their ministry. Sometimes your pastor may be aware of the troubles of a person in the congregation; other times you may know of someone's problems before your pastor does. Encourage your friend to contact your pastor, or, with your friend's permission, make the call yourself. (You definitely should consider contacting your pastor when your friend is dealing with unconfessed sin. Marriage, family, and spiritual problems are three other areas in which the pastor should be included.)

Sometimes you may want to stay involved with your friend even though he or she is seeing your pastor. Coordinate your efforts so that you don't duplicate or contradict the other's counsel. Working with your pastor is particularly important when helping the type of person who goes from one person to another and tries to get help from everyone. The saying "too many cooks spoil the broth" can be true in counseling!

Respect your pastor's role as shepherd of the flock. Your pastor may welcome your assistance or may view it as an intrusion. No matter what helping relationship the two of you agree upon, you can always help by praying for your pastor.

The second type of Christian helpers are psychologists, psychiatrists, counselors, and social workers, who work either inside or outside the church. Depending on their particular field, most have at least a master's degree in counseling or psychology, and some are trained in both psychology and theology.

Do you know the Christian counselors in your community? Some may be listed in the phone book as pastoral counselors; others advertise as counselors with a Christian perspective. Your pastor should also be able to recommend a counselor. Several organizations of Christian counselors also could provide you with the names of qualified counselors in your area (see Appendix A for a list). Whichever counselor you encourage your friend to consult, make sure that you have carefully investigated his or her qualifications. The counselor should be someone who holds the Bible as the Word of truth and uses it as the standard by which he or she counsels.

The third type of professional Christian helpers are those that your friend can meet through reading. Many noted Christian counselors have written books that can help people deal with their problems. (See the Supplementary Bibliography and the For Further Reading sections for books that deal with their problems. Familiarize yourself with some of these so that you can draw upon this resource as necessary.)

Non-Christian professionals. Is it ever appropriate for your friend to get help from a non-Christian? This question is difficult to answer. Some Christians believe that counsel from a nonbeliever can never be helpful; other Christians disagree. There are significant arguments on both sides of the debate.

Obviously, a non-Christian helper will operate from a set of beliefs different from a Christian's. Research shows that all counselors' values will be reflected in how they interact with their clients and in how they counsel. Therefore, if your Christian friend receives help from a non-Christian, the counsel may conflict with your friend's principles and beliefs. In fact, the counsel may be counterproductive and may hinder your friend's walk with the Lord. Therefore, it's best that help provided by a non-Christian is under the oversight of the pastor or elder of your friend's church.

On the other hand, Christian professionals haven't researched every area of mental health. They may lack the understanding in such areas as family therapy, how to treat eating disorders, or the best approach to drug addiction. In some areas non-Christian psychologists have done more research than Christians have and therefore can offer some insights that Christian professionals may lack.

Sometimes our friends will not be able to find help from Christian professionals. Such may be the case if your friend needs treatment in a hospital. If a Christian mental health hospital is not available to your friend, he or she will need to get help from the psychiatric unit of your local hospital, or he or she might need a longer visit at a psychiatric facility. The decision and arrangements for in-patient treatment should be made through a psychiatrist or other medical doctor.

In considering the question of using non-Christian mental health professionals, we need to avoid two extremes. We don't want to give Bible platitudes that superficially exhort our friends without considering their entire situation.[3] But we also don't want to secularize the answers to psychological, emotional, and spiritual problems. Obviously, non-Christian professionals won't have the complete answer since they don't recognize that our spiritual needs are met in the Lord Jesus Christ. But when help for our friends' specific needs aren't available from a Christian, our friends may need to get help from a non-Christian.

How to Get Your Friend Additional Help

How can we tell our friends they need additional help without making them feel rejected, abandoned, or like a "mental case"? From the beginning of our conversations, we must let our friends know that we may not be the best helper for them. Always keep open the possibility of directing a friend to another helper. Make this a joint decision. Together the *two of you* will decide whether or not your help is adequate.

Second, refer with love and hope. We encourage our friends to get help from someone else *not* because we dislike them, but because our care extends to securing the best help available. Think of it this way: if your friend John had a sore throat, you'd be happy to give him a cough drop. You wouldn't volunteer to take out his tonsils unless you were a qualified surgeon!

As always, your tone of voice is important since it communicates the message your friend receives. "I think you might benefit from talking to someone else" can be said kindly and hopefully or with pity and frustration. If you are unsure how your message is received, go back and check it out. Don't leave the subject until you are sure that what you *intended* to say is what *has been heard*.

Third, find an appropriate helper. Go over the information in chart #4 with your friend and find out what services your community offers. Talk to your pastor as well as to other people in the helping professions and figure out what alternatives are available. (Often doctors, lawyers, and school personnel are familiar with community social services.) Your friend should then consider the various possibilities and decide which one to follow.

If your friend seems hesitant, be understanding. Often the first step into a counselor's office is the hardest. Be empathic but don't be pushy. Don't make the appointment for your friend! The decision and choice must be your friend's, not yours.

Fourth, stay in touch with your friend. Don't just give out a phone number and say, "Here's someone who can *really* help you with your problems." Stay involved and encourage your friend to stick it out. Stand alongside your friend, but don't interfere with the counseling. Since you are no longer the primary helper, your friend should be working on his or her problems with the counselor and should not be repeating them to you.

Now, how do *you* feel when you decide your friend needs additional help? Do you feel ashamed that you haven't been able to help more? Are you disappointed in yourself? Is your pride hurt? If you're going to help others, you must be able to refer without punishing yourself or feeling as if you've failed.

What if your friends refuse to seek additional help? Their refusal may indicate that they don't want to admit their real needs and problems. Or they may find it safer to talk to you rather than to reveal their problems to a complete stranger. (Besides, lay helpers are always available, and our services are free!) If you get the impression that any of these reasons are stopping your friends from seeking professional help, give them this feedback. If your friends continue to refuse professional help, then it's time to be more direct. Don't end the friendship, but don't allow conversations to focus on your friends' problems. Your friends may get the message and find more appropriate help. See the chart below for a review of these suggestions.

CHART #5: DO'S AND DON'TS OF REFERRAL

DO'S

DO refer when you feel your help is no longer effective.

DO refer when your friend's problem is more complicated than you can handle.

DO refer when you lack the skills to help your friend.

DO refer when you react in ways that interfere with helping your friend.

DO accept your own limits and refer without guilt or shame.

DON'TS

DON'T refer with rejection or frustration.

DON'T refer with despair or hopelessness.

DON'T refer and communicate that something is wrong with your friend.

DON'T refer and then abandon your friend.

LOOKING ONWARD: THE BIG PICTURE OF HELPING OTHERS

A recent radio announcement promoting health care claimed that "If you prevent a problem, then you don't need a cure." Most of us try to maintain our *physical* health: We brush our teeth to prevent tooth decay; we yield ourselves to painful needles to prevent measles, smallpox, and tetanus. But do we take similar precautions in order to prevent *emotional, spiritual,* or *psychological* problems?

If "an ounce of prevention is *really* worth a pound of cure" then taking the time to prevent problems is worth *sixteen* times more than a cure. Unfortunately, by the time a person with emotional needs goes to a professional, it may be a long road back to emotional health.

Preventing emotional and spiritual problems isn't as easy as preventing disease. We've gotten very comfortable with sweeping emotional problems under the rug. If we neglected to brush our teeth, people would soon be unpleasantly aware of us. If we hide our anger, jealousy, hurt, or fear, we think the effects are not quite as noticeable.

What does it take to prevent emotional and psychological problems from occurring? How can we, as trained lay counselors, promote mental and emotional health? We'll consider three levels of prevention: helping our friends before problems occur; helping them after problems occur by working to lessen the impact of the problems; and then helping them return to normal activities after a serious problem is over.[4]

Prevention at the Preproblem Level

Smokey the Bear reminds us that "Only *you* can prevent forest fires." So we dutifully put out our fires *before* they destroy our favorite campground. But that assumes that a fire has already been started. How can we prevent an emotional "fire" from being lit in the first place?

The first line of defense: ourselves.   First, we can help prevent problems in our own lives. Having participated in this training, we should have some basic tools to help us handle our own problems better. We have learned how to apply the gospel to our own lives: how to *confront* our sins, weaknesses, and limitations and how to receive God's *comfort,* forgiveness, love, and acceptance. Our emotional, psychological, and spiritual health is vastly improved when we put these truths into practice.

In addition, if we live according to God's Word, we have the assurance that things will go well with us (Deut. 6:18, 24–25). This, of course, is not a simple formula for success but rather a statement about the way God has ordered the world. Therefore, the way to spiritual peace and emotional health is by leaving behind what is contrary to God and embracing His ways at a deep, personal level.

The second line of defense: our family and friends.   Second, we can help prevent problems in the lives of our close family and friends. Incarnating the gospel begins here. Our new listening and speaking skills will enable us to relate more sensitively and lovingly to those around us. Our helping skills are the tools we use to build solid, meaningful relationships. These relationships, in turn, are instrumental in preventing problems from occurring.

As we draw close to others, we gain access to speaking the

truth to them. We not only win the privilege of demonstrating God's love to them, but we also call them to love God and follow Him. Fewer people would need professional counselors if we were daily encouraging our loved ones to build their lives around Jesus, to stay close to Him, to say no to the superficial attraction of sin, and to maintain their original confidence and faith in Christ (Heb. 3:1, 12–14). As a result of this encouragement, our friends' lives will more closely reflect God's purpose for them (Heb. 10:24–25). Obeying the principles laid down in God's Word will bless our lives, our families, as well as all our relationships.

The third line of defense: our churches. As a committed body of believers, the church has a great potential to be both a helping and a healing community. If churches would serve their members as God has directed in His Word, fewer emotional and psychological fires would need extinguishing.

We can maximize the church's resources for wholeness and healing in a number of ways. First of all, we should be sincerely committed to loving our brothers and sisters (John 13:34–35; 15:17). Our love for one another should create an atmosphere of acceptance so that the church becomes a place where people feel at home and can comfortably be themselves. The church is to be like a family: a place where I can trust that I will be known, loved, and accepted for who I am; a place where I don't have to hide my tears, sins, fears, or failures; a place where I don't have to be embarrassed or ashamed to ask for help; a place where I don't have to wear a mask of "I'm fine, thank you" if I have just received bad news. At the same time, the church also should be a place where others will hold me accountable to Christian values; a place where a brother or sister will lovingly put me back on the path of following Jesus if I begin to stray away.

Education is another aspect of prevention within the church. A high school Sunday school class on dating and marriage could prevent poor decisions later on; a class on communication skills for married couples could prevent marital and family problems, a seminar for couples facing retirement could prevent unmet expectations and disappointment. Sermons that tackle topics like how to handle conflict in a Christlike way, the Christian understanding of death, or how to deal with temptation also can prevent problems. As churches assume their significant role in problem prevention, they would be fighting fires before they had a chance to ignite and spread.

Prevention at the Problem Level

What can we do if a fire has already been lit in our friend's life and we see it burning? What kind of prevention is effective then? Just as a fire fighter works to contain a fire, we also can work to prevent our friends' problems from affecting the rest of their lives or the lives of the people around them.

In order to see what our role is at this level of problem prevention, let's return to Donna, the teenage girl we met in chapter 11. Obviously Donna already has a problem—she is pregnant. In what ways can you help her now? You can't undo the pregnancy, but you can help Donna face the consequences of her sin. Without condemnation and judgment, you can walk alongside her now, preventing her from making other poor decisions. By accepting her and listening to her, you can help her see her options. You can help her work through the list of problems she made when the two of you first talked. In all these ways, you are preventing Donna's pregnancy from ruining her whole life or the lives of her baby and boyfriend.

Prevention at the Postproblem Level

What can park rangers do *after* a fire has consumed a large part of the forest? They prevent fires by making sure the last flame is completely out, by redoubling their prevention efforts, by investigating the causes of this fire, and by planting new trees to replace the destroyed ones.

In the same way, we must make sure that our friends' problems are completely "out." Has Donna gotten the help she needed, or is she just brushing the sparks away to be taken care of later? If she decides to marry Alan against her parents' wishes, a new fire may break out very soon.

Second, we must find out what started the problem in the first place. Often God uses trials and difficulties to bring us back to Himself. Donna needs to think about why she got so deeply involved with Alan. What need was she hoping he would fulfill? How can she avoid future mistakes and further sin? Answering these questions might help her to reconsider marrying Alan.

Third, we must help plant new activities, decisions, and behaviors to replace the destructive ones. Although Donna's life will change significantly (whether or not she keeps the baby), her life is not over. Helping Donna to figure out what she wants to do with her life after the baby is born will encourage her to start over again. She may choose to complete high school and receive job training; she may plan to meet with other new mothers to discuss child care. Eventually, she might be able to help other pregnant teenagers—in this way planting a new "forest" on the ashes of the old.

ONE FINAL WORD

Your job as a helper began before you read this book. It will continue your whole life. I hope that you will take along the many skills you've learned in this book. But most of all, I pray that you will take along the apostle Paul's encouragement to the Philippian church:

> And this is my prayer:
>> that your love may abound more and more in knowledge
>>> and depth of insight,
>
> so that you may be able to discern what is best
>> and may be pure and blameless until the day of Christ,
>
> filled with the fruit of righteousness
>> that comes through Jesus Christ—
>
> to the glory and praise of God.
>
> —Philippians 1:9–11

PERSONAL AND PRACTICAL

Study the Scriptures

1. Think about someone in your church who appears to be left out of the mainstream of activities. Develop a plan for how you will reach him or her. Read Romans 12:9–16 and 15:1–7 and list at least five different suggestions of how to love. Which of these will you try to implement with this person?

2. Read James 5:13–16, 20. In what two ways can we be involved with one another in the church? How are either of these related to problem prevention?

3. Read Paul's instructions to the church in 1 Thessalonians 5:14–15. According to Paul, what six things can

we do to help each other? How do these actions prevent problems?

For Thought

1. Think of a friend whom you were unsuccessful in helping. Try to remember how you felt. Did your own emotional reaction to your friend or your friend's problem prevent you from being an effective helper?

2. Think of another friend with whom you fell into a rescuing pattern. What indicated to you that you were rescuing? Why did you begin to rescue? How else could you have responded?

3. Are you working on "fire prevention" in your family and with your friends? Think of the people with whom you are close. Have you ignored any subtle clues that they are unhappy, hurt, confused, or scared? Think about new ways that you can respond to them.

For Practice

Read the case below and answer the following questions:
- What were Bruce's main problems?
- How does he seem to hide from true knowledge of himself? Is he guilty of something? What do you think he might feel ashamed about? Does he have problems accepting himself or others? What might he be ignorant of?
- If you were Bruce's close friend, how could you have helped him? What helping skills would you have used?
- If you were only an acquaintance of Bruce, how would you have been able to tell that he needed help? How could you have helped him then?
- What should be the church's role in helping him?

BRUCE

Bruce, twenty-nine, is the elder of two children. He lives at home, while his younger sister left home when she was seventeen. Bruce is very close to his parents; in fact he appears to be overly dependent on them. He would like to be married, but he gets very nervous around women. Since he feels that he has nothing to say to them, he ends up going out of his way to avoid social contact.

Bruce attends your church but is not a member. Over the last few years he has made repeated confessions of faith, but he doesn't seem to understand the gospel fully. He isn't involved in church activities.

Bruce tends to blame others for not befriending him and bitterly complains that his life is passing him by.

NOTES

[1] Some of the material in this table was adapted from the *Diagnostic and Statistical Manual of Mental Disorders Third Edition Revised* (Washington, D.C.: American Psychiatric Association, 1980). Reprinted by permission.

[2] Adapted from Gary Collins, *How To Be a People Helper* (Santa Ana, California: Vision House, 1976), p. 111.

[3] See Jay Adams, *Ready To Restore* (Phillipsburg, New Jersey: Presbyterian and Reformed Publishing Co., 1981), pp. 63–65.

[4] Gerald Caplan and Henry Grunebaum, "Perspectives on Primary Prevention: A Review" in Harry Gottesfield, *The Critical Issues of Community Mental Health* (New York: Behavior Publications, 1972), p. 128.

☦

INDEX

LEADER'S GUIDE

HOW TO USE THIS GUIDE

This guide is designed for use in two settings: the group training to become official lay counselors and the Bible study (discipleship group, etc.) studying *Friendship Counseling* in a small group. The first group should be led by a trained professional counselor. The second group may be led by any person sensitive to group dynamics and the learning process.

Each of the thirteen lessons in this guide corresponds to the chapters of *Friendship Counseling*. Each week the group members will read one chapter and answer the questions in the Personal and Practical section at the end of each chapter. Ask group members—especially those using this study as a lay counseling course—to record their answers, responses to case studies, reflections, and notes in a notebook or journal. The group members should come to the meeting prepared to discuss their answers and to participate in the group activities outlined in this Leader's Guide. Each participant will be expected to come to class with a Bible, the text, the notebook, and sometimes a concordance.

Schedule at least an hour for each group meeting. An hour and a half or two hours is even better—especially if your group members are training to become lay counselors. The extra hour gives your group the needed time to practice their helping skills, and it gives you, the leader, time both to observe the participants' growth and to give needed encouragement and guidance. Briefly review the chapter by answering a few of the questions in the Personal and Practical section or highlighting the main topics covered. Then choose some group activities from this Leader's Guide. Because these activities provide important hands-on learning opportunities for the participants, you will want to use as many as possible for each meeting. Be flexible. Certain exercises or questions will take more time than is suggested; others will take less. Don't be afraid to adapt these activities to the needs of your group. Spend a few minutes at the end of each meeting for discussion, questions and answers, and prayer. If you are not able to finish all the exercises in this guide, assign some of the discussion questions for homework.

Be aware that the size of your group will influence the dynamics of the class. A smaller group (five to nine people) will allow for more personal disclosure, confrontation, and feedback between group members. A larger group (ten to twenty-five people) may inhibit some people but will encourage a wider range of questions and more varied group interaction.

As you lead the group, try to use many examples from your own experiences of helping others. Feel free to include your failures as well as your successes. Ask people from the group for experiences they have had in helping people. Encourage them to share both kinds of stories as well. Later on in lessons 6–10, you'll use these cases as examples when demonstrating the various helping skills.

One of your most important jobs as the group leader is to model good helping skills. Be attentive and ask open-ended questions. Use active listening and "I statements" appropriately. Don't rescue group members if they get stuck when helping someone; allow them the opportunity to learn through these experiences. Be sure to highlight good helping responses between group members.

Feel free to break a large group into smaller groups of approximately four people for the discussion times. This is particularly helpful when group members don't know each other and may be afraid of answering questions in a large group. You may want to assign a leader for each smaller discussion group. These leaders will be responsible for assigning Scripture verses, preventing the group from bogging down on any one particular question, and reporting back to the larger group.

In the beginning of the course, you also may want to assign partners. This will encourage accountability as group members help measure each other's progress by giving feedback throughout the course. The experience of giving and receiving feedback runs parallel to the helping experience. In this way the group member finds out what it feels like to be on both the receiving and giving end of helping a friend.

Prepare for every group meeting by praying for each one of the participants. After the first meeting (or after the screening interview if you are beginning a formal lay counseling training program), you should have a good idea of why each person is taking the course and what he or she hopes to learn and accomplish. Pray that God will enable all the group members to reach their goals and to grow as Christians. Ask God to help you be an effective helper to each one.

I give special thanks to Julie Roland, Madeline Arrell, the students at Westminster Theological Seminary who gave input into this material, and all the people who took this course and gave me feedback. They are the ones who helped me become a more sensitive teacher, thus making this a more helpful Leader's Guide. I also wish to thank Judy Brown, a parent education coordinator, who gave me permission to adapt her active-listening ball-toss exercise.

1

WHO IS GOD AND WHO ARE WE?

LESSON GOALS

1. To set the tone for the entire thirteen weeks. A relaxed friendly atmosphere is best. Discuss how the training will be a learning and growing experience for everyone. Emphasize the confidentiality of the group.
2. To discuss the nature, purpose, and goals of the course. This will depend on the participants of your group and the purpose of your specific group.
3. To have all members introduce themselves—including you.
4. To review the foundational principles of chapter 1.

ICEBREAKERS

Directions: Choose one or two of the following exercises to help group members relax and get to know each other. (Time: 15–30 minutes)

1. Ask all group members to introduce themselves and give some personal information including past counseling training, religious background, present occupation, and expectations for the course. They should also share the most embarrassing or funny thing that happened when they were trying to help someone.
2. Assign people to the partners (preferably someone they don't already know) with whom they will work during the course. Have them spend a few minutes getting to know each other. Going around the room, have each person introduce his or her partner to the group.
3. Have everyone answer the following questions: "Why do you want to help others?"; "Do you think that in some way you are trying to make yourself feel better by

helping others?''; ''Can people want to become helpers for the wrong reason?''

4. Have group members share the goals they wrote down at the end of chapter 1. (This exercise can be combined with #1 or #3.) Ask each group member to be prepared to share at the next meeting the answer to this question: How will you know when you have reached these goals?

DISCUSSION QUESTIONS

Directions: Form small groups. Assign each group one of the questions listed below as well as one of questions 2–5 from Study the Scriptures in chapter 1. Allow 10 minutes for each group to work together on the answers. Reassemble to hear everyone's answers. (Time: 30 minutes)

1. What is mankind's nature? Why? What are some of the results of the Fall? Find examples for each consequence or problem listed in the text.

2. What are some of our basic needs? How are these needs usually met? How do people meet their needs in sinful ways?

3. Discuss the problem of evil in the world. How does that effect the friends we are trying to help? List examples of different types of evil and the problems that evil precipitates.

4. How does the problem of ignorance surface in the lives of our friends? Give specific examples. How have you tried to help these friends?

2

JESUS, OUR MODEL COUNSELOR

LESSON GOALS

1. To help group members identify how the person and work of Christ influences them as Christian helpers.
2. To encourage more interaction among group members so that they will feel comfortable working and sharing together.

ICEBREAKER

Form small groups or have members work with their partners. Have participants review the goals they set last week and share how they will know when they have reached their goals. Take turns praying for each other's goals. (Time: 10 minutes)

DISCUSSION QUESTIONS

Directions: Form small groups and assign several of the questions listed below to each group. When the time is over, reassemble and have a "reporter" summarize the small group's answers to the entire group. (Time: 30 minutes)

1. Read Matt. 20:29–34 and Luke 17:11–19. Name at least six aspects of Jesus' response to the blind men and the lepers. What are the similarities and differences in how He responded to the two groups? How does this apply to your role as a helper? Think of the last time someone asked you for help and you didn't stop to listen to him or her. What hindered you?

2. Read John 15:12–13, 17. What does Jesus teach about loving each other? How can you demonstrate love and acceptance to your friends?

3. Read Matt. 9:20–22. How did Jesus show compassion to this woman? What was special about this incident?

4. Read Matt. 19:16–24. What did Jesus confront in the rich young ruler's life? List examples of misplaced priorities you see in a friend's life. How would you confront him or her?

5. Review Luke 10:38–42 and read John 11:1–26. List the problems Jesus identified in Martha's life. How did Jesus confront her?

6. Read John 6:26–40. What attitudes did Jesus confront in the Jews? What problems did He identify? Has someone ever come to you for the wrong kind of help? What did you do? In the light of Jesus' example, what could you have done differently?

7. Compare John 4 with Luke 24. Look specifically for the actions people took in response to Jesus. What does this tell you about the action stage of the helping process?

8. Read John 9:1–12. The blind man's past could have been an excuse for his present situation and a barrier to future growth. Consider how Jesus focused on healing him rather than allowing him to dwell on excuses for not changing. What application do you see in this for your role as helper?

LARGE GROUP ACTIVITY

Directions: In order to see more clearly how Jesus interacted with the people He met, act out some situations that helpers might encounter today. Feel free to add more situations to the list below. Have one person role-play the person described below and have another role-play how Jesus might have responded. Encourage help from other members of the group. (Time: 30 minutes)

How would Jesus have responded to:

1. A man diagnosed with AIDS.

2. A teenager who has run away from home, claiming that her parents treat her brothers and sisters better than they treat her.

3. An unbeliever who always badgers you with obnoxious questions and who tries to trick you into getting angry so that you'll blow your cool as a Christian.

4. An unemployed husband who lies around the house, watches TV, and drinks beer all day long.

5. A homosexual caught with his lover.

6. A person who hangs on to you, looking for emotional as well as material handouts.

7. A woman who constantly criticizes and belittles her husband.

8. A young woman who always appears disheveled, has poor personal hygiene, and follows you around at church.

Encourage everyone to bring a concordance to the next group meeting.

3

THE HOLY SPIRIT, OUR HELPER

LESSON GOALS

1. To help group members become more acquainted with the work of the Holy Spirit in their lives as well as in the lives of their friends.
2. To enable group members to see how they can use Scripture when helping their friends.

DISCUSSION QUESTIONS

Directions: Form three small groups. Assign the first group numbers 1–6, which refer to the word *parakaleo;* assign the second group 7–12, which refer to the word *noutheteo;* assign the third group numbers 13–17, which refer to the word *dunamoo.* A concordance is helpful for this exercise.

Group members should read the passage, then put the passage into their own words in the column marked *Paraphrase.* Under *Application,* they should write *either* what this passage teaches them about being a helper or how they could use it when helping a friend. (Try to think of a specific situation in which to use the passage.) Reassemble the group and review answers. (Time: 30 minutes)

SCRIPTURE	PARAPHRASE	APPLICATION

1. 2 Cor. 1:3–6

2. 2 Cor. 2:4–8

3. Matt. 5:4

4. 1 Thess. 4:13–18

5. 1 Thess. 5:11, 14

6. Heb. 3:13

7. Rom. 15:14

8. Col. 3:16

9. Acts 20:31

10. Col. 1:28

11. 1 Cor. 4:14

12. 2 Thess. 3:15

13. Luke 5:17

14. Acts 1:8

15. Rom. 15:13

16. Phil. 4:13

17. 2 Tim. 4:17

GROUP ACTIVITIES

A. Discuss the following: In what ways did studying the different helping roles that Jesus and the Holy Spirit have change your mind about your role as a helper?

B. If time permits, encourage partners to share their answers to questions 3, 6, and 9 from the For Thought section of chapter 2. (Total time: 15–30 minutes)

4

A HELPER'S SPIRITUAL INVENTORY

LESSON GOALS

1. To be a model of appropriate self-disclosure and good communication skills. Read Heb. 13:7 and 1 Thess. 1:6. Remember, as the leader, you are the main person to model good helping skills for your group!
2. To create a safe environment in which group members feel free to discover and share about themselves.
3. To study the biblical characteristics of an effective helper.
4. To help group members become aware of the helping temptations they personally face.

DISCUSSION QUESTIONS

Directions: Briefly review the Study The Scriptures exercise from the text, highlighting the characteristics of effective biblical helpers. Then have participants meet with their partners to answer the following questions. Upon completion, partners should share the results of the Spiritual Inventory evaluation form as well as their answers to question 4 from the For Thought section of the text. Encourage them to spend a few minutes praying for one another. (Total Time: 30–45 minutes)

1. Read Luke 18:10–14. What does this parable teach us about the attitude we should have as helpers? When have you acted like a Pharisee? How could you prevent this attitude in yourself?

2. Read Gal. 6:1–10. Name at least nine characteristics of a biblical helper.

3. What are the six helping gifts listed in Rom. 12:7–8?

4. Read Ps. 101:6. What does this say to you as a helper?

GROUP ACTIVITIES

A. *Directions:* Have group members share the personal gifts and abilities they listed as they read chapter 4. You can list them on a blackboard or overhead projector. This exercise will help group members recognize each other's skills when they see them exhibited later on during the role-plays. (Time: 15 minutes) From Howard Stone's *The Caring Church* (San Francisco: Harper & Row, 1980), p. 30.

B. *Directions:* Before the group meets, copy the following list of helper temptations onto small pieces of paper. Assign participants to groups of twos and give each group one of the temptations to dramatize. One person acts as the friend in the situation; the other acts as the helper who is tempted. Both should try to illustrate the situation through their words, tone of voice, and body language. Group members who play the role of helper should consider a question such as, "How would pride affect what I say and how I come across?" The rest of the group guesses which temptation is being demonstrated and tries to recall other situations when they might face a similar temptation. (Time: 30 minutes. Note: The sex of the characters can be changed, if necessary.)

1. *"Holier than Thou."* Helper is tempted by pride and subtly communicates "I'm better than you."

   Situation: Your friend's son is caught shoplifting.

2. *"Let Me Hear the Gory Details."* Helper is tempted to gossip and to help for curiosity's sake and subtly communicates, "Tell me more, I'm fascinated."

   Situation: Your neighbor wants to leave her husband since she discovered that he has been having an affair.

3. *"Here Comes the Judge."* Helper is tempted to judge the other person and subtly communicates, "You're wrong."

   Situation: Your co-worker is living with his girlfriend and relates how his Christian parents can't understand the arrangement.

4. *"Let's Get Together Sometime."* Helper is sexually attracted to the friend being helped and subtly communicates, "I find

you attractive. Let's get together to talk again, I think you *really* need my help."

Situation: Your friend starts telling you about the problems he's having with his wife.

5. *"Where Is That Escape Hatch When I Need It?"* Helper is tempted to avoid the friend's problem and subtly communicates, "I'm uncomfortable with this topic. Let's talk about something else."

Situation: Your friend wants to tell you about how he has felt since his son killed himself.

6. *"Paste-A-Verse."* Helper is tempted to overspiritualize a problem and subtly communicates, "Just simply pray and trust God."

Situation: Friend's brother was just injured in a serious motorcycle accident.

7. *"God Is Too Busy for You."* Helper is tempted to underspiritualize a problem and subtly communicates, "God probably can't help you with that problem; you have to deal with it on your own."

Situation: Friend just lost his job.

8. *"Oh, You Poor Thing."* Helper is tempted to rely on one-sided information and therefore to jump to conclusions. Helper subtly communicates, "Of course you're right. The other person must be wrong."

Situation: Teenager complaining about how strict her father is and how he always beats her.

9. *"Let Me Do It for You."* Helper is tempted to encourage overdependency on the helper and subtly communicates, "Lean on me, I'll take care of you. I know how to run your life better than you do. Just trust me."

Situation: Friend asks you for advice on everything: how to talk to his mother-in-law, how to raise his children, how to ask his boss for a raise.

10. *"Super-helper to the Rescue."* Helper doesn't know his or her limits and subtly communicates, "I can solve all your problems."

Situation: Friend isn't sure where next month's rent will come from, and there's no food in the refrigerator. Helper feels compelled to loan the friend money to take care of these problems.

11. *"I Need You To Love Me and Need Me."* Helper helps in order to gain approval, love, and a feeling of being needed and subtly communicates, "You must like me and always need me."

Situation: Your friend is depressed, so you work hard at cheering her up. You buy her flowers, take her meals, and babysit her children.

12. *"Mary, the Martyr."* The helper wants to be paid back and subtly communicates, "After all I've done for you, you're not even thankful."

Situation: You frequently put yourself out for your friend who seems to get into one problem after another. You've tried to help her quit smoking, intervened in fights with her husband, and talked her out of killing herself.

13. *"I Can Top Yours."* Helper is tempted to take the focus off of the friend and subtly communicates, "That's not as bad as what happened to me."

Situation: Your friend is about to lose his job because he refuses to cheat like everyone else.

5

TAKE STOCK OF YOUR HELPING SKILLS

LESSON GOALS

1. To examine each group member's problem-solving style and to assess his or her helping skills at this point.
2. To review the first two parts of the book.

GROUP ACTIVITIES

A. Have group members meet with their partners and review the skill evaluation forms together. They should also share the results of their problem-solving checklist. Encourage them to reevaluate their goals and pray about any new insights they may have had about themselves. (Time: 15–30 minutes)

NOTE: If your group represents people who are to become formal lay counselors in your church, you may want to review all the evaluation forms. People who consistently scored high on the Obstacles sections may need to be encouraged to seek counseling help for themselves.

B. *Directions:* In the large group, review the two main categories of problems presented in the text: those lay helpers are equipped to deal with and those they need to refer. Ask group members to give examples from their own experiences of problems that fit into these different categories. Then ask them to think whether the person with the problem was hiding, wrestling with guilt or shame, experiencing a form of pride, having a problem with acceptance, suffering from a lack of information, tempted by some sort of evil, or facing a physical crisis. (Time: 15–30 minutes)

DISCUSSION QUESTIONS

Directions: These either can be answered in the large group or can be used with small groups. (Time: 15–30 minutes)

1. What does *noutheteo* mean? Using a concordance, find three references for the word "admonish" (NASB, NIV). What do you learn from these passages about being a helper?

2. What does *parakaleo* mean? Using a concordance, find three references for the word "comfort" (NASB, NIV). What do you learn from these passages about your role as a helper?

3. What does *dunamoo* mean? What does it tell you about your job as a helper?

4. Name three temptations you think you might experience in helping someone. How can you guard against these situations?

5. How can you tell the difference between putting Band-Aids on a problem and really helping a person work through a problem? Give examples of each.

A WORD ABOUT ROLE-PLAYING

The remaining lessons help group members begin to learn the helping skills. Much of their learning will be from role-playing. Don't hesitate to change the sex of the characters in the suggested role-plays. In the same way, group members can take off from these suggestions and ad-lib as they go along.

Your good-natured approach is an important tool to counter the resistance that will probably surface in reaction to role-playing. Be empathic towards group members who feel shy, but don't allow them to "cop out" from practicing their new skills. Encourage group members to associate the characters with someone they really know. When they are the helper, they should try to picture a real friend they are trying to help. When they are the friend, they should think of someone who has experienced something similar. Role-playing is often the most difficult but valuable part of the course.

Watch out for people who always volunteer to do the role-playing and thereby dominate the group. Encourage their participation but not to the exclusion of others.

It's helpful to begin each practice time by demonstrating one of the role-playing situations yourself. This breaks the ice and gives the participants an example of how to implement their new skills. Then divide the group up into smaller groups of threes. One person assumes the role of the friend with the problem. The second person, the helper, practices the skills learned in that lesson and the previous lessons. The third person is the observer who uses the Role-Play Evaluation Sheet found at the end of the Leader's Guide to give feedback to the helper.

Before the group meeting, photocopy enough evaluation forms for each group member to have several. It's also a good idea to review these forms with the group ahead of time so that they know what to observe. After the role-playing, the observer should let the helper keep the evaluation. Helpers should avoid trying out skills that are to be covered in future lessons. Keep the same groups for the sake of continuity and trust, unless the group is not interacting well. (When you organize the groups, mix talkers with quiet people.)

During the practice time, walk around the room and observe the different groups. Try to critique each group member. Gently point out areas that need correction. For example, many beginning helpers try to jump in and solve their friend's problems immediately. If you see this, ask the helper how he or she could respond differently. If you see someone get stuck, offer suggestions like, "Why don't you try active listening?" or "You could ask. . . ." to get a helper on track again.

Keep each role-play to about fifteen minutes and encourage everyone to try each of the three roles at least once. Remind students that their goal is to practice the particular helping skill, not necessarily to solve their friend's problem.

Ask a volunteer to role-play one of the situations in front of the entire group. If you have the equipment available, tape the role-playing. (Both video and audio taping are good training tools.) This way students have the chance to evaluate their strengths and weaknesses further.

When group members ask questions about specific cases, encourage them to think about what they have already learned and how they can apply that information. This encourages them to figure out answers to their own questions and prevents you from rescuing them!

6

LOVE AND WELCOME: THE FOUNDATION FOR HELPING

LESSON GOALS

1. To teach and demonstrate biblical acceptance.
2. To introduce role-playing, explaining how it is a chance to try out helping skills in a safe environment.
3. To review the biblical principles presented in the text.

GROUP ACTIVITIES

A. Practice Attending Skills

Directions: Form groups of two (or ask people to use their partners). In each pair, choose one person to be person A and another to be person B. Instruct person B to begin a normal conversation, and instruct person A to pay attention to what person B is saying (by leaning forward slightly with relaxed and open posture while maintaining eye contact). Instruct person A to stop attending to person B at some point in the conversation (person A can appear distracted, fidget, interrupt eye contact, switch subjects, or have a closed posture). After a few minutes, have group members reverse roles. Afterwards reassemble into the large group and ask the following questions. (Time: 15 minutes)

1. What was this experience like for you? How did you feel when you were attended to? How about when you were not attended to?

2. How did you feel when you were paying attention to the other person? How did you feel when you were not attending? Which was more comfortable for you? Is there some aspect of attending to another person that makes you feel uncomfortable? Why?

3. For practice, keep track of your interactions with your friends. When do you pay attention to them and when do you stop listening?

B. Practice Empathy Skills

1. *Directions:* Before class, write out the feeling words listed in the next two exercises on slips of paper. Begin this activity by handing a slip of paper to each person. Group members must silently act out the emotion while other group members try to guess what emotion is being portrayed. Actors should think of a time that they felt this emotion and consider how that feeling affected their body posture, body movements, and facial expressions. (Feelings expressed in similar ways are suggested in the parenthesis. These synonyms are also acceptable.) If group members fail to guess an emotion, try to find out why. Perhaps the actor has difficulty showing that particular emotion, or the group is not reading him or her well. (Time: 30 minutes)

Feeling Words: defeated (failure); shocked (stunned, surprised); contented (relaxed, peaceful); frustrated (exasperated); excited (joyful, happy); sad (depressed, grieved); anxious (worried, nervous); confident (self-assured); angry (furious); fearful (suspicious); playful; embarrassed (guilty, ashamed); hurt (pained, anguish); critical (judgmental, harsh).

2. *Directions:* Assign each group member a different emotion from this second set of feeling words. This time, the actors must communicate the feeling by their tone of voice while the group guesses what they are feeling. Using the following statement: "Tom called me today," the group member should try to "sound" the feeling that he or she is assigned. Once again, the actor should focus on a time that he or she felt like that and act as if the feeling is present right now. Group members should close their eyes to screen out all other nonverbal data.

Feeling Words: annoyed (irritated, exasperated); angry (bitter); worried (anxious, unsure, afraid, doubtful); rejected (hurt); kind (caring); surprised (shocked); hopeful; great (wonderful); indifferent (apathetic, bored); jealous (suspicious, competitive); proud; disappointed; critical (harsh).

C. Role-Play

Directions: Form groups of threes and have group members take turns acting out the roles in the six situations listed below. The helper needs to focus on showing love, acceptance, and understanding to the friend. Photocopy the Love and Acceptance Evaluation Sheet found at the end of the Leader's Guide. The observer uses this evaluation sheet to give feedback to the helper. Group members may not be able to practice each skill in each role-play. (Time: 30–45 minutes)

1. Several years ago you and a friend planned to go into business together, but at the last minute you pulled out of the deal. Now you're in trouble financially, and you hope your friend to whom you are now talking will help you out.

2. To secure a promotion in your company, you would have to falsify reports about meeting your sales quota for the year. You are talking to a relative about the situation.

3. You're a college senior and have a boyfriend who has asked you to marry him. However, your parents strongly disapprove of him because he's not a Christian. You are talking to a friend who has known you for several years.

4. Your wife just left you after fifteen years of marriage. You have two young children who are asking where mommy is and when she is coming back. You are talking to someone in your Bible study group.

5. Your grandmother is dying of cancer, and as far as you know, she's not a Christian. You're also upset because you have never shared the gospel with her. You are talking with a Christian medical professional whom you just met.

6. You are caught smoking pot at school. At the same time your parents find out that you are close to failing several subjects. You are talking to your youth group advisor.

DISCUSSION QUESTIONS

Directions: If you have extra time, consider one of the following questions:

1. Review Study the Scriptures from chapter 6. Ask group members which Scripture verses were particularly important to them.

2. Review the eight practical ways of helping someone. Think of times when you *did not* handle a situation correctly. What went wrong and why?

3. Ask group members to define the *opposite* of biblical acceptance. Talk about the many ways that we might unknowingly
   communicate rejection, such as avoiding a person, rolling our
   eyes, scowling. (Total time: 15–30 minutes)

7

LEARN TO LISTEN: THE FIRST LEVEL OF HELPING

LESSON GOALS

1. To encourage group members to learn how to listen for
   the *content, feelings,* and *implications* of their friends'
   messages. This will enable them to ask more penetrating
   questions directing their friends toward biblical thinking
   and action.
2. To demonstrate how active listening clarifies and defines
   people's problems at the same time that it shows
   understanding and acceptance.
3. To show group members how to integrate active
   listening into their normal conversations.

ICEBREAKERS

1. Begin the group time by talking about something that is
   happening in your life. Afterward ask group members to
   write down the content, feelings, and possible implications of what you said. Compare their answers. How are
   they the same or different? Did different group members
   hear different aspects of your message? Review the

concept of listening filters and how that influences the messages we receive.
2. Review the active listening response and make sure that everyone understands each component. Demonstrate some good active listening responses as well as some responses that cut off communication. Be sure to integrate active listening responses into your teaching so that your group can see how it is an effective form of communication. (Total time: 15–30 minutes)

GROUP ACTIVITIES

A. Active-Listening Ball-Toss

Directions: Bring three small, easy-to-catch, different colored balls to the group. (Soft children's balls work well.) With a piece of masking tape label one "closed response," one "active-listening response," and one "next question."

Have the group form a circle with their chairs. Explain that you're going to read a statement and then throw out the three different balls. The person who catches the ball labeled "closed response" must give a response that would stop communication. (This is usually a judgmental response—the easiest to give!) The person who catches the ball labeled "active listening" must give an active-listening response. The person who catches the third ball must ask an open-ended question that pursues the possible implications of the original statement. Group members can help each other out. After you've read the first statement and the class has responded, let the group members throw the balls to one another for the rest of the exercise. This exercise is not only a good teaching tool, but it's also a lot of fun! (Time: 30 minutes)

1. "I feel so lousy all the time. My course work is harder than I expected, so I put off doing it. Of course, nothing gets done. I feel like hanging it all up. I mean, why bother even trying? I can't do anything right away."

2. "Cheryl just took the kids and walked out and said she was never coming back! I can't believe she would do this to me!"

3. "I've never told anyone this before. It's hard to even talk to you. I just had to get it off my chest. You see, I've been having an affair for three years."

4. "I feel so fat, but I can never stick to a diet. No wonder no one ever talks to me. They probably think I'm just a fat slob and no one wants to be friends with a slob!"

5. "Frank and I just aren't getting along these days. We disagree on everything, and he never listens to my opinions any more. Sometimes I think I would be better off without him."

6. "They're posting the lay-off list at work tomorrow. What if my name is on it? What will I do? How will I support my family?"

7. "Do you really think that God forgives *everything*? I feel like my abortion can never be forgiven."

8. "Bill and I never talk anymore. He works, comes home, has dinner, reads the paper, watches TV, and goes to bed. I feel like I'm married to a zombie! What happened to our marriage?"

9. "The doctor told Beth that after this last miscarriage we really shouldn't try to have kids. She's so angry at God, and I don't blame her."

10. "I don't know what's wrong with Philip. He's always so busy with his friends that we never do anything together anymore."

11. "I get so nervous every time I have to speak in front of a group. My mouth goes dry and I can't even find my voice to speak. I feel like a fool."

12. "Things just haven't been the same for me since mom died. Why did God take her from me?"

13. "I don't want an abortion, but I'm just ready to start college, and I can't go to school pregnant. And if my parents find out, they're going to kill me! What will their church friends think of me? What should I do?"

14. "I can't talk to my parents at all. They just don't understand what it's like to be a teenager today."

15. "After all those times I messed up, I finally got my driver's license!"

B. Active-Listening Role-Playing

Directions: Form groups of threes. Each person takes turns at being the helper, the friend with the problem, and the observer. The helper should practice asking open-ended questions and using active listening, alternating these responses as it fits the conversation. The friend acts out the situation described, and the observer uses one of the Role-Play Evaluation Sheets to give feedback to the helper. Groups should spend approximately 10–15 minutes with each role-play and 5 minutes for the observer and friend to give the helper feedback. (Time: 45 minutes)

1. You are angry with your friend (the one who is helping you) because you feel left out of her life ever since she got married. "I don't understand what has happened between us. I thought we were friends!"

2. Your teenage son just got caught skipping school. Last week you found cigarettes in his jeans. You ask your neighbor, "What's wrong with kids today? I would never have tried this stuff when I was his age!"

3. You just went through a painful divorce after your husband left you. You are talking on the phone to a friend who doesn't go to your church: "I can't stand how everybody at church looks at me differently now. I feel as if I'm a marked person!"

4. You are a father of three teenage children. You say to a co-worker, "The kids never listen to me anymore. I yell and they just ignore me."

5. You're sixty-two and thinking of retiring. You mention to a co-worker, "I feel like my life is over now. What's left for me?"

6. Your newborn child is born retarded. You are talking to a friend from church: "I can't believe that a loving God would do this to us."

Note: If your group prefers, members can use real-life situations that they are experiencing now, instead of the role-playing examples above.

8

SPEAK THE TRUTH: THE SECOND LEVEL OF HELPING

LESSON GOALS

1. To integrate the "I statements" formula into normal conversations.
2. To integrate the speaking skills of feedback, self-disclosure, affirmation, and finding the big picture into a total helping response.

ICEBREAKERS

Discuss a time that someone did not speak the truth in love to you. How did the other person come across? What was not loving in his or her approach? How did it make you feel? (Time: 15 minutes)

GROUP ACTIVITIES

A. Speaking-skills Ball-toss

Directions: Relabel the three balls that you used for lesson 7, marking the first, "When you," the second, "I feel," and the third, "I statement." This is the same exercise that you did with active listening, except the group will take the following statements and revise them using the "I statement" formula. Have the group form a circle. You read a statement and then toss the balls. The person who catches the first ball will label the other person's behavior; the person who catches the second ball will label the speaker's feelings or thoughts; and the third person will give the full "I statement." Again, if someone gets stuck, encourage everyone to help out with the answers. After you've thrown the first balls, the group members throw them to each other for the rest of the exercise. Remind the class that these statements may be legitimate confrontations. *How* they are said will determine whether or not they are heard. (Time: 30 minutes)

1. "You spend too much money on yourself and don't give enough to the Lord."

2. "Can't you leave me alone? Your constant chatter is driving me nuts!"

3. "You're so busy with all your church activities that you never have time for me anymore."

4. "You mean to tell me that you invited your friends from work without even consulting me first?"

5. "You don't care how you look when we go out. What do you think other people think when they see you dressed like that?"

6. "It was really stupid to blow up at your boss like that. Now look where it's got you."

7. "What a mess this kitchen is! I can't stand even walking into it!"

8. "You're never around anymore. I can't help it if our friendship isn't what it used to be."

9. "Don't you think you should have a little more self-control? I mean, another piece of cake was overdoing it a little, wasn't it?"

10. "Everything always goes so well for you. You could never understand how bad my life is."

11. "Your laziness gets me furious!"

12. "You never trust me."

B. Speaking-skills Role-playing

Directions: Form groups of threes and role-play the following situations. Once again each person should take a turn at being the friend with the problem, the helper, and the observer. The friend begins with a statement based on the problem described below. The helper responds with one of the speaking skills: "I statements," feedback, self-disclosure, giving the big picture, or affirmation. Helpers also should continue active listening as they try to help their friend identify and take responsibility for the problem. Walk around the class and help students who get stuck. Make sure they don't move on to problem solving yet! (Time: 45 minutes)

Note: If your group used personal experiences in the last lesson, they could continue with those situations rather than using the ones listed below.

1. Everyone else seems to have it better than you. Other people get promoted when you stay in the same job; others serve on important committees when you're never asked to do anything. It looks to you as if God really hasn't given you a fair share in life. But when someone tries to encourage you, you frequently respond with "Yes, but" or "I can't." Your helper is a long-time friend who has heard you talk about this before.

2. You are talking to a friend in the church about the problems you are having in your Bible study. The leader says that you are too critical and that you always find fault with other people's contributions. You don't understand why other Christians don't see things the way you do.

3. Your life is a mess: your boss is mad at you for a silly mistake you made; your roommate asked you to move out; your diet isn't working; and the car your brother sold you needs repair. Even God doesn't seem to be coming through on His promises to take care of you! You're talking with a co-worker after work and having a hard time seeing your responsibility in any of these situations.

4. You are thirty-five and single. A non-Christian divorced person starts paying a lot of attention to you and you find yourself attracted to him (her). You date for two months and the relationship quickly becomes serious. You are talking to someone from your Bible study.

5. You are a teacher and have been unemployed for a year. You just completed further course work in education without doing very well. You can't understand why you can't get a job as a teacher since that has been your dream for a long time. You are talking to a relative.

6. Your mother, with whom you weren't very close, died six months ago. Your neighbor asks how you are doing since you talk about her death a lot. You say that you are very sad, but, in truth, you don't act upset. It appears that you are looking for attention more than you are mourning your mother.

DISCUSSION QUESTIONS

1. Review the cases from the Personal and Practical section of chapter 8. What were the sins involved in each situation? How did the people hide from seeing their own problems? Did they feel guilt and shame? How did pride manifest itself? Was there a problem not accepting self or another person? Was information lacking? How did the problems of evil affect these people? How would you try to minister both comfort and confrontation to these people?

2. What obstacles might you meet in speaking the truth to a friend? Consider both your own difficulties as well as any resistance your friend might show. (Total time: 15–30 minutes)

Note: At the end of the meeting, have students write down one or two situations they have difficulty confronting. Use these as case examples for the next lesson.

9

CONFRONT BIBLICALLY

LESSON GOALS

1. To encourage group members to practice biblical confrontation.

2. To review that the way God has dealt with us models the way that we are to help others.

GROUP ACTIVITY

Directions: Highlight the techniques of confrontation by role-playing before the group a situation that you have talked about in previous meetings. Then form the same groups used in the last lesson. The groups should resume their role-playing at the point at which they left off last time—either continuing the conversation or assuming that this talk is a follow-up to the previous one.

The friend begins with a statement based on his or her problem. The helper should gradually work into confrontation, following the rules in the text. Once again, the helper's goal is not to solve the friend's problem but to make sure the friend is taking responsibility for his or her problem and is ready to change. Encourage the friends not to be helped too easily. That gives the helpers more realistic opportunities to practice their feedback, "I statements," and confrontation skills. (Time: 45 minutes-1 hour)

DISCUSSION QUESTIONS

1. Discuss with the group the ways that God has dealt with us. In what ways does the helping process (as described in the last four lessons) parallel God's interaction with us?

2. Review the words *parakaleo* and *noutheteo* from lesson 3. What two themes of the counseling process did each represent? How have you seen them represented in the last four lessons? What aspects of the counseling process would you consider parakletic? What aspects nouthetic? In what ways are they joined together?

3. If you have extra time, review the Study the Scripture section from the text. (Time: 30 minutes)

10

DIRECT TOWARD ACTION: THE THIRD LEVEL OF HELPING

LESSON GOALS

1. To help group members learn how to encourage their friends toward action.
2. To encourage group members to integrate Scripture into the help they give.
3. To further develop the characteristics of a biblical helper.

GROUP ACTIVITY

Directions: Now that it's time to put all the helping skills together, the "helpers" will get a chance to see some action! Have group members use the situations from the previous two lessons, imagining that this is the third time they are talking to their friend. The helper should use the Ten Steps Towards Taking Action from the text to develop a specific plan of action. They also should indicate how they will follow up on the help they give.

Observers should look at whether the helper is doing more of the problem solving than the friend. Have the groups discuss what was said after about fifteen minutes of role-playing. As you observe, encourage helpers to consider what Scripture verses they might use as they help their friend. They can read either a specific verse or paraphrase an appropriate passage, depending on the situation. (Time: 45 minutes-1 hour)

EXTRA ROLE-PLAYS

The following situations can be used to supplement the cases that are already provided. (They can be used in addition to or as alternatives to the previous role-plays.)

Situation: You are confiding to the leader of your Bible study that you just lost your second programming job in three years. You feel like it's no use trying to find another job because you'll probably lose that one, too. You say, "I can't seem to make anything work. My bosses always pick on me, no one seems to like me wherever I work. I guess I may as well resign myself that I will never be a computer programmer."

Situation: You are angry with yourself because the third woman in a row just refused to go out with you. In your anger, you call yourself names ("You're a no good fat slob!"); overeat ("What's the use anyway, I may as well enjoy myself."); or put the other person down ("I'm never going to call another woman again! They're all a bunch of snobs!"). You are talking to a friend from church.

Situation: You are nervous in new situations and are very worried about how others perceive you. You think about this a lot and as a result have difficulty speaking in groups of people. You say to a close friend, "I feel so embarrassed. I feel like crawling into a hole whenever someone asks me a question. I'd rather die than say the wrong thing!"

DISCUSSION QUESTIONS

1. Review the three situations listed above. What were the problems these individuals faced? If there was sin involved, what was it? In what ways did they hide? Were there experiences of guilt and shame? How did pride surface? Was there a problem with not accepting self or another person? Was information lacking in any of the situations? If they were Christians, what kind of problems did they seem to have in relationship to God?

2. Discuss the different ways that helpers can use the Bible. What extremes do helpers need to avoid? Point out how helpers need to be compassionate and understanding at the same time that they communicate God's truth. (Total time: 15–30 minutes)

11

CRISIS INTERVENTION AND INITIATING HELP

LESSON GOALS

1. To help group members apply their helping skills to the processes of crisis intervention and initiating help.
2. To review the goals that group members set in the beginning of the course.

ICEBREAKERS

1. Have members meet with their partners briefly to review the goals they set in lesson 1. Are they still working on them? If not, why not? Have their goals changed?
2. Back in the large group, ask for volunteers to describe a crisis in their life and talk about what helped them through it, what didn't help, and why. (Total time: 15–30 minutes)

GROUP ACTIVITIES

Directions: Form groups of threes for the following two sets of role-plays. Each person should get at least one chance to be the helper, the friend needing help, and the observer in each set. In the first set, the friend begins the role-play; in the second, the helper begins. In each situation ask group members to consider:

- What is this person feeling and why?
- What are the first things you would do to help?
- What further steps would you take?
- How would you use active listening, "I statements," and feedback?
- What plan of action is necessary?
- How would you communicate hope?

- How and when would you follow up on this person?

A. Role-Playing for Crisis Intervention (Time: 30 minutes)

1. Your sister-in-law's baby is born with Down's syndrome. She can't seem to shake her depression and is barely taking care of the child, her house, or herself. Your brother calls you and asks you to talk to her.

2. A neighbor's son runs away from home. She is frantic as she calls you on the phone after finding a note saying that he was fed up with the family arguments and so decided to leave.

3. Your best friend's wife is seriously injured in a car accident. He receives the call at work and turns to you for help.

4. Your friend calls you sobbing and hysterical. She finally blurts out that she was raped on the way home from work.

5. Your father is forced into early retirement. Your mother tells you that he either lies around watching TV or locks himself in his room while he works on his "affairs." She begs you to talk to him.

6. Your Sunday school student's father dies, and she is feeling very angry with God. Her aunt told her that it is sinful to be angry and that she should just trust God.

B. Role-Playing for Initiating Help (Time: 30 minutes)

1. You have a friend who is frequently discouraged and calls you to tell you his problems: he can't get along with people at work, his job isn't going well, and he feels lonely and discouraged. He says he would like to be a more positive person but he talks in terms of "nothing good ever happens to me." You want to help him but are reluctant because he has resisted your help in the past.

2. You heard in church that Marianne, thirty-five, just miscarried her second baby. You are at the hospital visiting her.

3. Your married business partner starts dating one of the secretaries in your office.

4. You see an acquaintance crying during church.

5. You read in the local paper that a friend from high school just filed for divorce. He is forty-five and has three kids. You decide to give him a call to see how he's doing.

6. You have a friend who is a practicing homosexual and who considers himself a Christian. You pray about the situation and decide to talk to him.

Discussion Questions

1. When do you think you need an invitation before stepping in to help a friend? Under what circumstances don't you need one?

2. When was the last time that you experienced personal risk in helping in a crisis? In retrospect, were you the best person to offer help in that situation? Why or why not?

3. What types of people do you avoid offering help to because you feel uncomfortable when you are with them?

4. Role-play a person in crisis and have group members try to help you. You can pick either a real situation from your own life or one of the following: you have been mugged or raped; your car was burglarized; you just heard that your spouse has cancer; your son was born with brain damage; or you are thinking about killing yourself. (Total time: 15–30 minutes)

NOTE TO LEADERS: Be aware that emotional issues like death, rape, abuse, or life-threatening illnesses will bring up a lot of feelings for group members. Be prepared to spend some time talking about personal incidents. With their permission, use group members' experiences as material for class discussion and role-playing.

12

HELPING NON-CHRISTIANS AND PEOPLE FROM OTHER CULTURES

LESSON GOALS

1. To encourage group members to think about how to apply their helping skills when talking to non-Christians and people from other cultures.
2. To develop sensitivity to the problems of cross-cultural counseling. To become aware of the time, effort, and energy that goes into cross-cultural helping.

ICEBREAKERS

1. Ask several group members to talk about their pre-Christian experience. What did Christians do or not do that helped them in coming to believe the gospel?
2. Ask several group members to talk about their own cultures and what they think might be helpful in reaching people from a similar background. (Total time: 15–30 minutes)

GROUP ACTIVITY

Directions: Role play the following situations. Encourage the helper to try to get inside the other person's shoes and to understand the experience from his or her perspective. Once again, form groups of threes. Have group members take turns being the helper, the friend, and the observer. (Time: 45 minutes)

1. Your non-Christian friend is very angry because his fiancée left him. He asks you to help him "get even" with her for dumping him.

2. You have befriended a Vietnamese family that moved into your neighborhood six months ago. The mother seems very unhappy to you, but when you ask her what's wrong, she just shrugs her shoulders and answers, "Nothing."

3. Your non-Christian brother and his girlfriend are coming for an overnight visit. They expect to sleep in the same room.

4. You have a friend who is in college and who has been depressed ever since his brother died in a motorcycle accident. Before this death, he asked a lot of questions about God. Since then he hasn't wanted to talk about Christianity.

5. The sixteen-year-old boy who lives next door confides that his girlfriend is pregnant. He wants to know where they should go for an abortion. Neither he nor his girlfriend are Christians.

6. A Brazilian family begins attending your church. You invite them over for dinner and during the conversation, the wife tells you that she has been very frustrated because she can't find a good maid. She's not used to having to take care of everything herself and feels at a loss in knowing how to manage the household.

DISCUSSION QUESTIONS

1. How would you help a friend who does not want to change? Think about a homosexual who is comfortable with his sexual "preference" or a woman who won't do anything about her drug-addicted husband who beats her and their children.

2. In what ways can you open your life to someone from another culture? Are there people from other cultures to whom you could reach out? How could you do this?

3. Consider how Jesus talked to the woman at the well. He took an ordinary event and turned it into an opportunity to tell her the gospel. What opportunities for evangelism do you have in your day-to-day experiences with non-Christians? (Total time: 15–30 minutes)

13

LOOKING UPWARD, INWARD, AND OUTWARD: A REPRISE

LESSON GOALS

1. To have group members complete their self-evaluations through personal inventory and feedback from other members.
2. To practice the skills of referral and prevention.
3. To encourage group members to consider the ways they will use their helping skills in the future.

ICEBREAKERS

With their partners, have group members compare the results of the Evaluate Your Skills evaluation with the feedback they received from the observers in the role-plays. Compare these self-evaluations with the ones completed in lesson 5. Encourage them to talk about the ways they have changed or stayed the same. Are there any patterns to their progress or lack of progress? (Time: 15 minutes)

GROUP ACTIVITIES

A. Referral Role Playing

Directions: Form groups of threes and role-play the situations listed below. At what point should the helper decide to bring in another helper? What other services do these friends need? How should the idea of referral be introduced? How should the helper follow up with this friend? (Time: 30 minutes)

1. Your daughter's friend, Terri, is fourteen years old, 5'3", and weighs ninety pounds. When she comes to your house after

school, she is very picky about what she will and will not eat for a snack. Your daughter tells you that Terri confided to her that at home she eats huge amounts of ice cream, pretzels, and cookies and then makes herself vomit. Terri is at your house when you decide to talk to her.

2. Your friend Alan calls you late one night. He's obviously had a few drinks and isn't talking too clearly. His wife is threatening to leave him because of his drinking. All he can think about is "ending it all" because "why should I bother going on if she's going to leave me?"

3. Your friend Marie tells you about her latest shopping spree in which she bought everyone in the family new clothes and shoes. She says that it makes her feel good to shop. She is talking a mile a minute and can't sit still. You're a little surprised by her behavior since the week before she was pretty down in the dumps. You've noticed that this isn't the first time that her moods have changed so much in such a short period of time.

B. Prevention Role-Playing

Directions: Before role-playing the situations below, have group members think about the following: What is going on with this person? What problems should you look for? What are you trying to prevent? What resources would you suggest to this person? (Time: 30 minutes)

1. Betty is a single parent of a thirteen-month-old boy. You observe that ever since Sammy was born, Betty's attendance at church has been very irregular. When she does come, she refuses to leave him in the church nursery and always keeps him with her. When you ask her how she's doing, she smiles and says that everything is wonderful since Sammy was born: they go shopping, out to dinner, and even to the movies together! You are concerned about Betty's relationship to her son and decide to talk with her.

2. Paul is a teenager in your youth group who appears very sullen and angry. You find out that his father left home when he was twelve and he has had to help out by working after-school jobs ever since. He brags that he can't wait until he is sixteen and will be able to drop out of school and get a "real" job.

3. Whenever you visit your friends Jeff and Lorraine, they always seem to be in the middle of a fight. Although they quickly "make up" and laugh it off, you wonder what is really going on.

DISCUSSION QUESTIONS

1. Have group members review the social services available in your community. If you are not personally aware of them, invite a knowledgeable social service person to talk to the group.

2. Ask group members to discuss how they can be more effective in reaching out to people in their church or neighborhood. Brainstorm about new ways of showing Christ's love. It can be as simple as each person greeting one person or family whom they don't know and inviting them home for dinner after church, or organizing a block party to get to know your neighbors.

3. With their partners, have members write out how they plan to use their helping skills in the future. Have them also discuss the helping skills they plan to continue working on and how.

4. Have group members take turns sharing what they've learned during the last thirteen weeks. Specifically, invite them to comment on how they have or have not reached their goals.

5. Have group members summarize their feedback to one another using the observations from the role-play exercises. If the group is small (up to ten people), this can be done as an entire group. If your group is large, form smaller groups.

6. If this is the beginning of a lay counseling training program in your church, take time to plan for future classes.

7. End with a time of prayer for one another. (Total time: 30 minutes–1 hour)

LOVE AND ACCEPTANCE EVALUATION SHEET

1. Helper uses prayer appropriately. _____

2. Helper pays attention to his or her friend. _____

3. Helper maintains good eye contact. _____

4. Helper seems relaxed and at ease. _____

5. Helper has an open posture. _____

6. Helper withholds judgment and advice. _____

7. Helper demonstrates understanding and empathy. _____

8. Helper touches his or her friend. _____

9. Helper offers concrete ways of helping the friend. _____

10. Helper demonstrates an attitude of forbearance. _____

11. Helper communicates trust and confidentiality. _____

ROLE-PLAY EVALUATION SHEET

Observer _____

Helper _____

Directions: Use the following evaluation form for the role-plays in Part III. The observer gives feedback to the helper by placing slash marks in the blanks corresponding to the number of times the helper exhibits each behavior. Sample responses can also be recorded. The numbers in the parentheses refer to the chapter in which the skills are discussed. New skills are added in each consecutive role-play. Some of the responses listed below are *not* helpful. Which ones are they?

1. Helper pays attention to his or her friend. _____ (6)

2. Helper looks away from his or her friend. _____ (6)

3. Helper seems relaxed and at ease. _____ (5)

4. Helper touches his or her friend. _____ (6)

5. Helper seems nervous. _____ (5)

6. Helper accurately paraphrases the content of his or her friend's statements. _____ (7)

7. Helper accurately reflects his or her friend's feelings. _____ (7)

8. Helper seems to understand the implication of his or her friend's statements. _____ (7)

9. Helper paces his or her responses. _____ (6, 7)

10. Helper asks a series of questions without pausing for an answer. _____ (7)

11. Helper asks probing questions that gain more information without making his or her friend uncomfortable. _____ (7)

12. Helper asks questions that are answered simply with yes/no answers. _____ (7)

13. Helper is open and undefensive. _____ (6, 7)

14. Helper is helpful and encouraging. _____ (4, 6, 8)

15. Helper understands his or her friend's viewpoint. _____ (6, 7)

16. Helper uses "I statements." _____ (8)

17. Helper gives advice. _____ (9, 10)

18. Helper is comfortable with silence. _____ (7)

19. Helper talks about his/her own experience. _____ (8)

20. Helper gives good feedback. _____ (8)

21. Helper changes the focus of the conversation. _____ (8)

22. Helper shows warmth and empathy. _____ (6, 7)

23. Helper is patient. _____ (4, 5, 6, 7)

24. Helper seems overly curious. _____ (4, 5)

25. Helper encourages his or her friend to appropriate action. _____ (10)

26. Helper suggests appropriate referral. _____ (13)

27. Helper uses Scripture appropriately. _____ (9, 10, 12)

28. Helper suggests some ways he or she will follow up. _____ (10, 11)

OTHER COMMENTS:

Permission to copy this form for training purposes only is hereby granted by the author.

APPENDIX A

HOW TO FIND A CHRISTIAN COUNSELOR

If you are having difficulty finding a Christian counselor for yourself or a friend, the following national organizations can provide names and address of counselors in your area. Since each of these organizations reflect a slightly different professional orientation, individual counselors may vary. Before recommending any particular counselor to a friend, talk to your pastor and contact the individual counselor to find out his or her specific views on Christian counseling.

Dr. Harold Ellens, Executive Director
Christian Association for Psychological Studies
26705 Farmington Road
Farmington Hills, MI 48018

Dr. Robert R. King, Jr.
Christian Association for Psychological Studies
P.O. Box 789
Blue Jay, CA 92317

National Association for Christians in Social Work
Box 84
Wheaton, IL 60187

Dr. Eyrich
National Association of Nouthetic Counseling
c/o Kirk of the Hills Presbyterian Church
12928 Ladve Road
St. Louis, MO 63141

APPENDIX B

SCRIPTURE VERSES FOR USE IN COUNSELING[1]

2 Timothy 3:16–17

Hebrews 4:12

The following list of Scripture verses is not exhaustive but rather suggests some passages you can use when helping a friend. You may want to add verses that you have found helpful for yourself or the people you've helped. Encourage the people whom you help to write down their favorite verses also.

As you refer to these Scripture verses, keep in mind that when people are struggling with personal or family problems, they may have difficulty appropriating God's promises. Begin by acknowledging God's promises *and* your friend's feelings. Move on to studying the verses that describe trusting God's faithfulness, and then look at particular passages that speak to your friend's problems.

Anxiety: Ps. 43:5; Matt. 6:31–32; Phil. 4:6, 19; 1 Peter 5:7.

Bereavement: Deut. 31:8; Ps. 30:5, 11; 119:50; Eccl. 3:4; Phil. 3:8; 1 Thess. 4:13–18; Rev. 21:4.

Comfort: Ps. 91:14–15; Lam. 3:22–23; Matt. 5:4; 11:28–30; John 14:16, 18; 2 Cor. 1:3–4.

Conflict resolution: Matt. 5:23–25; Luke 17:3–4; Eph. 4:26–27.

Death: Ps. 23:4; Ps. 116; Isa. 25:8–9; Rom. 14:8; 1 Cor. 15:20–27; 2 Cor. 5:1–9; Phil. 1:21; 1 Thess. 5:9–11; Heb. 9:27.

Developing confidence: Ps. 27:3; Prov. 3:26; Eph. 3:6–12; Phil. 1:6; 4:13; Heb. 10:35; 1 Peter 2:9.

Difficulties: Rom. 8:28; Heb. 5:8; 12:7–11; Rev. 3:19.

Disappointment: Ps. 54:4, 55:22; John 14:27; 2 Cor. 4:8–9.

Discouragement: Josh. 1:9; Ps. 27:14; 43:5; John 14:1, 27; 16:33; Heb. 4:16; 1 John 5:14.

Faith: Rom. 4:3; 10:17; Eph. 2:8–9; Heb. 11:1–12:1; James 1:3, 5–6; 1 Peter 1:7.

Fear: Ps. 27:1; 34:4; 46:1–2; 56:11; 94:19; Prov. 3:25–26; Isa. 51:12–13; Rom. 8:31; 2 Tim. 1:7; 1 John 4:18.

Forgiveness of sin: Ps. 32:1–5; Ps. 51; Ps. 103:3, 10–12; Prov. 28:13; Isa. 1:18; Isa. 53; Isa. 55:7; Rom. 8:1; James 5:15–16; 1 John 1:9.

Forgiving others: Matt. 6:12, 14; 18:21–35; Mark 11:25; Eph. 4:32; Col. 3:13.

Friends and friendliness: Prov. 18:24; Matt. 22:39; John 13:35; Gal. 6:1, 9–10.

God's love: Jer. 31:3; John 3:16; 15:9; Rom. 5:8; 8:38–39; Eph. 3:17b–19; 1 John 3:1.

God's provision: Ps. 37:3–4; Isa. 58:11; Matt. 6:33; 2 Cor. 9:8–9; Phil. 4:19.

Growing spiritually: Eph. 3:17–19; Phil. 1:6; Col. 1:9–11; 3:16; 1 Tim. 4:15; 1 Peter 2:1–2; 2 Peter 1:5–8; 3:17–18.

Guidance: Ps. 32:8; Prov. 3:5–6; Isa. 30:21; 48:17; 58:11; John 16:13.

Help and care: 2 Chron. 16:9a; Ps. 37:5, 23–24; 55:22; Ps. 77; Ps. 91:4; Heb. 4:16; 13:5b–6; 1 Peter 5:7.

Hope: Job 19:25–26; Isa. 40:31; Jer. 29:11–13; Rom. 5:3–5; 8:24–25; 15:4.

Loneliness: Deut. 33:27a; Josh. 1:5; Ps. 23; Ps. 27:10; 23:25–28; Isa.41:10; Matt. 28:20; Heb. 13:5.

Love one another: Matt. 5:39–48; Luke 10:30–37; John 15:12–17; 1 Peter 4:8.

Obedience: 1 Sam. 15:22; Ps. 111:10; 119:2; John 14:15, 21; 1 John 3:22–24.

Peace of mind: Isa. 26:3–4; John 14:27; 16:33; Rom. 5:1; Phil. 4:6–7; Col. 3:15.

Persecution: Matt. 5:10–11; 10:21–22; Acts 5:41; Rom. 8:17; 2 Tim. 3:12; 1 Peter 2:20.

Praise and gratitude: 1 Sam. 12:24; Ps. 34:1–8; 51:15; Ps. 100; Ps. 107:8–9; 139:14; Eph. 5:19–20; Heb. 13:15.

Protection from danger: Ps. 23:3–4; 32:7; 34:7, 17, 19; 61:1–4; 91:11; 121:3, 8; Isa. 43:2; Rom. 14:8.

Return of Christ: Luke 21:35–6; Acts 1:11; 1 Thess. 4:16–18; Titus 2:13; 1 John 3:2–3.

Sickness: Ps. 41:3; 103:3; Matt. 4:23; James 5:15–16.

Sin: Isa. 53:5–6; 59:1–2; John 8:34; Rom. 3:23; 6:23; Gal. 6:7–8.

Sorrow: Isa. 53:4; John 16:22; 2 Cor. 6:10; 1 Thess. 4:13–14; Rev. 21:4.

Strength: Ps. 27:14; 28:7; Isa. 40:29, 31; 2 Cor. 12:9; Phil. 4:13.

Suffering: Acts 14:22; Rom. 8:18; 2 Cor. 1:3–5; 5:1–9; Phil. 1:29; 3:10; 2 Tim. 2:11–12; 1 Peter 2:19; 4:12–13, 16; 1 Peter 5:10.

Temptation: 1 Cor. 10:12–13; Heb. 2:18; James 1:2–4, 12–14; 1 Peter 1:6–7; 2 Peter 2:9; Jude 24.

Trusting God: Ps. 18:2; 37:5; 40:1–4; Isa. 12:2.

Victory: Ps. 98:1; Rom. 8:35–37; 1 Cor. 15:55, 57; 1 John 5:4; Rev. 21:7.

[1] Adapted from Selwyn Hughes, *Helping People Through Their Problems* (Minneapolis: Bethany House, 1981), pp. 184–85 and Jay Adams, *The Use of Scriptures in Counseling* (Phillipsburg, New Jersey: Presbyterian and Reformed, 1975), pp. 93–104.

SUPPLEMENTAL BIBLIOGRAPHY

The following books are additional resources on the topic of both lay and professional Christian counseling. They are in addition to those books already referred to in the text.

CHRISTIAN COUNSELING

Collins, Gary. *Christian Counseling: A Comprehensive Guide*. Waco, Texas: Word Books, 1980.

Helping People Grow: Practical Approaches to Christian Counseling. Santa Ana, California: Vision House, 1980.

Crabb, Lawrence J., Jr. *Basic Principles of Biblical Counseling*. Grand Rapids: Zondervan Publishing House, 1975.

Narramore, Clyde. *The Compact Encyclopedia of Psychological Problems*. Grand Rapids: Zondervan Publishing House, 1984.

Vitz, Paul. *Psychology as Religion: The Cult of Self-worship*. Grand Rapids: Wm. B. Eerdmans Publishing Company, 1977.

White, John and Blie, Ken. *Healing the Wounded: The Costly Love of Church Discipline*. Downers Grove, Illinois: InterVarsity Press, 1985.

Wright, H. Norman. *Crisis Counseling: Helping People in Crisis and Stress*. San Bernardino, California: Here's Life Publishers, 1985.

The following books are those you might consider recommending to friends. In this way they will meet some other recognized Christian counselors.

MARRIAGE AND THE FAMILY

Adams, Jay. *Christian Living in the Home*. Grand Rapids: Baker Book House, 1972.

Marriage, Divorce, and Remarriage. Phillipsburg, New Jersey: Presbyterian and Reformed Publishing Co., 1980.

Christenson, Larry. *The Christian Family*. Minneapolis: Bethany House Publishers, 1970.

Crabb, Lawrence, Jr. *The Marriage Builder*. Grand Rapids: Zondervan Publishing House, 1982.

Dobson, James. *What Wives Wish Their Husbands Knew About Women*. Wheaton, Illinois: Tyndale House Publishers, 1975.

Fennema, Jack. *Nurturing Children in the Lord*. Phillipsburg, New Jersey: Presbyterian and Reformed Publishing Co., 1977.

Murray, John. *Divorce*. Phillipsburg, New Jersey: Presbyterian and Reformed, 1961.

Ray, Bruce. *Withhold Not Correction*. Phillipsburg, New Jersey: Presbyterian and Reformed Publishing Co., 1978.

Schaeffer, Edith. *What Is a Family?* Old Tappan, New Jersey: Fleming H. Revell Co., 1975.

Welter, Paul. *Family Problems and Predicaments: How To Respond*. Wheaton, Illinois: Tyndale House Publishers, 1977.

Wheat, Ed and Gaye. *Intended for Pleasure*. Old Tappan, New Jersey: Fleming H. Revell Co., 1977.

White, John. *Parents in Pain*. Downers Grove, Illinois: InterVarsity Press, 1979.

HANDLING ONE'S EMOTIONS

Seamands, David. *Healing of Damaged Emotions*. Wheaton, Illinois: Victor Books, 1981.

Swihart, Phillip. *How To Live With Your Feelings*. Downers Grove, Illinois: InterVarsity Press, 1977.

HANDLING SUFFERING AND DIFFICULT TIMES

Erickson, Joni. *Joni*. Grand Rapids: Zondervan Publishing House, 1976.

Erickson, Joni, and Estes, Steve. *A Step Further*. Grand Rapids: Zondervan Publishing House, 1978.

Lewis, C. S. *A Grief Observed*. New York: Seabury Press Inc., 1963.

Skoglund, Elizabeth. *Coping*. Glendale, California: Regal Books, 1979.
Yancey, Philip. *Where Is God When It Hurts?* Grand Rapids: Zondervan
Publishing House and Wheaton, Illinois: Campus Life, 1977.

EVALUATION OF
THE TEXT

1. Which exercises did you or your group find most helpful? Please include what was most helpful about these exercises.

2. Which exercises were not helpful to you or your group?

For what reason(s):

a. Unclear directions

b. Lack of time

c. Inappropriate for group

d. Too repetitive

e. Other:

3. If you could delete something from the text, it would be .

4. If you could add something to the text, it would be .

5. How did you use the text?

6. Did you use the Leader's Guide? If so, in what capacity?

7. Other comments?

I would love to hear your feedback. You may write to me at this address:

Carol Lesser Baldwin
c/o Zondervan
1415 Lake Drive, S. E.
Grand Rapids, MI 49506